CW01035100

BEFORE
MRS BEETON

For Hugues

BEFORE
MRS BEETON

Elizabeth Raffald, England's Most Influential Housekeeper

NEIL BUTTERY

PEN & SWORD
HISTORY

AN IMPRINT OF PEN & SWORD BOOKS LTD.
YORKSHIRE - PHILADELPHIA

First published in Great Britain in 2023 by
PEN AND SWORD HISTORY
An imprint of
Pen & Sword Books Ltd
Yorkshire – Philadelphia

ISBN 978 1 39908 447 5

Typeset in Times New Roman 11/14.5 by
SJmagic DESIGN SERVICES, India.
Printed and bound in the UK by CPI Group (UK) Ltd.

Pen & Sword Books Limited incorporates the imprints of Atlas, Archaeology,
Aviation, Discovery, Family History, Fiction, History, Maritime, Military, Military
Classics, Politics, Select, Transport, True Crime, Air World, Frontline Publishing,
Leo Cooper, Remember When, Seaforth Publishing, The Praetorian Press,
Wharncliffe Local History, Wharncliffe Transport, Wharncliffe True Crime and
White Owl.

For a complete list of Pen & Sword titles please contact
PEN & SWORD BOOKS LIMITED
47 Church Street, Barnsley, South Yorkshire, S70 2AS, England
E-mail: enquiries@pen-and-sword.co.uk
Website: www.pen-and-sword.co.uk

Or
PEN AND SWORD BOOKS
1950 Lawrence Rd, Havertown, PA 19083, USA
E-mail: Uspen-and-sword@casematepublishers.com
Website: www.penandswordbooks.com

Contents

Acknowledgements

This is a book about Elizabeth Raffald, one of the most significant people in British culinary history. She is almost forgotten, yet her ideas about what British food is, and should be, still stand today. Her story needs to be told, so I thank Pen & Sword for agreeing to let me tell you about this wonderful, creative and indefatigable woman. I am indebted to my copy-editor Cecily Blench for her support and constructive criticism of the manuscript.

My thanks to Lord and Lady Ashbrook of Arley Hall and to Annika Flower for making me so welcome at Arley, for sparing the time to show me around, and for allowing me to view the Arley Hall archives. I am grateful to Charles Foster for permitting me to see his personal Raffald archives and research, and to the garden staff of Arley Hall for showing and teaching me about the gardens as they were in the eighteenth century.

I am most grateful to Suze Appleton, Sam Bilton and Mary-Ann Boermans for sparing the time to chat and give me their insights into Elizabeth's life and legacy, as well as pointing out many of the pitfalls when attempting to recreate eighteenth-century foods.

I thank Katherina Reiche and Mary Sheahan for supplying excellent research skills when mine had failed. I am also indebted to Ellie Huxley for going through the rigmarole of making Mrs Raffald's calves' foot jelly so I didn't have to. And on the subject of research, may I thank the wonderful, knowledgeable, patient and friendly staff of the Archives, Family and Local History section of Manchester Central Library. Those microfilm consoles began to feel like a second home.

Lastly, a great big thank you to my family for their continuing support, and to Hugues Roberts, not only for his excellent editing skills and criticism of the text but also for his unfaltering emotional support.

Introduction

I first came across Elizabeth Raffald in the same way as I usually come across great British cookery book writers, and that's via author Jane Grigson. It was 2008, and I was a year into the seemingly impossible self-imposed task of cooking every recipe in her classic tome *English Food*.[1] Jane includes recipes by several other well-known cookery writers such as Mrs Beeton, Eliza Acton, Hannah Glasse and Alexis Soyer, but it was Elizabeth who stood out. Jane wrote a potted history of Elizabeth in the introduction to her recipe for orange custards. It read:

> The majority of the best cookery books in this country have been written by women (or by foreigners). And of this energetic tribe, the most energetic of all was Elizabeth Raffald. Consider her career. She started work at fifteen, in 1748, ending up as housekeeper at Arley Hall in Cheshire. At thirty she married. Eighteen years later she was dead.

Jane then went on to list her achievements in those eighteen years: she owned two food shops, created the first register office (a domestic servants' employment agency), ran two inns,[2] collated Manchester's first street and trade directory, financed two newspapers, married 'an unreliable husband', had fifteen (or sixteen) daughters, and lastly wrote her influential cookery book *The Experienced English Housekeeper*.[3]

I was intrigued. How could anyone have achieved so much in so little time? I purchased the 1997 edition of *The Experienced English Housekeeper*, published by Southover Press and updated with modern spelling and a helpful glossary by Raffald historian Roy Shipperbottom. Inside he wrote a short, but wonderful, comprehensive and evocative biography of Elizabeth, showcasing her achievements. I also saw her recipes for the first time. I cooked a few and found that not only did they still work, but they were delicious. And whilst there are certainly a fair number of bizarre recipes in there, I was surprised just how many are recognisably British: curd tart, Yorkshire pudding, beef and oysters, trifle, jugged hare. All British classics. What I didn't appreciate at the time was just how forward-thinking and cutting edge she was: in those pages is the germ of a modern British food culture that's endured for two and a half centuries.

I rummaged deeper into her history and found her book ran to over twenty editions, was a standard wedding gift for new brides, and popular enough even for it to be printed in North America. Elizabeth was a household name. Jane Grigson even missed out a few of her achievements. We can add to the list: a cookery school for young ladies, a catering service for the well-to-do of Manchester and the surrounding area, and – if the sources are to be believed – she was the author of a book on midwifery and exorcised a building of a turbulent, terrifying spirit.

Almost single-handedly, and from a domestic servant's background, she gained national notoriety with her book and regional acclaim by bringing the business community of Manchester together in ways never before imagined. The people of Manchester knew this, and she was well remembered in the city a century after her death. In life, Elizabeth preferred to play her achievements down, describing herself as 'a confectioner, a convenient but inadequate title'.[4]

Understanding the historical backdrop to Elizabeth's life is key to understanding her life choices, successes and failures. It informs us particularly of the changes to Britain's social history with regard to class, gender and the north-south divide. Elizabeth lived right in the thick of what is known as the 'long eighteenth century', a broader and more meaningful historical distinction than the arbitrary dividing lines of calendars. It begins with the Glorious Revolution of 1688 and the twin reign of William of Orange and Mary Stuart, and it ends with the Battle of Waterloo in 1815.

Within this period, the modern cultural identity of Great Britain was formed, with the union of England and Scotland in 1707. It was a time of great commercial and imperial expansion: the English, then British, empire was liberally peppering itself across the surface of the globe, whilst at the same time increasing its domestic productivity. Integral to this were the improvements in its infrastructure with the creation of an extensive canal network. For those in the North-West of England, this came in the form of the Sankey, Liverpool and Bridgewater canals. It was a great symbiosis; empire and homeland providing for and fuelling each other.

This *industrious* revolution came before the industrial revolution kicked in and it began to transform Britain from a rural nation into an urban one; as a result, 'Britain [would become] the most dynamic area of urban development in Europe or possibly the world.'[5] With this great transformation, Great Britain became a main player on a new world stage, and because this was a world of colonisation and expansion of several European nations, it meant that Britain interacted more politically with continental Europe than at any other time in its history. Elizabeth would embrace these huge sweeping changes and use them for her financial gain because with the long eighteenth century came an explosion of wealth and all of the trappings that came with it. The most important of these, of course, from Elizabeth's point of view, was food.

From the experience she gained in employment in stately homes of North-East England, and then in her shops and catering businesses, she wrote a cookery book that helped form an idea of a modern British cuisine. Elizabeth was an artist, and she created her art from the exciting exotics of the empire and home-grown produce, brought to her by Britain's agricultural revolution. 'The Georgians', as Clarissa Dickson Wright tells us, 'had an enormous impact on our food, our way of cooking it, our way of consuming it, our way of serving it, and even the times of day when we eat it.'[6] Elizabeth's influence is embedded in it: her ideas about good British food and how it should be prepared are captured in *The Experienced English Housekeeper*. It informed a country then and continues to do so today.

But it was Elizabeth's personal story that got me hooked: her rapid, exciting and seemingly unstoppable rise that would be followed by a tumultuous fall. The complex of businesses, the directories and the cookery book that brought her fame and riches and great social standing so that she was 'highly regarded by the most respectable people of Manchester'.[7] In the space of two years, all would be gone. Her husband John, the handsome and charismatic head gardener of Arley Hall, is identified as the cause; for it was his alcoholism, overspending and mismanagement that were to blame. Elizabeth's life is about so much more than a cookery book.

That Elizabeth's life has a rise and fall narrative helped me with the organisation of the book, and I have, somewhat unsurprisingly, split it into two halves, 'Rise' and 'Fall'. The chapters broadly follow her chronology via the establishments she lived and worked in. 'Foundations (1733–1760)' follows the young Elizabeth Whitaker and her life in domestic service as cook and kitchen maid in Yorkshire and Lincolnshire, including England's second city at the time, York. 'Arley Hall (1760–1763)' looks at Elizabeth's life as housekeeper to the Warburtons of Arley Hall in Cheshire, and the role of the upper servant class in particular. It is at Arley she meets and marries John Raffald. At 'Fennel Street (1763–1766)', Elizabeth gets her catering business and shop off the ground and starts Manchester's first register office for domestic servants. Her time at 'Market Place (1766–1772)' was her period of great personal industry. The list is impressive: her 'normal school for ladies', not one, but two, editions of *The Experienced English Housekeeper*, and the first edition of her *Directory of Manchester and Salford* were all created here. This is her rise.

In 'The King's Head (1772–1779)', her upward trajectory continues, at least in the first couple of years. There, the Raffalds manage and run an upmarket inn and tavern, events space and stable yard. But then things take a downward; a turn from which she barely recovers. Did John cause this, or had Elizabeth simply bitten off more than she could chew? Either way, they end up in 'The Exchange Coffeehouse (1779–1881)', a ramshackle establishment in a dangerous and dark corner of the Shambles area of Manchester. Here, she tries to make ends meet by working a stall at the Manchester races. In 'Suddenly Gone', I recount the circumstances surrounding her death and its aftermath for John, her daughters, but also for Manchester and her cookery book.

I have interspersed these chapters with aspects of Elizabeth's life that sit outside of her chronology: In 'Feeding the Upstairs', I look at the lengths housekeepers such as Elizabeth went to in feeding their employers, the vast amount of work and industry required of not just her, and her kitchen staff, but also the head gardener, who was tasked to grow tropical fruits at great expense. Arley Hall is a case study, of course, but many other stately homes had similar setups. They didn't all have Elizabeth though, or her unique, showstopping desserts and table decorations. There is a chapter devoted to *The Experienced English Housekeeper*: its contents, her writing and its marketing, and its success.

Her recipes are not just discussed in this chapter but are also dispersed throughout this book. I do this for three main reasons: to demonstrate the effort that went into making food that today would either be outsourced or be the work of moments; to highlight the similarities and differences between British cuisine then and now; and lastly to show how her own life informed the book itself. After all, she does tell us her *receipts* (*recipe* is a French word, by the way) 'are truly wrote from my own Experience'.[8] 'The Exorcist and the Midwife' takes a look at some achievements attributed to Elizabeth that may or may not be apocryphal.

In the final chapter, I discuss Elizabeth's legacy: something I once thought was forgotten. I was wrong, and there *are* people who know about her and continue to be inspired by her and her achievements. I argue too that we are still affected by the ripples she has left in Britain's food culture – whether we are aware of her or not – because it was she, and a few other women of the long eighteenth century, who created what we think of today as modern British cuisine. For those of you interested in the process of cooking eighteenth-century food, and how one may go about recreating it in a modern kitchen, I have included an appendix of recipes updated for modern measures, ingredients and equipment. Here, I go through some of the terminology, and identify the pitfalls one comes across when cooking eighteenth-century food today.

There is an elephant in the room that I need to address, because I am sure you're thinking: if she was so great and so influential, surely we would all know who she was, there would be a gleaming statue on a plinth in Manchester city centre, or a building named after her or something like that. There would be books and documentaries written about her, and her cookery book would still be in print, you know, like Mrs Beeton. It's a fair point, and there are a variety of reasons, but one – and it is possibly the largest one – is that Elizabeth's book came before the door-stopping volume that is *Mrs Beeton's Book of Household Management* in 1861. A colossus of a book so popular and comprehensive, it blew all others out of the water. How did this happen? You'll have to wait and see.

But this book is not just about Elizabeth Raffald: for social historians, her Manchester and Salford directories are gifts that keep on giving, and I never tire of looking at them. She wrote three editions, three comprehensive snapshots of life from the 'Inhabitant of the least Consequence' to the wealthy country tradesman. They tell us so much about life in a large industrial town just as it was riding the great and terrible swelling wave of the industrial revolution. The detail contained within its pages is wonderful, and I have enjoyed dipping into it to help build up a picture of life in Manchester in the latter half of the eighteenth century. Indeed, I have explored a great deal of social, local and world history to understand the world that formed Elizabeth and the world she would form. Of course, I devoured many other cookery books of the era and looked at the history of housekeepers and domestic servants, but there were so many other things about which I did not expect to need to know: the agricultural revolution, women's rights, publishing and copyright law, gentlemen's clubs and societies, the horse races, the defeminisation of midwifery, and the paranormal, to name but a few. Of course, after reading this book, I hope you become as enthused as I am about Elizabeth Raffald, but I hope too that you leave understanding more about the daily life of people whose biographies cannot be pieced together in a time of relentless industrial growth where the everyday folk are forgotten. Elizabeth helps us remember: in her directories they are there, name-checked, complete with their trade and the street upon which they lived and worked.

I couldn't have pieced Elizabeth's life together without the wonderful primary and secondary sources available today, both online and at Manchester's Central and John Rylands libraries. Elizabeth's own words can be found in her cookery book and her directories, as well as the many notices she placed in Joseph Harrop's *Manchester Mercury* newspaper. Her writing is always very formal in these contexts, but nevertheless, she does disclose some opinions and provides some insight into the difficulties she faced. There are no records of her private thoughts and feelings still extant; the Raffald family bible is now unfortunately lost. However, local historian, archivist and journalist John Harland managed to capture a great deal of Raffald family history, lore and legend in the 1840s when he interviewed Elizabeth's 92-year-old nephew Joshua Middleton and Elizabeth's granddaughter 'Mrs Munday', daughter of her youngest, Anna. From these interviews and his own research, he put together a series of articles that were published in the *Manchester Guardian*. They were later published as parts of a wider history of Manchester called *Collectanea Relating to Manchester and Its Neighbourhood, at Various Periods* in 1867. Harland tends towards the dramatic and has a somewhat flowery writing style, which is delightful to read but forces one to take some of what he says with a pinch of salt.

There is little known of Elizabeth's life before Manchester, except for what can be found in the Arley Hall archives, which contain dozens of invaluable receipts, notes, lists and other information from the hall in the eighteenth century. They are an interesting snapshot of life behind the scenes in a large stately home, written by the people who lived and worked there. The archives are online for all to see, painstakingly scanned and labelled by Arley Hall historian Charles Foster. Many of the daily receipts, lists and notes Elizabeth wrote in her hand are there to view. Charles has written several books about Arley and the history of Cheshire and industrial Britain. He has also written much about Elizabeth after she left the Warburtons' employment for Manchester; indeed, the inhabitants of Arley Hall have always been very proud of their association with Elizabeth. Then there is the aforementioned Roy Shipperbottom, who wrote two biographies of Elizabeth: one I have already mentioned, and the other is a paper found with a collection of others presented as part of the *Proceedings of the Oxford Symposium on Food and Cookery*. Sadly Roy passed away in 1997, just before the reprint of *The Experienced English Housekeeper* was published. His two relatively short pieces are dense and contain essential details I would not have otherwise known. Roy and Charles became friends and wrote regular correspondence throughout the 1990s and up until Roy's death, letting each other know of any new juicy morsels discovered about Elizabeth or her family. In my research, I was lucky enough to be allowed to view these letters and Charles's other archived notes regarding Elizabeth in Arley Hall's beautiful library.

Finally, and most recently, there is the work of Suze Appleton who, in the mid-2010s, became somewhat obsessed with Elizabeth (this seems to happen to anyone who researches her) and considered, quite rightly, it a travesty that Elizabeth has evaporated from the British conscience. Over the space of four years or so, she set about collecting all of the primary and secondary sources she could, including key writings from Messrs Shipperbottom and Foster, newspaper clippings and church records and compiled them in several books regarding Elizabeth and her work. They have been essential in telling Elizabeth's story and this book would be a much slimmer volume without Suze and her excellent detective skills.

Other books were essential in my research: *The Domestic Servant Class in Eighteenth Century England* by J. Jean Hecht (1956) and *Servants: English Domestics in the Eighteenth Century* by Bridget Hill (1996) are both classic works in their field that really helped me imagine the daily life of domestic servants in the eighteenth century. Troy Bickham's *Eating the*

Empire (2020) is an excellent, detailed overview of Great Britain, its empire and its food, especially with regard to cookery book writers including Elizabeth. For getting to grips with eighteenth-century Manchester, there is John Sanders' succinct, comprehensive and evocative *Manchester* (1967). There are several other key texts and there is not space enough to list them all here, but they are referenced in the notes section at the back of this book.

Elizabeth's rise and fall story is a compelling one in itself, but it is not a piece of obscure local history: it informs us of so much of daily life, not just in Manchester but any industrial British town. Nor is it a niche titbit of food history; the eighteenth century was the crucible in which modern British food culture was forged, and Elizabeth was integral to it. Grandiose claims these may appear to be, but what will hopefully become very clear as you read this book is that Elizabeth Raffald should be remembered, should be better known, and should certainly be revered and lauded as Britain's defining cookery writer. One thing is for sure: the quality and extent of Mrs Beeton's household management would have been much, much poorer without the ground-breaking work of this most experienced of English housekeepers.

RISE

Chapter 1

Foundations (1733–1760)

Doncaster and its surrounding area in the first half of the eighteenth century was a grim place indeed. It was still largely medieval in its infrastructure: small, claustrophobic, ramshackle wattle and daub homes lined the narrow streets, groaning under the pressure of an expanding populace. The roads were pocked with potholes and the blocked sewerage system choked up with human effluent and garbage. It was dangerous to walk the streets after dark, lest one was jumped upon and mugged, or worse. Yet amongst the outdated medieval squalor – like many other towns in England in the first half of the eighteenth century – new streets, homes and municipal buildings, all equipped with decent drainage, were being created. Doncaster was on the cusp of a great change that was less of an *industrial* revolution and more an *industrious* one: a peak time for cottage industry, where people spun and wove wool and flax at home or in small groups to make fabrics to sell to clothiers, tailors and haberdashers. Doncaster attracted people from the countryside, not quite in the droves that the industrial revolution would attract, but in significant numbers nonetheless. The work was hard, monotonous and time-consuming, and many were left destitute.

It was into this world that Elizabeth Whitaker was born, in what seems to have been a loving home in Wadworth, just south of Doncaster in the South Riding of Yorkshire on 8 July 1733.[1] Little is known of her early years, but we do know that her parents were named Joshua and Elizabeth, and she was the second of five daughters. The eldest was Jane, ten years Elizabeth's senior, then Sarah, Ann and Mary, the youngest.[2] Joshua Whitaker's role in the community was teacher. We know not whom he taught, but we do know that he tutored his daughters well; under his tutelage, all could read and write and could speak conversational French,[3] a skill Elizabeth would use to great effect in her later career. Their good education put the Raffald sisters head and shoulders above their peers at a time when the level of literacy for the country was only around a third, with the north of England very much lagging behind the south.[4] Elizabeth's youngest sister Mary, to whom she was very close, trained early in the art of confectionery. Confectioners were highly sought after, being 'the most highly regarded of all tradesmen involved in the preparation of food', and confectionery promised those skilled with great wealth and social standing; indeed, confectioners were very much in demand in the houses of the aristocracy.[5] Unfortunately for Mary, she had little chance of rising to such dizzying heights; only men ran the confectionery kitchens of royalty, but there was the potential to work under them. Mary likely taught Elizabeth, giving her a grounding in the craft:[6] candying, making preserves and jellies, such as 'marmalet', as well as a range of cakes and biscuits. It was hard work, and something considered very simple today was quite the opposite in the eighteenth century, as Elizabeth's recipe for 'common Biscuits' from *The Experienced English Housekeeper* demonstrates:

> Beat eight Eggs half an Hour, put in a Pound of Sugar beat and sifted, with the Rind of a Lemon grated, Whisk it an Hour 'till it looks light, then put in a Pound of Flour, with a little Rose Water, and bake them in Tins, or on Papers, with Sugar over them.[7]

Skills such as these set Elizabeth in good stead for 'fifteen years [in service to] great and worthy Families in the Capacity of a House-keeper' in Yorkshire and Lincolnshire.[8]

***

Life in domestic service in the eighteenth century was not quite the *Upstairs, Downstairs* set-up one might expect it to be; in fact, the system was still somewhat medieval, in that the relationship between master and servant was closer and kinder and with a more familial feel. It wouldn't be until the next century that total segregation of employer and employee would become the norm and relationships became austere and focused heavily upon contractual obligations.[9] Of course, there were contracts written in the first half of the eighteenth century to the benefit of both parties, but alongside these were obligations that were not written down, obligations that were latterly lost. It was expected that the master of the house – and by extension, the mistress – should be like a parent to their servants and cater not just to their corporeal needs – board, clothing and food – but also to their spiritual needs, allowing and encouraging everyone to regularly attend church or Sunday school. A good employer provided moral guidance too and made sure even the lowliest footboy or chambermaid was, at the very least, taught to read.

That these needs were met as standard was, unsurprisingly, a big attraction, and for many, acquiring a position in domestic service provided a real refuge from poverty.[10] However, in return, servants were expected to express not just gratitude toward their employers but also humility, lowliness, meekness, submissiveness, gentleness, respectfulness, a good temper and – let's not omit this one – fearfulness. And if that wasn't enough, they were also expected to put their all into serving their employer and his family. In other words: your life was not your own. And so '[d]espite this spiritual rhetoric of *choosing* obedience, the domestic servant remain[ed] dependent and bound.'[11] This was a contract that had been nurtured for centuries, a medieval model of domestic service that worked and depended on the two classes living together, under the same roof, with servants working and sleeping cheek-by-jowl with their employers. As social historian J. Jean Hecht remarks in his detailed thesis on this relationship: 'it is clear that the medieval tradition of family feeling retained a certain amount of vitality. A good servant was as likely to receive more from his master than was called for by actual contract.'[12]

By the time Elizabeth entered service, this relationship was starting to erode. The cause of this erosion was an increase in demand for servants at a time when the urban population was rapidly growing in size, with sections of it growing richer, attracting rural domestic servants, keen to live perhaps a more exciting life in the bigger towns and cities, which had become foci of trade, commerce and great wealth; Britain's empire was expanding, as were the profits of plantation owners, traders and merchants. There were the investors too, who invested shrewdly in these businesses and found themselves making tidy profits, allowing them to climb a few extra rungs on the social ladder. The thriving empire also made tradesmen like shipwrights, stationers and blacksmiths substantially better off from providing goods required for its expansion. These newly middle-class households found themselves in a position where they could afford servants. Everyone could afford staff, it seemed, if this excerpt from a letter in a 1756 edition of *The London Magazine* is anything to go by:

> There is scarce a mechanick in town who does not keep a servant in livery, which is an insistence of pride and luxury of very late date. Liveries were formerly given only by noblemen and gentlemen, to distinguish what family servants belonged to … But, what was then [in Richard II's time] a distinguishing garb, is now the indiscriminate cloathing of almost every domestick of the male gender.[13]

The distribution of such households was not spread evenly about the country; most of this new money resided in London, and it was this uneven distribution that drove the detrimental effect upon traditional master–servant relationships in the rest of the country because, as the century wore on, more of the servant and would-be servant class moved away from the country seats of their employers to the city. The familial relationships that both employer and employee had benefitted from and worked so hard to maintain were destroyed. And they were leaving their rural homes in droves; approximately 5,000 individuals per year.

The exodus was such that in London, one-third of households had live-in servants and one-thirteenth of the London population was made up of live-in domestic servants.[14] Servants would become such a common luxury by the 1770s that Prime Minister Lord North saw fit to impose a tax of one guinea upon every male servant. The tax became somewhat weightier in 1785, when William Pitt the Younger increased it to between a guinea and £3.[15] But because neither side knew the other well, there was no time to build up the old relationships of the countryside; instead, there was distrust and uneasy reciprocity. Sadly, many of those who did travel to London found it hard to get work in domestic service, and when they did, they were treated poorly. A significant proportion became homeless or resorted to prostitution, living in terrible conditions. This increased the death rate considerably and pulled even more from their countryside homes. For the landowners in the Yorkshire and Lincolnshire countryside, a labour vacuum developed; the gravitational pull of London was so strong it took away the children of their tenant families, once their source of servants, who now filled the often meagre servants' quarters of London's middle classes.

For those who did continue to work in service in the more rural parts of the country, like the young Elizabeth, there were many opportunities, and good, reliable staff were highly sought after. There are no records of the houses in which Elizabeth worked in the first twelve of the fifteen years she spent in domestic service, but we can guess with a certain degree of assurance that her excellent education, natural intelligence, and her aptitude for pastry work and confectionery meant she was quickly snapped up as a kitchen maid by one of any number of upper-class houses looking for trustworthy folk who wanted to quickly climb the career ladder with honesty and pride; a sort of worker that seemed to potential employers to be in very short supply. As people were desperate for staff, employees held the bargaining chips, and they pressurised employers into providing extra perks which would never have been part of the contractual agreements in the old medieval model.

The traditional perquisites of working in domestic service were very much derived from the Middle Ages; every member of staff could expect to be provided with small beer – a very low-alcohol drink, packed with nutrition unlike modern beers and ales.[16] In addition, every man received a pot of stronger ale, and every woman, a pint. They were fed well but were unlikely to have been indulging in the 'good eating' of their betters, unless they were eating the leftovers from the previous day. For servants, it was more about quantity over quality: cheap, plain fillers such as boiled suet pudding and boiled beef or mutton. If the household were travelling to another town and found themselves in unfamiliar territory, staff were given cash so they could frequent the local inns, taverns or bakeries and purchase their food there – an exciting, rare and fleeting opportunity of freedom.

Servants expected to receive clothing from their employers, at least those who were 'on show' such as footmen, pages and valets. Others who were less seen usually had simple clothes made for them in-house. The families' hand-me-downs were really coveted: typically, the upper servants of the houses – that is stewards, housekeepers and valets – expected to receive the employer and his family's old or unwanted clothes to wear when not working. Lower servants, in series, were handed down the upper servants' hand-me-downs. Several other items were considered fair game for staff to take and sell on at a small profit: candle ends were melted down, and animal bones and fat, including that in the dripping pan, were sequestered and sold on to various manufacturers of soaps and candles. Even urine and 'night soil' – i.e. human faeces – were sold to producers of saltpetre, an essential chemical for food preservation, gunpowder and tanning.

Any item that found itself unwanted by the employer and could be sold, worn or utilised in some way, the servants had first refusal over. Savvy servants were therefore furnished with many of their masters' luxuries, either because they were given it, or because they had purchased or traded items with other servants. Other items often added to the list were damaged or broken silver, brass and copper items.[17] As a consequence, servants began 'to imitate the manners and clothing' of their superiors.[18] Quite quickly, servants began to covet other luxuries – especially those of the empire – previously only available to the well-to-do: tea, and sugar with which to sweeten it, and to a lesser degree, coffee and chocolate. At first, they demanded the rights to used tea leaves, but soon they wanted virgin leaves. As MP Thomas Alcock wrote in 1752: 'It is now usual with the Female Servants to insist on Tea in their Agreement, and to refuse serving where this is not allowed,'[19] and meticulous diarist Parson Woodforde scribbled on 3 June 1778, '[t]wo servant maids came to me this morning and offered their services to me. I agreed with them both and they are to come to me here Midsummer day next. One of them is to be an upper servant and … I am to give her … tea twice a day.'[20]

Employers agreed to these terms readily, but this tendency for servants to attempt to better themselves via another's contractual obligation was just the thin end of the wedge, and servants developed tastes considered well above their station. Alcock observed: 'And when from Servants they go to be poor Men's Wives, we may naturally suppose they carry the same expensive Appetites and Habits with them, which being propagated by Example to the Offspring, the Evil becomes still more epidemical.'[21] Empowered servants began to take liberties, and soon wine, tea and sugar were considered fair game for the taking, kitchen maids stole butter and sold it on to the community and many a light-fingered kitchen boy was caught filling his boots with expensive pies and sweetmeats.

Things had become so bad by 1780 that servants accused of stealing from their employers made up a third of all English court cases. The servants were very much in the driving seat: 'God help the Georgian employer who didn't provide' the appropriate perquisites for '[i]nsults and ill-treatment were the certain rewards of those who failed to give generously.'[22] Some resorted to getting one over on their parasitic staff by darkening used tea leaves with burnt toast – or worse, lead blacking – to pass them off as new. Others paid them cash rather than extras, and even extended it to food, leaving their staff to procure their own food and drink, forcing them to shop more modestly and hold back on their extravagances. This came at a cost, as it forced servants who received only board and wages to spend more time away from the employer's house, making them more independent.[23] In the end, the most typical approach was to keep wages and perquisites finely balanced: if there were few perks, one expected to be paid more and *vice versa*. This worked well, but because employees remained in demand, there was always pressure to increase both wages and benefits.

Relationships were further eroded by the introduction of vials – cash tips – that were given out to employees by visitors as they were about to leave their host's home. They were expected to tip everyone, though in some houses, only males were allowed to receive them. The giving of tips was very much a British phenomenon, and it came as quite a shock to foreign visitors, who frequently complained of the expense associated with simply visiting somebody else's house; and pity the poor the middle-class gentleman or lady who was really feeling the pinch trying to keep up with the Joneses, having to turn down invites because of the embarrassment of not being able to cough up the appropriate staff vials once dinner and drinks had concluded.[24] The origin of the system of tipping is unknown, but Bridget Hill suggests it may have been simple ostentatiousness by showing off one's wealth when visiting others, or that it stemmed from the admittance that many visitors felt the servants employed by their hosts were not paid enough. However it started, by the second half of the eighteenth century, it was completely out of hand. In response, a movement against the payment of vials gained traction and swept the country. By the closing decades of the century, the giving of tips had largely died out.[25]

The breakdown of the filial relationship between employer and employee made them physically, as well as socially, distant; servants' rooms, once close to their masters', or sometimes even within the same room, were moved to separate servants' quarters, 'built for the gentry in which the strict segregation of servants from family was assumed',[26] preferably out of sight in the attic or cellar. It is no surprise, therefore, that once one found a staff member of fine moral character who understood less cynically the relationship between servant and master, they would be held in high regard and kept close. For some, working in domestic service was about more than fleecing the boss out of as many of their food items and valuables as possible. Rather it gave them purpose, and 'the employment of servants was a way of defining oneself socially as not being working class.'[27] This certainly applied to the proud, hard-working Elizabeth, and one assumes she had great role models in the various kitchens within which she worked who demonstrated to her the importance of a good work ethic; she didn't care about short-term gains (though one expects that she did not turn them down), she was much more interested in climbing the ladder as far as possible.

There were several downsides to domestic service, however: being employed in the isolated houses of the countryside, set away from the local town, meant living a life confined to their own quarters and the house's grounds.[28] Those who did live near a town were often disallowed from leaving their employers' house lest they took some of their hard-earned cash and got plastered in the local tavern; anything with the potential to cause any kind of embarrassment to the master and mistress had to be avoided, much to the detriment of their staff's freedom and mental health. Any servant who did cause the family embarrassment could have their contract broken and be out on their ear. If this description by a correspondent in the *London Chronicle* in 1791 is anything to go by, the threat of dismissal loomed over them like the Sword of Damocles:

> a servant, though never so attentive and industrious, lives in continual dread of their [employer's] displeasure upon every trivial offence, and lives in fear of not only being discarded from their service, but also of being deprived of that which is the only recommendation to his future subsistence, which recommendation consists in a good character.[29]

Many were 'let go' on grounds of ill health and many were not paid well enough to save if there ever was a significant period of poor health, forcing a great number of cast out individuals into sex work. Servants were often dismissed with poor references, or none at all, something that was required when applying for new vacancies. This led to a black market in counterfeit testimonials, which provided individuals of 'false character' opportunities to get into people's homes.[30]

Those who were not fired were habitually 'caned, cuffed and slapped'[31] and English law provided masters with the power to do so: 'As for stubborn and unruly Servants, the Law of England gives Masters and Mistresses

Power to correct them; and Resistance in a Servant is punished with severe Penalty.'[32] Often damages were paid to servants if the beatings they received were considered excessive. Poor treatment such as this was more common in London and the other major cities, where relationships were more contractual and conditions more cramped. Yet those employed in service often tried to remain so for two main reasons: first, the life of free labourers who worked the factories and had to pay rent, buy and cook their own food and support their families. The work was gruelling and poorly paid, with a diet correspondingly reduced to rough bread, dripping and onions. These 'free' workers were trapped not by overzealous masters but their poverty, and service was viewed as the lesser of two evils.

The second reason is that with all of their perks and vials, many servants could use their employers as a bank. Some servants did not need to draw any wages at all, and with many servants earning an additional £12 to £15 per year in benefits alone, they could leave service with a tidy sum. Compare this to a labourer in a factory, who earned £12 a year in total *and* had a family to support and rent to pay.[33] The labouring poor viewed domestic servants with a certain amount of disdain; like leeches, they were 'valueless to the community [and] contributed little or nothing to the common welfare.'[34] Of course, that didn't apply to all, and those who left service in a positive manner, as Elizabeth would, escaped this stigma and inserted themselves very successfully into the bosom of their community.

***

Whatever skills Elizabeth began her career with, she most certainly had skills above that of the lowliest female kitchen worker, the scullery maid, whose role was to keep the kitchen and its ancillary rooms clean. Next up in the female hierarchy were the kitchen maids; in large houses, there would have been several of them, all of different ages and levels of experience. Then there was the cook, whose wages were very dependent upon the types of food they were proficient in cooking: a 'good plain cook' who produced everyday food was paid a good deal less than one who could create more elaborate dishes.[35] Most kitchens employed a man-cook; he usually did the same work and had the same responsibilities as the female cooks, but by virtue of his gender was paid considerably more. If he was French or skilled in the French method of cookery, he could be paid triple that of a female cook.[36] If they showed the appropriate skills, female cooks could move up to the role of housekeeper.

Another male presence was the butler, who was 'custodian of the wines and liquors' and was accountable for their preservation. He also served the wines and was in charge of the pantry and buttery as well as the glass and plate.[37] Other female roles within the realm of lower servants included chambermaids, who dusted, polished, swept and cleaned upstairs and saw to the making of beds in the morning and the warming of them in the evening. Some large houses had laundry maids and dairymaids. In smaller houses, many of these roles were outsourced or combined and given to the maids and cooks. Most hard-working of all was the maid-of-all-work, employed as the only female member of staff and expected to fulfil all of the roles listed above. All of these women were the 'unseen', people who worked downstairs, or if found upstairs dressed in a way that they would blend into the background. They were therefore kitted out in plain, dowdy and often distressed clothing – unlike the footmen, stewards, butlers and valets, who dressed in fine livery. This seems terribly demoralising; of course, all lower servants were expected to be subservient, but for these numerous invisible women the expectation was greatest.

The tasks expected of kitchen maids and cooks were wide, varied and often gruesome. Some tasks have changed little or not at all: chopping, peeling, plucking, scaling, poaching, mixing and kneading. But the work required in the making of a smooth soup – a task of mere seconds with a modern food blender – by pushing the contents of one's stockpot through a sieve with only a ladle and one's own elbow grease was no mean feat. Nuts, spices and rock-hard sugarloaves ground and sifted by hand; the seeds of raisins individually picked from each dried fruit – no seedless grapes here – pounds of which were used in cakes and puddings; cooked meat and fish pounded into pastes for potting; and egg whites whisked to stiff peaks with nothing but bundles of stripped feathers. There were other tasks not required at all today: fattening caught wild game birds for the table as well as, of course, dispatching them oneself. This did not stop at birds, as Elizabeth's recipe 'To Roast a Pig' informs us:

> Stick your Pig just above the Breast-bone, run your Knife to the Heart … put your Pig into a Pale of scalding water half a Minute, take it out, lay it on a clean Table, pull off the Hair

as quick as possible … take off the four Feet at the first Joint, make a Slit in its Belly, take out all the Entrails … when you roast it, put in a little shred Sage and a Tea spoonful of Black Pepper, Spit your Pig, and sew it up, lay it down to a brisk Fire … a large one will take an Hour and a half … then take a sharp Knife, cut off the Head, and take off the Collar, then take off the Ears and Jaw-bone, split the Jaw in two, then lay your Pig Back to Back on your Dish, and the Jaw on each Side; the Ears [on] each Shoulder, and the Collar at the Shoulder, and pour in your Sauce and serve it up.

To ensure there was as little waste as possible, offal and other odd bits were used in other 'made dishes' or as garnishes: the brain provided the basis of the pig's sauce, and the trotters, heart, liver and lungs were cooked and the meat chopped to make a mincemeat.[38] The blood was made into black puddings (using the intestines as casings, of course), and the bladder dried and used to seal pots of preserved fruits and vegetables.

Work in a large kitchen was focused around the fireplace (or places). The slow move from the medieval fuel combination of charcoal and wood to charcoal and coal, and the filthy soot it produced, meant saying goodbye to the old layout of a single large central fire in the centre of the room, its smoke drawn out via a hole in the roof above it. The thick black smoke had to be instead extracted via a narrow chimney stack built into the sides of the kitchen, cleaned by chimney sweep boys, often obtained from workhouses or purchased from parents.[39] Upon the fire was a stack of roasting spits, turned by clockwork, or more often a poor spit boy, shielded from the heat by a fireguard. The fire would also have had cauldrons placed on trivets or hanging from chains, used for cooking large volumes of soup or stew, but more often to cook several different things at once; bobbing about in the hot water of a cauldron might have been bag puddings (such as pease pudding), meat joints wrapped in cloth, and various jars and jugs – water and thinly sliced beef for beef tea, or strongly flavoured food such as smoked fish and game – the jugged kippers and hare of old.[40]

If one's employers kept up with kitchen technology, one might have been able to simmer more complex sauces or sauté vegetables on the top of an iron range cooker. 'When built into the wall of the kitchen, their cast iron facades had a central firebox fitted with a door to control the draught … Inside, a series of narrow ledges was provided along each side to support moveable oven shelves'[41] for baking meats, pasties (not the handheld snacks of today, but entire joints of meat wrapped in pastry and baked) and other baked goods. Some were also fitted with highly polished metal screens, so any heat that escaped from the back of the oven was reflected back into it, rather than lost straight up the chimney.[42] Often, a water tank sat on the other side of the range's oven, capturing more heat in the water for cooking and cleaning tasks.[43] They were quite an investment to fit, but these ovens were very heat-efficient and helped to diminish the size of the fuel bill significantly. It was excellent for the cooks too, less dangerous and much more controlled, allowing for more precise cooking and evermore dainty sweetmeats.

In kitchens without a range, delicate sauces were still expected, so cooks and kitchen maids had to hold their saucepans directly over the heat, hands wrapped in cloths to prevent serious burning, as is shown in the frontispiece illustration of the fourteenth (1750) edition of Eliza Smith's classic cookery book *The Complete Housewife*.

Having next to no information about Elizabeth's formative years in service, it looks as though she entered service at fifteen as a kitchen maid in 1748, and emerged twelve years later, fully formed as a reputable, honest and strong-headed housekeeper of a large stately home. We can only assume, therefore, that she did not arrive in that role amongst the other upper servants of Arley Hall entirely without managerial experience, and she very likely worked as housekeeper in a smaller house belonging to the gentry or upper-middle class. In order to progress comparatively quickly – the role of housekeeper was usually only given to mature, experienced women – she must have been a very quick learner, as well as efficient organiser, skilled cook and formidable presence. It seems remarkable that she was to – or was seen to have the potential to – take on this role at twenty-five years of age or probably younger. Little can be gleaned from her own writing, and the only specific mention of her life in domestic service before Arley crops up in *The Experienced English Housekeeper* in her recipe for roast ruffs; wading birds found in the coastal wetlands of most of England, which are particularly abundant in the country of Lincolnshire:

To roast Ruffs and Rees

These Birds I never met with but in Lincolnshire, the best Way to feed them is with White Bread boiled in Milk, they must

have separate Pots, for two will not eat out of one, they will be
fat in eight or ten Days; when you kill them, slip the Skin off
the Head and Neck with the Feathers on, then pluck and draw
them; when you roast them, put them a good Distance from the
Fire, if the Fire be good, they will take about twelve Minutes,
when they are roasted, slip the Skin on again with the Feathers
on, send them up with Gravy under them ... and Bread Sauce,
in a Boat, or crisp Crumps [sic] of Bread round the Edge of
the Dish.[44]

One thing we do know is that Elizabeth spent a great deal of her time in
the city of York, which, by the mid-eighteenth century, was considered to
be England's second city culturally. York had had a considerable downturn
since the Reformation; its population stagnated somewhat since the armies
of the Civil War and interregnum had dispersed, leaving behind a small
but significant number of the gentry. Therefore, the tradespeople who
tended to be found in the city were 'luxury craftsmen, shop [owners] and
service personnel'. In 1715, there were (amongst others) eight apothecaries,
eighteen gardeners, nine cooks, fifty-nine innholders and one vintner.[45] This
was great if you were a member of the upper class or part of the newly
solvent middle class, but the city offered little to anyone of the 'lower sort'.

In the 1730s, several buildings were erected in the city to attract other
members of the gentry and aristocracy, and York became widely known
as an excellent leisure town, a place where one could experience a bit of
high-end rest and relaxation. The jewel in its crown was the Blake Street
Assembly Rooms, which was built in 1732 and headed a 'cluster of projects
in the early 1730s aimed at equipping York with a first-rate ensemble of
up-market leisure institutions'. Others grew up around it, including the
New Theatre in 1744, which attracted some of the greatest actors of the
day.[46] Establishments such as this were key to York's success because they
offered a real taste of culture and civility, the likes of which could only be
found in London, and to a lesser degree, Bath. However, it could take four
days to travel to these places, so York was providing a real service to the
upper classes of the North, selling 'three related notions: civility, sociability
and improvement'. Viewing it through the eyes of the eighteenth-century
gentleman or lady, urbanity meant true civility. 'Civility was considered an
inherently urbane phenomenon, and there was a conscious policy to distance

it from the values of unreconstructed nature.' It was fashionable and it was progressive; at least from the narrow viewpoint of the upper classes: indeed, '[t]he emphasis in civility upon the distinction between mind and body, brain and brawn, man and beast, was part of this attempt to drive a wedge between the learning and the labouring classes.'[47]

With its diverse complement of fashionable shops, York became a hub of fashion and quite the place to be seen, and women made up 60 per cent of its visitors. Prior to this, many ladies living in the north of England had never seen the horseraces or indeed a fair, for that matter.[48] These young women, in turn, attracted gentlemen who were on the lookout for wives; hopefully with a decent dowry. In short, York was 'a marriage market', and it forced the men of Yorkshire – known for their rough plain-speaking – to up their game and behave in a more civilised manner.

A significant population of the well-to-do demanded a suitably large population of domestic servants, and by the 1750s, York contained the highest concentration of servants outside the West End of London, of which 'an astonishingly high proportion [were] female domestic servants, a service activity which accounted for nearly three-quarters of all female employment in the city.'[49] A good proportion of these would have been ladies-in-waiting or housekeepers accompanying urbane ladies, but a great number lived and worked in York on short-term contracts, supporting or replacing visitors' domestic staff during their vacation. We do not know in which capacity Elizabeth was working during her time in York, but the chances are that she worked both types of job. The competition for contracts such as these was ruthless, and there must have been plenty of disreputable domestics with the gift of the gab who were in to make some quick money and get their hands on some top-drawer contractual perquisites. Obviously, having a good reputation could help one to get ahead of the competition, but how does one do that? Luck, shrewdness and tenacity are all helpful, but to be consistently successful you need *connections*, and luckily for Elizabeth, she had Seth Agur on her side. Agur was her agent and ran a domestic servants' registry from his luxury food store and greengrocers in the Stonegate area of the city,[50] a business model she would replicate in Manchester. Agur was an influential member of the community and a 'subscriber to the Freemasons'.[51] In short: a man to know. Elizabeth and Seth's business relationship would surely have been a fruitful and symbiotic one: he found her good work with the best of the gentry in the great houses of the North, and she purchased his luxury foods for the kitchens of those great houses.

> The most expensive provisions were, as we would expect, those items intended for the dessert. All the usual suspects appear in the invoices: provisions needed for the preparation of wet and dry sweetmeats, the single, double and treble refined loaf sugar, also individual supplies like morrels, trouffles, macaroons, prunelloes, candied oranges, orange chips, small comfits, white candy, cherries, clear cakes, apricot tart and French plumbs.[52]

The greatest inspiration in her early career was Monsieur Seguin, a Frenchman who ran a high-class confectioner's shop in Minster Gate. He was a highly skilled pastry chef who used the best ingredients and adopted innovative techniques to make delectable patisserie that could not be bettered in the city. According to a handful of surviving receipts, amongst his supplies at Christmastime were crystallised fruit, meringues, candied citrus zest, coloured sweets, waffles, orange flower water, shortbread and sugar figures.[53] Cheesecakes were particularly popular, and were often made from curd cheese, rather than cream cheese as they typically are today:

> To make Curd Cheese-cakes
>
> Take half a Pint of good Curds, beat them with four Eggs, three Spoonfuls of rich Cream, half a Nutmeg grated, one Spoonful of Ratafia, Rose or Orange Water, put to them a quarter of a Pound of Sugar, half a Pound of Currants well washed and dried before the Fire, mix them all well together, and bake it in Petty Pans with a good crust under them.[54]

Monsieur Seguin had a particular flair for edible table ornaments for banquets and replicating these marvels would become Elizabeth's *modus operandi*; she learnt the skills required to produce excellent French foods, but then applyed those skills in a more economical way to English cooking. We can assume with confidence that Elizabeth got to know Monsieur Seguin because she kept and maintained many contacts in the city; years later, when looking for subscribers to her cookery book, she appealed to the high-class confectioners, cooks and housekeepers of York.

In a dozen years, Elizabeth Whitaker had become skilled and well-regarded enough to take on the position of housekeeper, but it would be achieving that position at Arley Hall in Cheshire at the end of 1760 that would allow her to progress and develop her talents further. These productive twelve years in service in the North-East of England were but a primer, and she would go on to plan and cook banquets fit for kings, whilst avoiding the expensive and superfluous frivolities of which French chefs, in her opinion, were very much guilty. But that is not all; at Arley, she found a true and lifelong friend in the mistress of the house, Lady Elizabeth Warburton, and love in the form of the handsome head gardener, Mr John Raffald.

Chapter 2

Arley Hall (1760–1763)

Elizabeth Whitaker travelled the 120-kilometre route across the 'atrocious rutted roads from Doncaster to Arley Hall in Cheshire',[1] arriving in the first few days of December 1760. Arley Hall is a large stately home and the Warburtons, who resided within it, an 'old major gentry' family headed by the fourth baronet of Arley, Peter Warburton.[2] The family had owned land in the region since the twelfth century, and the hall in which he and his family dwelled was built in the fifteenth century by his ancestor Piers Warburton.[3] Because Arley Hall was so large, it had a suitably large number of domestic staff.

Like most houses, it had evolved from the medieval set-up of communal living: the master and mistress, their family and members of the lower gentry living alongside not just the domestic staff but also families who farmed, grew flax and made textiles. But as this way of life began to degrade, farmers moved out into accommodation and paid their rent in cash rather than in the fruits of their labour. Textile-making and flax-growing ground to a halt, as production became centralised in the cities and industrial towns. This trend continued until the 1750s when Sir Peter Warburton abandoned 'the last vestiges of the system of self-sufficiency'.[4] As on-site production fell, there was a marked increase in the number and diversity of local suppliers and national traders. In 1626, there were over 200 cattle at Arley, but by 1750, this had fizzled down to a mere twelve dairy cows, and the lion's share of the meat was bought from Thomas Gately, a local butcher, at an annual cost of £225. Similarly, the house bought in grain – mainly wheat, but also barley and oats – from local dealers or at local markets, though a little was still cultivated on site by tenant farmers.[5]

At the same time, the north of England was going through a transformation from which the Warburtons would benefit greatly; Arley was already strategically built, nestled close to the rivers Mersey and Weaver and therefore had always benefitted from the choice of goods available, but in the 1750s and 1760s, with the extensive construction of the canal network,[6] waterways came within ten kilometres of Arley, transporting essential industrial materials such as coal, timber and lime in such quantities that prices dropped significantly. As a result, wages increased by up to 50 per cent.[7] This was no accident: Sir Peter's father (also named Peter) sat on the committee that rebuilt and modernised the Weaver navigation works.[8] Arley, like most of Cheshire, was benefitting from the burgeoning industrial revolution, and although there were not quite the extensive numbers of staff that the Warburtons would have enjoyed in the late Middle Ages, the house certainly boasted a decent set for the time.

It must have been quite a daunting prospect to enter Arley Hall as housekeeper; even if Elizabeth had held that same position in other residences, it is very unlikely that she would have had experience of managing such a large house. She was far away from Doncaster, from her support network and her excellent connections in York. Indeed, it rather begs the question: how on earth did Elizabeth manage to get this position in the first place? Alright, she was hardly still wet behind the ears, but after just a dozen years of domestic work and at the age of only twenty-five, it doesn't seem like enough time to achieve either the appropriate 'age and experience' or the 'gravity and decorum' required of the post in such a large private house.[9]

It is possible that she simply saw the position advertised in Seth Agur's register office, assuming, that is, the Warburtons visited York regularly enough; it certainly would make sense to seek female staff there, seeing as it had such a large pool of them. Alternatively, she may have already been working as a housekeeper in a smaller house, and felt ready to move on to a more challenging role – she was ambitious and very able. Perhaps the master or mistress of a house in which she worked knew the Warburtons and that they were looking for a housekeeper themselves; verbal recommendations are the best kind of testimonial, after all. These would both be perfectly credible scenarios if Arley were in Yorkshire or Lincolnshire, or at least a neighbouring county. Instead, historians who have looked into Elizabeth's life point the finger firmly at John Raffald, the talented head gardener of Arley Hall as the catalyst.

John was appointed head gardener at Arley in January 1760, fresh from his apprenticeship with the renowned nursery and seedsmen Perfects of Pontefract. Mary Griffiths, the housekeeper, left abruptly and with little notice ('possibly after some row'[10]) in December. If this is correct, it seems that with little notice, and in somewhat of a whirlwind, Elizabeth was made housekeeper of Arley Hall. Elizabeth Raffald biographer Roy Shipperbottom believed that Elizabeth and John probably met and got to know each other in York – Perfects of Pontefract certainly traded in the city, and almost definitely would have supplied Seth Agur with at least some of his fancy fruits and vegetables.[11] They supplied Arley Hall too: there are several receipts from Perfects, including one for 'parcels' of fruit trees and seeds dated 11 August 1760. Whether their relationship was professional or romantic at this stage, we do not know, but either way, John was impressed by this keen, intelligent, forthright, yet sober young woman and saw her as a perfect match for Arley. Elizabeth's reputation must have preceded her to some degree because she was paid almost a third more than the outgoing housekeeper; a salary of £16, an increase from £12.6s.[12] It could be because wages at Arley were increasing in tandem with the rest of the country and its strong economy, or it might simply be that the position hadn't seen a pay increase in the time Ms Griffith was employed.

Entering Arley as housekeeper made Elizabeth one of the upper servants, sharing the top tier with the mistress's lady (or ladies) in waiting. Elizabeth was in charge of all the female members of staff below them, from the scullery maid to the chambermaids via the cook. All of the other upper servants were male: the valet, or gentleman-in-waiting, served the master directly; the house steward, Peter Harper, looked after the estate, making sure rents were collected, and kept the farmers informed of farming techniques and developments. The steward was the male counterpart to the housekeeper, and it was Peter to whom Elizabeth was answerable. As the highest-ranking male servant, Peter Harper earned a tidy £40 per year – two and a half times Elizabeth's salary. Despite the disparity in income, they were both considered a cut above the other staff members, enjoying a much greater deal of autonomy. The hiring and firing of staff was well within their power and it is likely that they dined separately from the other servants and enjoyed better quality food and drink. They also retained sleeping quarters close to the master and mistress after the others had been segregated in separate servants' quarters.[13] The next highest male earner was John Raffald, with his salary of £20; there was also groom Joseph Kay (£14), John Allen, farm foreman (£8), and Isaac Hind, gamekeeper (£6). Of the women, the next highest earner down from Elizabeth was Martha

Hutchin, the cook, who earned £10 per year. There were several maids, such as Elizabeth Golden, who earned £5 a year, and a family member – Ann Golden – who worked as dairymaid, earning just £3 a year.[14] Women were paid less, perhaps because they were unseen, but it is more likely it was simply because they were women.[15] Such stark differences between genders and the upper and lower servants were very much typical of the time.[16]

Because they were more seen, male servants wore appropriately showy livery, displaying their master's wealth by proxy. This fact held whether a servant was valet or footboy. Many of the liveried took liberties with the fact they were only really employed to look good and were often found drunk on the job, knowing they wouldn't be roped into doing any real work. These differences between the treatment of male and female domestic servants did not go unnoticed; Dr Samuel Johnson was once posed the following question:

> What is the reason that women servants, though obliged to be at their expense of purchasing their own clothes, have much lower wages than men servants to whom a great proportion of that article is furnished and when in fact our female house servants work much harder than the male?

Johnson, rarely found speechless, could not think of a satisfactory reply.[17]

It is difficult to tell how representative the drunk, lazy and light-fingered stereotype of servants – especially male servants – really is. Most accounts tend to include incidents and episodes where there was some kind of misbehaviour but are silent when it comes to praising good work. The reason is – and ask anyone who has worked in the hospitality industry, they will confirm this – that when everything is going well and the staff are well organised, no one notices; creating the illusion of calm is all part of the job. The trick is to make things seem effortless. Only when the veil slips does it get noticed.[18] As a result, there are fewer realistic representations of trustworthy staff. In novels and plays, they are often the butt of jokes – lazy, greedy, stupid or untrustworthy.[19] Typical, hard-working, humble servants are of very little interest to the playwright. However, there is one example that bucks this trend and that is William Hogarth's painting *Heads of Six Servants* (c.1750–55), a group portrait of three male and three female members of his own domestic staff. The painting – composed by an artist more famous for his often grotesquely satirised depictions of eighteenth-century life – is a rare 'glimpse of plain reality', showing clearly 'their heads held high with confidence and candour, and are obviously held in affection by their master.'[20] The three males are all of very different ages: a boy, presumably a page; Hogarth's elderly valet; and a middle-aged man, reckoned to be the coachman. The males have fancy clothes with a bit of colour: the valet and page wear mustard yellows and deep greens, and the coachman is attired in a striking black jerkin with white collars and tassels. He also wears a black periwig. In contrast, the women have their hair tied back and covered with modest white bonnets. The three women are made up of two housemaids and a housekeeper, though it is difficult to tell which is which, as all three are of a similar age and wearing similar, fawn-coloured clothing.

Upper servants and male servants both inevitably spent a large amount of their time around the master or mistress of the house and their family, and looked up to them and copied their employers' speech, accents and gestures. So effective were they that visitors sometimes couldn't tell the servants from the dinner guests. This had two negative consequences: first, many of the servants, who were proud to have such access to their masters' lives, began to develop a snobbishness and often looked down upon the local villagers.[21] Second, so keen were they to ape their masters' more refined behaviour, their masters felt their waiting staff's 'overtly watching gaze' everywhere they went. Feeling understandably uncomfortable, many felt they could no longer have private conversations without their staff listening in. Necessity is the mother of invention, and the response to this was the creation of the dumb waiter: now lords and ladies could receive their afternoon tea without interacting with any staff at all.[22]

The consequences were not all negative: it has been hypothesised that these servants acted as a conduit for social change. Many positive behaviours and habits were passed down through the ranks: courteousness, politeness, the importance of reading, and being more mindful of the welfare of children and animals. Because their staff mixed with the locals, these affectations dispersed into the working folk in the adjacent villages and towns, and soon 'it was possible to look back and marvel at how the lower classes had been transformed.'[23]

The precise role of the housekeeper was dependent upon the size of the house in which she worked, and as was typical of the time, her role was less defined compared to the nineteenth century. The following 1771 advertisement from an employer seeking a housekeeper to 'undertake the Management of a large Family of Fashion' is, however, representative of the scope of the knowledge and skills required of her:

> She must thoroughly understand in what Manner to supply a Table in Town and Country; she must be neat and orderly, a good Oeconomist, and have Authority to oblige the other Servants to be so; she must understand Pickling, Preserving, Potting, Salting Meat, and keeping all sorts of provisions, to order and keep a proper Supply of them, buying them, paying for and keeping regular account thereof, and every Thing under her.[24]

Were it a small house with a handful of servants, Elizabeth would have been in charge of the whole troupe, but for larger houses like Arley, responsibilities in ordering food were split between Peter Harper and herself, with Elizabeth ordering the more everyday store cupboard ingredients, fish and some game (fishmongers often had a side-line in game butchery). Elizabeth Whitaker's first food order, dated 26 December 1760, contained such food items as larks, woodcock, lobster, salt, tripe, pikelets (crumpet-like pancakes), butter and lemons. Other orders included items such as Seville oranges, candle snuffers and pipeclay. Peter Harper, on the other hand, wrote and kept the hall's hefty meat order and was in charge of the spices, ice for the ice houses, and tea; the latter of which was purchased from Thomas Twining of London, and Auley's of Manchester. He also managed the granary book; the order book for the house's cereal grains and flours, which included mainly 'milled wheat', plus barley, oats and bran used to feed the horses, pigeons and fighting cocks.[25] Arley Hall accounts reveal that he oversaw the purchase of nets used for fishing, catching windfall fruit and entangling gamebirds such as partridges.[26]

Elizabeth was also in charge of organising food for staff, and several lists of food items with their costs are still extant in Arley Hall's archives. In 1761 staff ate beef and mutton, sometimes veal, and more rarely, lamb. Other food items included salmon, 'fowls', bacon, 'milled wheat', cheese, bread, mustard, nutmegs, lemons, as well as a significant amount of lump, double refined and brown sugar.[27]

The housekeeper's role was not entirely managerial; aside from keeping a short rein on her female staff and making food orders, she was expected to spend a significant amount of time in the kitchen. One key responsibility was the preservation of produce – John Raffald's kitchen garden produced a bounty of food, which, if preserved properly, would keep the Warburtons and their servants eating seasonal produce all year round. Elizabeth spent the year turning garden gluts, excess food and left-over cooked meat and fish into a range of delicious products: pickles, jams and 'marmalets', cordials, powders, country wines and potted meat and fish.[28]

> To pot Ham with Chicken
>
> Take as much Lean of a boiled Ham as you please, and half the Quantity of Fat, cut it as thin as possible, beat it very fine in a Mortar, with a little oiled Butter, beaten Mace, Pepper, and Salt, put Part of it into to China Pot, then beat the white Part of a Fowl with a very little seasoning, it is to qualify the Ham; put a lay of Chicken, then one of Ham, then Chicken at the Top, press hard down, and when it is cold, pour clarified Butter over it; when you send it to Table cut out a thin Slice in the form of half a Diamond, and lay it round the Edge of your Pot.[29]

She was expected to have practical knowledge of distilling, transforming herbs such as lavender, pennyroyal and elderflower into sweet-smelling waters. She would have overseen the storing of apples in their lofts, the vegetables in cellars, covered in sand. It was labour-intensive and required constant vigilance, lest a whole harvest be spoiled.[30]

Nothing went to waste, and Elizabeth's clever home economics meant that the Warburtons could be more extravagant when required. It was a fine balance between frugality and opulence. Elizabeth had to create fancy desserts, cakes, confections and patisserie for the tea tables as well as her famous table decorations, in house. Making fancy confectionery and putting on a show was part of the job description of any housekeeper who found herself in a large home of the gentry, and in this field she excelled. As she says in the introduction to her book, 'I am not afraid of being called extravagant, if my Reader does not think I have erred on the frugal Hand,' going on to say, 'I have made it my Study to please both the Eye and the Palate, without using pernicious Things for the sake of Beauty.'[31]

As housekeeper, Elizabeth spent a significant proportion of her time liaising with Lady Elizabeth Warburton, or Lady Betty, as she was affectionately called.[32] Lady Betty was not a hands-off mistress, indeed, for the first ten years of her marriage to Peter Warburton, she *was* the housekeeper of Arley Hall.[33] The mistress of the house had to be confident her housekeeper could run a ship as tight as she would herself. The relationship Elizabeth Whitaker had with Lady Betty was a positive one; she respected her greatly, and Lady Betty trusted Elizabeth with the full range of duties expected of her. But their relationship was much more than just a professional one, and they obviously cared about each other immensely. After Elizabeth left Arley for Manchester, Lady Warburton visited Elizabeth's establishments several times, and Elizabeth visited Arley too, most significantly to seek Lady Betty's patronage of *The Experienced English Housekeeper* before she took the liberty of dedicating the book to her ex-employer. She wrote:

To the Honourable Lady Elizabeth Warburton.

Permit me honoured Madam to lay before you, a Work, for which I am ambitious of obtaining your Ladyship's Approbation, as much to oblige a great Number of my Friends, who are well acquainted with the Practice I have had in the Art of Cookery, ever since I left your Ladyship's Family, and have often sollicited me to publish for the Instruction of their House-keepers.

As I flatter myself I had the Happiness to giving satisfaction during my Service, Madam, in your family, it would be a still greater Encouragement, should my Endeavours for the Service of my Sex, be honoured with the favourable Opinion of so good a Judge of Propriety and Elegance as your Ladyship.

I am not vain enough to propose adding any Thing to the Experienced House-keeper, but hope these Receipts (wrote purely from Practice) may be of use to young persons who are willing to improve themselves.

I rely on your Ladyship's Candour, and whatever Ladies favour this Book with reading it, to excuse my plainness of the Style, as in Compliance with the desire of my Friends, I have studied to express myself so as to be understood by

the meanest Capacity, think myself happy in being allowed the
Honour of Subscribing

Madam,
> Your Ladyship's
>> Most dutiful,
>>> Most obedient,
>>>> And most humble Servant,

ELIZABETH RAFFALD.[34]

Looking over her dedication with twenty-first century eyes, it appears terribly sycophantic, the praise and humility trowelled on rather too liberally, but the dedication, and the words within it, served several purposes. First, it shows the reader that Elizabeth has good connections, and that – given her status as a servant – she is civil and polite, with a good vocabulary; some of those positive affectations servants sought to ape had obviously percolated down to Elizabeth. It also shows that Elizabeth respected the order of, and the hierarchies within, society. She may be using fancy words, and she may be civil, but she also acknowledges her plain and common ways, at least in comparison to Lady Betty and others of her ilk. Elizabeth is a woman of high ambition and great civility, but she knows her place, respects her betters and doesn't forget just how lucky she is to have worked for someone with as much 'Candour' as Lady Betty. After suitably bigging up her Ladyship, Elizabeth received her stamp of approval, thus convincing anyone who might be in two minds whether they should subscribe to her book; getting the thumbs up from one of England's most gracious and discerning ladies would be the clincher. With Lady Betty's assurance, author, patron and purchaser of the book all come off very well: Elizabeth knew exactly what she was doing.

Peter Warburton had married Betty, eldest daughter of the eleventh Earl of Derby, Edward Stanley, in 1746. Peter was in a very lucky position; his father was the youngest of two brothers, so was never expected to inherit the family seat. However, he found himself becoming heir after his own father passed away, and his uncle, the tenth earl, died without issue. The vast majority of younger sons and nephews of the landed gentry were never so lucky. They often had to eke out a rather meagre existence whilst, at the same time, being expected to assume the life and manner of an upper-class gentleman with the trappings to boot. On the surface, they lived well, but in reality, they lived in near poverty, always ready, willing and appropriately highly regarded, should the heir unexpectedly pop his clogs without issue.[35] The Warburtons moved into Arley Hall as soon as they were married, and had six children.[36] One assumes that running a large stately home and overseeing all her children became rather too much for one person to handle, hence the employment of a housekeeper.

It was typical for ladies, and therefore their housekeepers, to act as a moral authority to the female servants of the house. In reality, this meant doing their level best to prevent the female servants from having 'relations' with the male members of the household, wherever they sat in the social hierarchy. As a consequence, '[t]he lives of servants, particularly female servants, were subjected to an intense, and unhealthy scrutiny by the masters and mistresses.'[37] There were self-help books to aid in this aspect of housekeeping: '[Eliza] Haywood, for example, divides her text on servant maids into a series of warnings against Sloth, Sluttishness … Telling Family Affairs … Giving Saucy Answers [and] Being too Free with Men Servants and Apprentices.'[38]

So worried were ladies that their female staff would succumb to the advances of the males of both house and village that they expected the housekeeper to physically prevent the maids from leaving the premises to wander the grounds or, worse, going to the local tavern unattended. If there were rumours of liaisons, the housekeeper would resort to locking women in their rooms to protect them and their virtue. There are plenty of tales of women under the care of employers who did get pregnant – in one case, two servants became pregnant by the same footman – and many ladies were worried about their maids being sexually assaulted by members of the family. It was not uncommon for mistresses to instruct their housekeepers to only employ maids perceived to be plain or unattractive.[39]

Unfortunately, from a maid's point of view, the circumstances around how she became pregnant were unimportant; if the father was a member of the mistress's family, she would be dismissed, and if it were a member of staff, or someone from the local village, they would be expected to be married. This may not come as a surprise in a world where the legitimacy of a child was of extreme importance; it was the only honourable thing to do, whether the mother and father liked it or not. The problem was that it was also expected for married couples – or indeed single mothers – to leave domestic service. 'Employers were apprehensive that a married couple, particularly if they had children, would be as much concerned with their own family as their master's,'[40] so either way, the maid would be dismissed.

***

One member of staff that Elizabeth would have worked with closely was head gardener John Raffald. Peter Harper, the house steward, may have been in charge of sourcing goods produced on the estate, but Elizabeth would still have worked with John; she would have needed to know what vegetables were doing well and which ones John was having difficulty with that season, including the fancy exotic plants destined for display on Arley's banqueting table.

John was no typical head gardener. He is described as 'a fine, aristocratic looking man, well-informed, even learned it is said, and his knowledge of botany and floriculture was in that day considered marvellous'. He 'was an able botanist and was celebrated as a seedsman and florist, in which business his family had hereditarily been engaged in Stockport for two centuries'.[41] It appears that working at Arley was something of a dream job; John had been set to inherit the Raffald family business, but after receiving the offer of the position of head gardener, with much soul-searching, he rescinded his inheritance, deferring it to the second eldest Raffald brother, James.

When Elizabeth started her employment with the Warburtons, the two did not live in the same building because the Warburtons were living in nearby Aston Park in nearby Great Budworth, as Arley Hall was being updated 'from black and white half-timbered house' to a modern building complete with sash windows and brick façade.[42] Therefore there was just a skeleton staff at Arley, and making up one of their number was John.[43] Elizabeth, as housekeeper, went with the household to Aston, but received produce from Arley's gardens, including exotics and cut flowers. John spent considerable time at Aston Park planting trees and shrubs in pots as was *en vogue* in houses with little or no garden or grounds – after all, just because the Warburtons were not living at Arley, it did not mean they couldn't live well. When the Warburtons moved back to the revamped Arley in 1763, John and Elizabeth found themselves in each other's company a great deal more, and although the building was no longer in the medieval style, the living arrangements remained so, and therefore the two of them were not only working together, but also living together.[44]

At some point, they became romantically involved, and Raffald biographers have questioned the nature of their early relationship. There was a seven-year age difference between the two of them, and it has been suggested that the younger Elizabeth may have been somewhat 'overawed' by this devilishly handsome, talented and charismatic gent.[45] However, this age gap is not particularly great, and knowing Elizabeth's sober pragmatism and John's tendency to be emotionally led, if anyone was besotted, it more likely would have been John, not Elizabeth. Being conscious of Elizabeth's shrewd business sense, one might suspect the relationship was not only about love and romance; she no doubt saw the worth of having a talented husband with good connections in the horticulture industry.

Whatever the grounds of decision made between Elizabeth and John to marry, they planned their move, and Elizabeth her fledgling business, very well. One thing was clearly imbalanced between the two of them, however; Elizabeth – it seems – was beginning the first exciting steps on her entrepreneurship, whilst John – however sure he was of the successes that lay ahead – had given up his dream; a dream that he gave up his inheritance to pursue. Their decision to marry demanded they leave domestic service and begin their lives anew in Manchester. It made perfect sense to move there: they both had connections and John would have a job with the family firm waiting for him. Elizabeth could see too that whilst although Manchester was no highbrow York, it was certainly on the up.

According to the Raffald family bible, 'John Raffald married Elizabeth Whitaker, 3rd March, 1763' in the neighbouring town of Greater Budworth.[46] They remained as staff for a short time, as a new housekeeper and head gardener were found and shown the ropes. Arley Hall has the last receipt signed by Elizabeth Raffald – one of only two that bear her married name – dated 23 April 1763, the very date she and John left for Manchester.

Sad as they were to see them go, the Warburtons' noses had been put slightly out of joint because this was the *fourth* time they had lost a head gardener to a member of Arley staff. Suitably frustrated, the Warburtons took the sensible decision of building a cottage set away from the house, separating any future dishy head gardener from the rest of the staff. And if he *did* marry Arley staff, he would not be obliged to move away. Upon their leaving, the Warburtons lost two trusted and beloved members of staff: both creative, dependable, sober-minded, trustworthy and with good work ethic. Elizabeth had been happy to be unseen at Arley, peacockery was not in her nature, but when the two of them left the Warburtons for the cramped, noisy medieval streets of Manchester's Shambles, Elizabeth would be unseen no longer.

Chapter 3

Feeding the Upstairs

Keeping up appearances has always been of paramount importance to the upper classes, but in the mid-eighteenth century, it peaked. Status symbols had to be displayed alongside behaviours appropriate to one's levels of gentility and civility, with their complex system of manners, gestures, vocabulary and conversation. There was no aspect of one's life that wasn't scrutinised by the beady eyes of one's peers, whether it be the state of the footman's shoes or the way in which one held a wineglass. The Warburtons were no different, and a vast amount of their time and money was spent ensuring that they were on the leading edge of fashion in Georgian polite society. Lady Betty was regularly seen visiting nearby Knutsford and Warrington, driven by coach with a footman or her lady-in-waiting in tow. She ensured she was wearing the up-to-the-minute fashions of the day and spent her time perusing the beautiful shop windows, viewing an array of silks and ribbons, wigs and millinery, furniture and drapery. She was also seen taking tea and chocolate in the best houses in town.[1]

Lady Betty also visited other homes for low tea, an emerging tradition that had created yet another arena in which to be seen and judged. Over the course of the century, dinnertime had migrated from the late afternoon or early evening (depending on the time of year) to a fixed time of nine o'clock as the mass production of candles made it much cheaper to light one's dining room artificially. No longer was a family at the mercy of sunlight. They *were* at the mercy of their stomachs, however, and found they had to plug the hunger gap between lunch and dinner. There was pressure to be seen visiting others for tea and one might turn up to more than one teatime per day to engage appropriately in polite conversation, daintily sip tea from china cups and nibble little cakes and biscuits with an appropriate degree of restraint. Maintaining all of this nonsense was a clear signal to everyone else in the room that one had the money and could afford the time required to keep it up.[2]

Lady Betty took tea at Arley too and she would have expected a good spread, carefully laid out on trays with the appropriate teapots and teacups. Elizabeth made many of the dainty morsels herself, and devoted a whole chapter in her book to their production, in which she includes a great deal of practical advice such as: 'When you make any Kind of Cakes, be sure you get your Things ready before you begin' and 'if your Cakes have Butter in, take Care you beat it to a fine Cream'. She also recommends avoiding baking them in tins which 'burn the Out-side of the Cakes, and confine them so that the Heat cannot penetrate into the Middle of your Cake, and prevents it from rising'. Instead, she recommends that one should 'bake them in Wood Garths', essentially wooden frames set on trays that heat the cake more steadily and evenly.[3] Teatimes were a simpler affair than those of the Victorians and Edwardians; rich, creamy and oversweet foods were avoided, and the finger sandwich had yet to be invented. It wasn't a meal, after all, just something to keep one going until dinner. Teatime treats included bread, butter and jam, rice cakes, lemon puffs and 'Wiggs' (wedge-shaped enriched yeast cakes) and the very popular seed cake. Don't let the apparent simplicity of these foods fool you, they were time-consuming to produce and required practised judgement and a great deal of elbow grease to make well.

> To make a rich Seed Cake.
>
> Take a Pound of Flour well dried, a pound of Loaf sugar best and sifted, eight Eggs, two Ounces of Carriway Seeds, one Nutmeg grated, and its Weight of Cinnamon; first beat your Butter to a Cream, then put in your Sugar, beat the Whites of your Eggs half an Hour, mix them with your Sugar and Butter, then beat the Yolks half an Hour, put it to the Whites, beat in your Flour, Spices and Seeds, a little before it goes to the Oven, put it in the Hoop and bake it two Hours in a quick Oven, and let it stand two Hours.[4]

Often the rock-hard loaf sugar had to be broken, cracked, pummelled and ground by hand, could be an entire morning's work for one member of kitchen staff.

The Warburtons regularly travelled farther afield. Bath was a great favourite of the family, and it took the household four days to reach the city by coach. They expected to be provided with two hot meals consisting of roast meat and greens, stews and sweetmeats, each day they were travelling. When they visited others' homes, they got the opportunity to show off their generosity (i.e. wealth); when they visited Oulton Hall in Leeds, Peter Warburton instructed payment of excellent tips to the domestic staff. He was obviously well aware of the hard work done by the housekeeper because he paid her 10s 6d, more than any other member of staff. He gave the housemaid 7s 6d and the butler 5s. In total, he paid out the handsome sum of £2 3s to the domestic servants of Oulton.[5]

***

Anyone visiting Arley would see first the hall's grounds before they got to see any of the interiors or eat any of the food. In the eighteenth century, opulence had certainly extended to the gardens where small Tudor box gardens had given way to heavily reshaped and landscaped estate gardens. Peter and Elizabeth Warburton built 'a large romantic pleasure ground of shrubberies and walls on the east side of the house',[6] and even moved the entrance to Arley to the opposite side of the house, away from the fields and forest, so that guests could travel through the gardens, avoiding the land their tenants occupied. But the most important element of the grounds – at least from a housekeeper's point of view – were the extensive walled gardens inside which a vast range of exciting exotic fruits and vegetables were grown with great care, attention, skill and expense.

John Raffald was a well-respected member of staff at Arley Hall and his skills were appreciated and his salary of £20 reflected that. Having a head gardener with John's skill was essential for upper-class families like the Warburtons because by the turn of the eighteenth century, gardening and landscaping had become the 'new medium of competitive display'[7] and gardeners, seedsmen and nurserymen were highly regarded and very much sought after. These were the days of the great landscape artists Lancelot 'Capability' Brown and William Kent. There had been great developments in the grafting and pruning of fruit trees and garden technology: hothouses, forcing houses and greenhouses. In the countryside estate, seasonal fruits and vegetables were one of the few things not being outsourced and left to labourers to produce, and they were only purchased from a supplier if a crop hadn't grown successfully.

This technology effectively extended the seasons and brought forth exotic fruits that could never have been successfully imported. All of this tested the gardeners' skill, and produced a new type of gardener: the horticulturist, a 'word coined in English to describe this innovative, hybrid pursuit, which spoke to interests in botany, agronomics, natural history, aesthetics, and refinement'. This new science required a system of classification, gardeners needed to know which plants were related, and they needed to avoid confusion between similar, but unrelated species: for example, the 'buttercup' of temperate Europe is a completely different species to the 'buttercup' of North America. This need for consistency and order inspired the Swedish botanist Carl Linnaeus to introduce his Latin binominal system of classification in 1753.[8] Horticulture was a global phenomenon and new plants came flooding in from all around the ever-mushrooming British Empire, and landowners wanted to be seen with a good, showy and expensive mix of beautiful British plants and foreign exotics. Most people associate such endeavours as a Victorian pursuit, but its peak is very much Hanoverian; it was the eighteenth century, not the nineteenth, that gave us the quintessential English country garden.

Seedsmen and nurserymen did not just sell their seeds, seedlings and saplings to local well-to-do folk; they also pioneered early mail-order systems – a testament to their ingenuity and the hardiness of their cultivars. It was businesses such as these that were key to improving the economy of the country, allowing both cash and saplings to move about the land, widening the net that constituted the 'local economy'. John had deliveries from a huge range of nurserymen and seedsmen: two varieties of holly trees from George Geary;[9] honeysuckles, laburnums and sweet bay samples from Jack Nicolson;[10] dwarf apricots and 'cornelian' cherries, and 100 spruce firs and 200 'Scotch pine' from nurseryman John Holbrook; and 'Sellery', chervil, 'Yorkshire cabbage', clary, caraway and French sorrel seeds from London.[11]

John was highly skilled in the craft of horticulture and had great experience of cultivating plants at every stage of their development: germinating seeds, nurturing saplings, grafting and pruning trees, running a seasonal kitchen garden and landscaping the grounds. He wasn't just a great talent, but he also had excellent connections and grounding in the area. John came from a family of horticulturists: the Raffalds had lived in Stockport, a town on the northern fringes of Cheshire and bordering Manchester, for generations, and therefore the family had been specialising in horticulture well before the word had been coined. As the popularity and phenomenon spread north from London, the Raffalds were already ahead of the curve, and although the family does not seem to appear in histories of the subject of horticulture, they were nevertheless great pioneers and practitioners of the science. Another pioneer of the north of England was, of course, Perfects of Pontefract. One of the great things about horticulturalists – indeed it is probably the secret to their success – was that they shared not just their seeds and cuttings but also their skills and information, producing a vast communal knowledge bank. So, with natural talent, a family in the business and a top-notch apprenticeship, John was snapped up by the Warburtons after their gardener left their service in 1760.

***

Before the long eighteenth century, kitchen gardens were very sensibly established adjacent to the kitchen but now that landscaped paths, ha-has and ornamental plants wrapped themselves around a house's grounds, the vegetable garden, orchards and fruit bushes were moved; their functionary existence no longer befitting of a grand house. It may not have been so accessible, but away from the prying eyes of visitors and residents alike, the kitchen garden could grow greatly in size and complexity. Being away from the house, the gardens could be encapsulated inside tall brick walls, which would be an eyesore if built close to the house, making the garden appear more like a prison than a place of horticulture. The walls served several purposes: they hid all of the kit required of the garden itself such as forcing, hot and greenhouses, and they kept out much of the noise generated by the hive of activity carried out within; they prevented thefts of equipment and valuable plants; they provided shelter; and they 'maximize[d] warmth by absorbing heat which [was] subsequently released overnight', effectively extending the growing season.[12]

More ingenious methods of extending (forcing) a food plant's season were devised. Some garden walls were built with extensive eternal flues that could be stocked with charcoal to create 'hot walls'. Using these methods, the cultivation of many fruits previously only grown successfully in mainland Europe or South-West England, such as dessert apples and pears, peaches and apricots, figs and plums, was possible as far north as

Scotland.[13] Some methods were simple such as the earthing of soil or manure, which protected and blanched vegetables such as 'sparrow-grass', cardoons and celery. Others, such as rhubarb and seakale, were forced and blanched under earthenware bell jars or cloches. Squat glasshouses and melon houses brought forth melons and cucumbers.[14]

But the jewel in the crown of any kitchen garden was the hothouse because it allowed the growth of exotic fruits and vegetables from far-away continents. They were usually built backed up against the inside of an exterior garden wall, and at the rear of the structure small furnaces burned, heating a sophisticated network of flues and ducts. The interior was made humid with heavy watering and the intensive fermentation of rotting oak bark and horse manure.[15] At Arley, to create further humidity, the inside wall had built-in evaporating dishes, essentially long shelves of shallow trays warmed by the heat of the furnaces, that provided a large surface area and efficient evaporation of water. This produced consistent heat and humidity, important for the growth of tropical plants like the pineapple which only has a three-degree window in which it can fruit successfully.[16] Other fruits such as mangoes and paw-paws were also grown successfully. So well made and managed were these hothouses that if a late frost developed and killed off the delicate outdoor varieties like strawberries or apricots, the snug and humid hothouse plants happily survived.

As for the lowlier common vegetables – cabbages, radishes, onions and the like – they were planted in beds surrounding the gardens. All in all, a vast assortment of fruits, vegetables and herbs were grown; of such variety it would bewilder shoppers used to the restricted number available in supermarkets today.[17] In Elizabeth's list of seasonal produce in *The Experienced English Housekeeper*, even February's fare promised forced radishes, cardoons, beets, celery, cucumbers, asparagus, kidney beans, rocambole (a type of leek), salsify, skirret (a type of root vegetable prepared as one would carrot), a range of fresh herbs, plus pears, apples and grapes. Other soft fruits and exotics such as peaches, plums and pineapples were produced right up until October.[18]

***

It is easy to think that with all this effort and expense, the Warburtons must have been eating luxuriously all the time; scoffing game and other roast meats, gorging on exotic fruits and filling their faces with cream cakes and sweetmeats, washing them all down with French wines. Whilst it was certainly true that the Warburtons ate well, most luxuries were eaten in limited amounts. Arley Hall historian Charles Foster collated receipt data from the hall between the years 1758 and 1762 and found that each person, on average, consumed ten pounds' worth of food annually, the equivalent of around £2,100 today, the majority of which was spent on meat and animal products. Almost 60 per cent of the food budget went on 'large joints' of meat, an annual total of 206 kilograms, or a hefty 4 kilograms of meat per person per week. Each person put away 1.4 kilograms of cheese and 190 grams of butter per week. Altogether, 75 per cent of the food budget was spent on meat and animal products. As for the luxuries of the day, tea and sugar, 8.7 grams of tea (approximately 30 teaspoons) and 149 grams of sugar (the equivalent of 12.5 teaspoons of sugar) were consumed per person per week.[19] Sugar was found in non-negligible amounts in more than just tea and coffee, it was present in desserts and biscuits, candied fruits, preserves, country wines and other bought-in sweet alcoholic drinks such as the popular sweet, sherry-like drink 'sack', much beloved by Shakespeare's Falstaff.

For everyday dinners, the food was relatively plain; it was noted by Swede Peter Kalm that 'the art of cooking as practised by most Englishmen does not extend much beyond roast beef and plum pudding',[20] most of the sweet and rich foods being saved for banqueting events. Puddings contained little or no added sugar, typically being made up of flour or breadcrumbs, suet and dried fruit:

Bread Pudding

Take the Crumb of a Penny Loaf, and pour on them a Pint of good Milk boiling hot, when it is cold, beat it very fine with two Ounces of Butter, and Sugar to your Palate, grater [sic] half a Nutmeg in it, beat it up with four Eggs, and put them in and beat all together near half an Hour, tie it in a Cloth and boil it an Hour, you may put in half a Pound of Currants for a change...[21]

If a dessert course was served, fresh fruit would have been limited and there would have been no exotic fruits. Instead, there were preserved or stewed and spiced fruits made with a great deal less spice than the Tudors and Stuarts would have used. Sweetened drinks would have been served such as the popular syllabub, a mixture of sweet sack or beer (which would have been much sweeter tasting than it is today) and milk or cream, which was left to stand and curdle, so the top could be eaten with a spoon and the bottom drunk. Such drinks were made with the freshest ingredients possible:

> To make a Syllabub under the Cow
>
> Put a Bottle of strong Beer and a Pint of Cyder into a Punch Bowl, grate in a small Nutmeg and sweeten to your Taste, then milk as much Milk from the Cow as will make a strong Froth and the Ale look clear. Let it stand an Hour, then strew over it a few Currants well washed, picked, and plumped before the Fire, then send it to table.[22]

***

Modern horticulture was providing Arley with its fresh vegetables and fruits, but similar improvements in farming methods meant that fresh meat was now available all year round; livestock was no longer slaughtered and salted *en masse* in November, as there was food enough to feed them through winter. Fresh, uncured meats could be stored in cool larders, but very perishable foods were kept in the ice house; the first in England was built for Charles II, but from the early eighteenth century, they began to pepper the grounds of the wealthier houses of the gentry.[23] The ice house was used as a huge refrigerator, with fresh meat and fish hung above and around the ice blocks, though it did provide too the ice for making complex ices for the grand banqueting tables:

> Pare, stone and scald twelve ripe Apricots, beat them fine in a Marble Mortar, put to them six Ounces of double refined Sugar, a Pint of scalding Cream, work it through the Hair Sieve, put it into a Tin that has a close Cover, set it in a Tub of Ice broken small, and a large Quantity of Salt put amongst it, when you see your Cream grow thick round the Edges of your Tin, stir it, and set it in again 'till it all grown quite thick, when your Cream is all Froze up, take it out of your Tin, and

put it in the Mould you intend it to be turned out of, then put
on the Lid, and have ready another Tub with Ice and Salt in as
before, but your Mould in the Middle, and lay your Ice under
and over it...[24]

Dinner was served *à la française*, usually two courses made up of several dishes served at table at the same time; the modern dinner with individual courses – service *à la russe* – is a Victorian adoption. Dishes would have included boiled and roasted meat, puddings and vegetables. Sometimes the meat and vegetables were served together if the combination was well established like braised duck and peas, but more typically fresh vegetables were served in separate dishes to the plain meats, usually having been boiled and dressed in 'melted butter', actually a butter sauce, made by whisking chilled butter with hot water or stock, sharpened with a little lemon and stabilised with a little flour.[25] There will have been several pies, including mince pies, a food not just for Christmas, containing, as one might expect, grated apples, dried fruits, brandy and spices and a little sugar, but also chopped fresh beef suet (the fat around the kidneys of cattle) and boiled and chopped cows' tongues. During Lent, vegetable pies were popular.

In the daytime, a little food was provided for luncheon, a light meal eaten around noon and defined by Dr Samuel Johnson as 'as much food as one's hand can hold'.[26] Breakfast was served from nine or ten o'clock in the morning; they were not late risers – the Warburtons rose early, preferring to break their fast after a few hours' work. Each member of the household worked to their own schedule in the morning, so food such as kidneys, bacon and eggs were left out by the butler and footmen on top of small heaters ('chafing dishes') until around noon so they could eat when it suited.

Breakfast, luncheon, teatime and complex multi-dished dinners required a vast array of crockery for serving and display of all of the different foods and cutlery with which to eat it. Crockery became much more sophisticated, and delicate porcelain imported from China was seized upon at greatly inflated prices. This provided British potters with a gap in the market, and they diversified their earthenware to mop up a great deal of the demand. Josiah Wedgwood was the greatest innovator, because not only did he make beautiful pieces, but he unashamedly followed the British fashions of the moment, producing his highly collectable 'cauliflower-ware' and 'pineapple-ware' tea sets. The lower middle classes felt the pinch in this respect: Robert

Sharp, a schoolmaster in Yorkshire, was left somewhat depressed after feeling obliged to buy 'a dozen china cups and saucers' and accompanying paraphernalia even though he had nowhere to display it and had to store them in a basket, commenting 'if this be not encouraging manufacturers I know not what is!'[27] Some were useful such as the innovative gravy jugs containing a cylinder into which hot water could be poured, preventing the gravy from congealing into an unappetising mass.[28]

The kitchen was positioned well away from the dining room so that its clatter, cooking smells and shouts would not be detected in that island of serenity that was the Warburtons' dining room. This was particularly enforced during grand celebrations and dinners, each a wondrous feat of planning and coordination carried out unheard and unseen. It was hot and it was stressful, and Elizabeth was in her element, approving every dish before it was taken to table by footmen. Away from the hot ranges, sizzling spits and cursing cooks, the guests were helped to their seats by servants. 'Promiscuous' seating had recently become the standard seating arrangement, where guests sat alternately male, female, replacing the old system of seating where men and women at opposite sides of the table, as John Trusler tells us in *The Honours of the Table*:

> Custom, however, has lately introduced a new mode of seating. A gentleman and a lady sitting alternately round the table, and this, for the better convenience of a lady's being attended to, and served by the gentleman next to her. But notwithstanding this promiscuous seating, the ladies, whether above or below, are to be served in order, according to their rank or age, and after them the gentlemen, in the same manner.[29]

This new arrangement greatly improved the manners of the diners – especially the men, who had a tendency to get very drunk and boisterous.[30] Now, eating in female company, the male guests had to show restraint, tone down their language and be more inclusive in their conversation. That was the idea, anyway.

Guests sat at a beautifully laid table, decorated with cut flowers and lit by ornate candlesticks. The first course was usually already waiting for guests as they arrived, covered with cloches to prevent food from cooling too quickly or forming a skin. Small plates of biscuits and a few fresh fruits were dotted about, should anyone feel the need to nibble before the meal officially began. When everyone was sitting and ready, the cloches were removed by servants.[31] As they tucked into the first course, the butler and footmen kept diners' drinks topped up. Out of sight, a small army of servers and extra hired hands waited for the dishes to be finished, as the kitchen staff prepared the dishes for the second course. The atmosphere in the dining room was a relaxed murmur, glasses clinking as guests talked to old friends, or were introduced to new acquaintances. The silent staff, however, were on tenterhooks, because the dishes and cutlery had to be cleared, along with the tablecloth, ready to receive the second course.

At the very back of *The Experienced English Housekeeper*, Elizabeth includes some 'Directions for a Grand Table'. In the chapter, she acknowledges the stress of organising and successfully pulling off a large banquet: 'I, from long Experience, can tell what a troublesome Task it is to make a Bill of Fare to be in Propriety, and not to have Two Things of the same Kind.'[32] Before the long eighteenth century, it was perfectly agreeable to duplicate some dishes on the table. In fact, it was preferred; like their gardens, the Tudors and Stuarts preferred things symmetrically laid out. But now no two dishes could be alike, and bearing in mind each of the three courses at Elizabeth's example banquet was made up of twenty-five dishes, the complexity is eye-crossing. But Elizabeth was no charlatan; the majority of the recipes in her book had been tried and tested at Arley Hall, and she reassures the (probably befuddled and panicking) reader that it could be done: 'I have made it my Study to set out the Dinner in as elegant a Manner as lies in my Power.'

In her book, Elizabeth focuses upon a meal served in January because it is 'at that Season when Entertainments are most used and most wanted',[33] the highlight of the Christmas festivities being Twelfth Night on 5 January. It also serves to illustrate the surprising variety of ingredients available in the depths of winter, which was lucky for her, seeing as she had to organise seventy-five unique dishes for a single meal. It will come as no surprise that the table arrangement had to be meticulously planned, and the servers had to know exactly where each serving plate, dish or basket should sit.

Elizabeth provides diagrams showing the organisation of dishes for the first and second courses. The first course is made up of: mock turtle soup, broccoli, kidney beans, bottled peas, salad, house lamb, fricassee of veal, a small ham, sweetbreads, ox pallets, ducks *almonde*, boiled turkey, pigeon compote, chicken fricassee, haricot beans, beef olives, hare soup, *florindene* of rabbits, pork griskins, larded oysters, sheep's rumps and kidneys, cod sounds, French pye, lambs' ears stuffed with forcemeat and transparent soup. Several of these dishes represented what was termed 'plain cooking' i.e. roast or poached meats with vegetables and simple sauces like gravy.

Diners served each other at table and both lord and lady were expected to carve the meat for their guests. Carving was a highly regarded social skill, directly descended from the High Middle Ages when knights used the opportunity to show off their skills with a blade in a more genteel manner. A good carver was, then, chivalric, so the pressure was really on for hosts to slice their meats with deftness and restrained calm. But there was too a preference for smaller cuts of meat as the nation became 'more delicate' and more complex 'made dishes' were preferred; a French affectation, which led writer Rev. John Adams to opine in his *Curious Thoughts on the History Man* that 'the hospitality of the Anglo-Saxons was sometimes exerted in roasting an ox whole ... great joints are less in use than formerly; and in England, the enormous sirloin, formerly the pride of the nation, is now in polite families banished to the side board.'[34] Offal, such as ox palettes or giblet pie, was well represented at grand meals and had not developed the stigma it has today. No one would have batted an eye at recipes for calves' heads, pigs' trotters or lambs' guts.

To grill a Calf's Head

Wash your Calf's Head clean, and boil it almost enough, then take it up and hash one half, the other half rub over with the Yolk of an Egg, a little Pepper and Salt, strew over it Breadcrumbs, Parsley chopped small, and a little grated Lemon Peel, set it before the Fire and keep basting it all the Time to make the Froth rise; when it is a fine light Brown, dish up the Hash, and lay the grilled Side upon it.

   Blanch your Tongue, slit it down the Middle, lay it on a Soup Plate; skin the Brains, boil them with a little Sage and parsley, chop them fine, and mix them with some melted Butter [sauce], and a Spoonful of Cream, make them hot and pour them over the Tongue, serve them up, and they are a Sauce for the Head.[35]

Popular dishes were replaced with back-up dishes called 'removes', but guests did not eat some of every dish, nor were they expected to.

The centrepiece of Elizabeth's first course is mock turtle soup. Real turtle was still served at great banquets, but it was not always available, and very expensive when it did appear at market. It was therefore necessary to come up with an alternative that would be just as delicious as the real thing and so mock turtle soup was devised. The main difficulty in replicating real turtle was that the reptile's flesh was so delicious, and the various cuts of meat taken from it varied so greatly in both flavour and texture. For early versions of this soup, like that in Elizabeth's book, a calf's head was used including the tongue, ears (stuffed with forcemeat), brain and its sweetbreads (thymus glands). Other ingredients included truffles, artichokes, Madeira wine, lemon pickle, mushrooms, anchovies and Cayenne pepper.[36] Later versions such as that in Eliza Acton's 1845 cookery book, *Modern Cookery for Private Families*, various other meats were added to the calf's head such as beef shin and ham to more closely reflect the diverse flavours and textures of turtle meat.[37] Other made dishes made up part of the spectacle and theatre of the meal, though they seem both bizarre and macabre to the modern diner. Take 'Rabbits Surprised' for example:

> Take young Rabbits, skewer them and [stuff them as for roasted rabbits], when they are roasted, draw out the Jaw-bones and stick them in the Eyes to appear like Horns … stick a Bunch of Myrtle in their Mouths, and serve them up with their Livers boiled and frothed.[38]

And for 'Pigeons Transmogrified', pigeons are stuffed into hollowed-out cucumbers with heads sticking out with 'a bunch of barberries in their bills'.[39]

The second course contained a greater proportion of sweet dishes so amongst the roast woodcocks and stewed cardoons were sweetened dishes such as Snow Balls (baked apple dumplings covered in icing), transparent pudding (dried fruits and sweetmeats suspended in jelly), 'Globes of gold web with mottoes in them' and a fish pond made from jelly and flummery. There too was 'Burnt Cream', a dessert still beloved today, though it had yet to be called by its French name, *crème brûlée*, a name Elizabeth would no doubt have rolled her eyes at.

To make Burnt Cream

Boil a Pint of Cream with Sugar and a little Lemon Peel shred fine, then beat the Yolks of six and the Whites of four Eggs separately, when your Cream is cooled, put in your Eggs, with a Spoonful of Orange Flower Water and one of fine Flour, set it over the Fire, keep stirring it 'till it is thick, put it into a Dish, when it is cold, sift a Quarter of a Pound of Sugar all over, hold a hot Salamander [a type of grill] over it till it is very Brown and looks like a Glass Plate put over your Cream.[40]

In the third course, '[f]inally, the English sweet tooth was rewarded, as it had been now for a long time, with a dessert of jellies and sweetmeats and perhaps also fruits, nuts and cheese.'[41] Elizabeth suggests for a January menu four different made ices (presumably utilising the Northern English winter weather), as well as diverse dried and brandied fruits, plus nuts and olives. Outside of wintertime, there would have been a wonderful display of John Raffald's fresh forced seasonal fruit and exotics, with the pineapple sitting in all its glory in the very centre of the table.

Elizabeth really flexed her creative muscles in her table decorations that would dot the second and the dessert course: a 'Dish of Snow', poached apples covered in meringue; 'Black Caps', apples roasted dark immersed in custard ('a pretty little corner dish').[42] One of the particularly hot and dangerous jobs was the creation of spun sugar nests for banqueting tables – so hot that Elizabeth makes a very important health and safety announcement, making it plain how dangerous it could be in her introduction to Chapter VII of her book, 'Observations on making Decorations for a Table':

> When you Spin a Silver Web for a Desert [sic], always take particular Care your Fire is clear [i.e. very hot], and a Pan of Water upon the Fire, to keep the Heat from your Face and Stomach, for fear the Heat should make you faint.

It was important to make your nests over a hot, focused fire to avoid being overwhelmed by the heat because 'if you spin a whole Desert [over a small grate], you will be several Hours in spinning it.'[43] But it was in her jelly and flummery desserts – edible sculptures – that made her stand out from all others in her field at the time. Elizabeth was carrying on the tradition of the medieval subtlety course: fountains of red wine, marzipan siege towers, and the most expensive of all, sugar subtleties; huge intricate sculptures of sugar. In the sixteenth and seventeenth centuries, sugar subtleties were bought and kept for reuse or were rented out, but now sugar was cheap enough for such sweetened delights to be eaten.

Jelly and flummery were the media of choice for eighteenth-century 'subtleties'. They were made from gelatine derived from calves' feet, ground hartshorn or, on fast days, isinglass extracted from the swim bladders of sturgeon. Flummery was a sweetened dish made from the boiling of cracked oat grains in water. The resulting opaque 'stock' was strained through cloth, flavoured and sweetened. Once cool, it set to a delicate jelly.[44] Elizabeth needed her flummery to form a wobbly, quivering but ultimately stable structure, and therefore made hers from almond milk mixed with calves' foot jelly, rather like a modern blancmange or panna cotta.[45]

Many of her complex creations were almost whimsical, such as her various *trompe d'oeil* dishes (literally dishes that 'fool the eye')[46] such as her 'Hen's Nest' or 'Cribbage Cards'. Even the simplest jelly or flummery took at least two days in its preparation. Elizabeth's procedure is thus:

> Put a Gang of [four] Calf's Feet well cleaned into a Pan with six Quarts of Water, and let them boil gently 'till reduced to two Quarts [this takes around seven hours], then take out the Feet, scum off the Fat clean, and clear your Jelly from the Sediment, beat the whites of five Eggs to a Froth, then add one Pint of Lisbon, Madeira, or any pale made Wine if you choose it, then squeeze in the Juice of three Lemons; when your Stock is boiling, take three Spoonfuls of it and keep stirring it with your Wine and eggs to keep it from curdling, then add a little more Stock and still keep stirring it, and then put it in the Pan and sweeten it with Loaf Sugar to your Taste, a Glass of French Brandy will keep the Jelly from turning blue in the frosty Air. Put in the outer Rind of two Lemons and let it boil one Minute all together, and pour it into a Flannel Bag and let it run [undisturbed for several hours] into a Bason, and keep pouring it back gently into the Bag, 'till it runs clear bright, then set your Glasses under the Bag and cover it lest Dust gets in.[47]

This was then flavoured and coloured further, depending upon the dish or decoration in question. For 'Eggs and Bacon in Flummery' one had to go through this rigmarole:

Take a Pint of stiff Flummery and make Part of it a pretty pink Colour with [bruised cochineal], dip a Potting-pot in cold Water and pour in Red Flummery the thickness of a Crown Piece, then the same of White Flummery and another of Red, and twice the thickness of White Flummery at the top; one Layer must be stiff and cold before you pour on another, then take five Tea Cups and put a large Spoonful of White Flummery into your Potting-pots on the Back of a Plate wet with cold water, cut your Flummery into thin Slices, and lay them on a China Dish, then turn out your Flummery out of the Cups on the Dish, and take a Bit out of the Top of every one, and lay in half a preserved Apricot, it will confine the Syrup from discolouring the Flummery and make it like the Yolk of a poached Egg: Garnish with Flowers.[48]

All of that work for 'a pretty Corner Dish for Dinner'.[49] Other complex delights include 'Gilded Fish', 'a Desert Island', 'a Floating Island' and the 'Moon and Stars in Jelly'. But her showstopper piece was 'Solomon's Temple in Flummery'.[50] The dessert 'required a specialist mould so would have been the invention of a potter rather than a cook', but it is in *The Experienced English Housekeeper* the recipe first appears in print. The moulds were complex with intricate domes and stairs, though they would become simpler over time.[51] Once Elizabeth, and her book, became the phenomena they were, recipes (often plagiarised with glaring typos) appeared in print regularly for several decades – imitated but never bettered:

Make a Quart of stiff Flummery, divide it into three Parts, make one Part a pretty pink Colour with a little Cochineal bruised fine, and steeped in French Brandy, scrape one Ounce of Chocolate very fine, dissolve it in a little strong Coffee, and mix it with another Part of your Flummery to make it a light Stone Colour, the last Part must be White, then wet your Temple Mould, and fix it in a Pot to stand even, then fill the Top of the Temple with Red Flummery to the steps, and the four Points with White, then fill it up with Chocolate Flummery, let it stand 'till next Day, then loosen it round with a Pin and shake it loose very gently, but don't dip your Mould in warm Water, it will take off the Gloss, and spoil the Colour; when you turn it out, stick a small Sprig or a flower stalk down from the Top of every point, it will strengthen them and make it look pretty, lay round it Rock Candy sweetmeats.[52]

These complex 'gargantuan meals' were the ultimate in refinement and home entertainment. And in this theatre, Elizabeth was the director: working the hardest and agonising over tiny details, but when the show was ready, she made sure she was unseen and let the lavishly laid table and its victuals speak for itself. It was about more than good dining too: '[t]able decorations and the design of particular dishes gave further opportunities for hosts to display an interest in imperial topics and distant places to provoke conversation. Table décor ... revealed hosts' tastes', not only that, hosts knew how difficult and time-consuming the foods were to make, 'providing further authenticity' and points of discussion,[53] creating an immersive experience for guests while Elizabeth, the creator, worked tirelessly with her staff out of sight and earshot in the hot, noisy kitchens.

Chapter 4

Fennel Street (1763–1766)

... if any one part of the country was in the van of the great change it was the small circle of Britain which had Manchester as its centre. (John Sanders)[1]

Elizabeth and John arrived in Manchester in the autumn of 1763 and immediately occupied their premises on Fennel Street in the centre of Manchester's vibrant town centre. They had left Arley Hall and the security servitude had provided them, but before leaving Cheshire, they both drew out their final annual wages, and any additional savings, to start their new lives as free citizens of Manchester. In 1760, Manchester was not yet a city (that wouldn't happen officially until 1847) but it had become a world leader in cotton manufacture, though, like the rest of England, its foundations were built on wool, and to a lesser degree linen and silk. It was a town on the up; in the seventeenth century, it was already the 'fairest, best builded, quickest, and most populous town of Lancashire' because of its early adoption of cotton working.[2] By the time the Raffalds arrived, the town had a rapidly increasing population of around 20,000 people.[3] Its textile industry was made up of many independent, usually filial groups, founded on a headstrong, antifeudal work ethic, meaning Manchester 'was free from guild restrictions, and was the home of many merchants who gave employment to the cottage industries'.[4]

In 1763, even though the coal-fuelled, steam-powered industrial revolution had not yet infiltrated the textiles trade, enough was produced for merchants and a few shrewd families to make tidy profits. In Elizabeth's 1772 *Directory of Manchester and Salford*, 25 per cent of listed businesses specialised in some aspect of textile manufacture; be it dyer, cutter, yarn maker, loom and shuttle maker or cotton merchant.[5] This does not include the many businesses that used their products, such as dressmakers, tailors and upholsterers. Elizabeth lists eighty whisters supplying Manchester with bleached linen, cotton and yarn, and in her 'LIST of the Country

TRADESMEN, with their Warehouses in MANCHESTER', almost all of the 119 names dealt in textiles; there were just four exceptions, two who dealt in paper and two that were not specified.

Raw cotton came from Britain's ever-growing empire and trading links. The work of processing raw cotton in textiles was difficult, time-consuming and took part in ramshackle, unsanitary conditions:

> Most of the cloth came from little family units, hunched together over primitive, hand-made machines in low-ceilinged, ill-lit rooms. It could ... take weeks ... to make a useful length of cloth, carding the raw cotton fibre into strands, spinning ... threads of yarn and twisting them ... on the flyer ... finally weaving usually performed by the head of the family. To him fell the laborious task. Slow processes all of them, and processes that made everyone ... yearn for speed and efficiency.[6]

Despite this, people moved into towns such as Manchester for this sort of work; their only option after the dismantling of the feudal system in the countryside made them 'free' and obliged tenants to pay rents many could not afford. The 'landless and the unemployed' joined the would-be domestic servants and drifted to the towns at the start of the great exodus which was to transform England from a rural to an urban society.[7] Anyone who could not afford to live on their meagre wages or found themselves surplus to requirements ended up on the streets or in the overcrowded workhouses.[8]

Manchester itself was relatively small and surrounded by countryside, so it was possible to purchase livestock, and there were attempts at keeping pigs and cows in the urban environment. Some families managed to keep a pig, a very efficient way to turn kitchen waste into edible protein; all good in theory, but often they were allowed to run free – or escaped – spreading chaos, eating almost anything into which they could poke their snouts. There was a similar problem with milk. Of course, some milk produced in the countryside could be fermented into cheese, but for fresh milk, the only option was to keep cows in towns inside buildings, there being insufficient space outside for them. In the first edition of her directory, Elizabeth lists five cow-keepers.[9] The poor heifers' lives were miserable and each one typically 'stood hock-deep in filth and lived in an appalling stench until she ceased to give milk. Then she went to the butcher's shambles.'[10]

The diet of these working-class neo-urbanites degraded greatly compared to their countryside contemporaries; without their own land, the varied peasant diet was becoming increasingly unachievable and the costs of wholemeal bread, ale, fresh milk and local cheese were ever-rising. The lack of space for anything other than a cauldron, and perhaps a bakestone, to use for cooking restricted them further, though some sent pies, hotpots or casseroles to the local baker's shop to be baked for a small fee. A huge variety of fresh fruit and vegetables were available, however, many of which were sold by the Raffald brothers on Market Place, but the vast majority of the working classes could not afford to purchase much beyond onions and root vegetables. Later, sustaining beer and ale would be exchanged in favour of poor-quality tea, sweetened by molasses. There would be repercussions: rickets and scurvy were commonplace, not only in Manchester but around the country, though it was felt most keenly in the northern English industrial towns.[11]

In Elizabeth's own lifetime, cotton imports into Manchester had swelled 150 per cent from 701 metric tonnes in 1730, to 1,755 tonnes in 1764. New technologies had vastly increased output. In 1733, John Kay's flying shuttle increased weaving rates so much the spinners couldn't keep up with demand. It would take thirty years before the spinning jenny would even things out, just as Elizabeth and John were settling into Manchester life. In 1765, the first weaving factory was opened by a Mr Gartside; others followed, of course, and the profits made by such men similarly exploded, the value of their cotton goods increasing from £13,524 in 1730 to £200,254 in 1764, a *fifteen*-fold increase.[12] So when Elizabeth set up shop, Manchester was well on its way to becoming a fully-fledged factory town, and the working poor were having to ditch their cottage industries to work in large factories.

The people of Manchester rioted at the introduction of the spinning jenny, knowing it had the potential to put many skilled employees and cottages industries out of work; they rioted in 1763 when corn prices were set too high; and did the same after a spate of overzealous 'military floggings'.[13] They knew the importance of good working conditions and humane treatment by their 'superiors'. They also knew, however, that all their superiors had at the forefront of their mind were their profits. Before the 1760s, textile workers had actually improved the working conditions of their underlings a great deal. Work began at six o'clock in the morning, but they had access to a heated back parlour, were given a hot breakfast at seven o'clock, two tea breaks, an hour for lunch and were allowed to leave at four o'clock to attend church.[14]

But this dignity would be stripped from the skilled weaver or spinner as their skills became redundant with increasing mechanisation, and with fewer staff to manage, factory owners stepped back from the work floor, leaving overseers to keep their wretched workforce toiling for thirteen hours a day. '[T]he magnates of the cotton world lived in rose-knotted, Georgian country houses … they looked out on a pleasant landscape of undulating turf backed by woods; only the rear windows gave onto the black, unlovely prospect of the mills, their reason for existence.'[15] From the factory owners' perspective, their workers were inferior to their machines because, as the engineer James Nasmyth observed a century later, 'machines never got drunk; their hands never shook from excess; they were never absent from work; they did not strike for wages; they were unfailing in their accuracy and regularity, while producing the most delicate or ponderous portions of mechanical structures.'[16] Employers' language reflected this shift in the relationship between worker and factory owner; the men, women and children employed, who were once called 'souls' were now merely 'hands';[17] the soul no longer a consideration. For those who had settled in Manchester from the countryside, their old way of life must have quickly become but a distant memory, their decision to move – or the necessity – viewed with regret. And of course, for those born in the town, it was the only life they would ever know, and '[a] child born at the start of that century into a cotton worker's family was conceived, raised and worn out before his time and died, in misery and wretchedness.'[18] This world of rich and poor, of struggles and riches, fancy eating and food poverty was the world Elizabeth would inhabit for the rest of her life.

Fennel Street was a bustling main street made up of a mixture of squat medieval wattle and daub buildings, three- or four-storey Tudor timber-framed structures, and a peppering of lanky modern brick constructions. It was situated adjacent to the ancient Collegiate Church of Christ – the site would eventually become home to Manchester Cathedral when the town became a city – it was close to the apple market, and a stone's throw away from the River Irwell, the dividing line between the twin towns, Manchester and Salford. To the south was the Shambles; small, cramped streets that made Fennel Street spacious by comparison. There was a variety of businesses in the area, but 'of particular interest to Elizabeth there was no shop that offered anything which could rival what she was about to offer; fine food and confectionery, table decorations and a supply of servants to fill the needs of men of thrusting ambition, new wealth, and unencumbered money.'[19]

We do not know what type of building Elizabeth moved into, but we can safely assume it was not small; the businesses she ran required space: there was the shop floor, storage space for ingredients and her produce, kitchens and living space for herself and John. That she also rented the spacious cellars to other businesses surely meant that she was not residing in a tiny wattle and daub affair. Living in and amongst the densely packed streets and buildings couldn't be more different to the pastoral splendour of Arley Hall, but Fennel Street was in a good location and the building gave her the space to get the wheels of her enterprise in motion while living within her means. Life on Fennel Street was unglamorous and unromantic, but it certainly was not a step back.

Elizabeth wasted no time in carving out her niche: with more people better off, and the already wealthy even richer, she had seen that Manchester's food culture simply wasn't up to the task of providing for these people, and she knew it would only be a matter of time before someone else came along to offer a similar service. Elizabeth, of course, knew every aspect of catering and cooking for almost any number of people, and she could advise gentlemen and ladies, or their staff, on the best foods appropriate both to season and budget. She hit the ground running with her fancy French dishes, impressive hot and cold roasted or poached joints, delicate pastries and showstopping table decorations.

Elizabeth could see there were more people with more money, and although their homes became more luxurious, the homes of the poor had made 'little or no progress since medieval times'.[20] There was a gap in the market; Manchester may not have been the stylish York or Bath, but there were plenty of *nouveau riche* hoping to climb the social ladder with the aim of becoming landed gentry. Such a venture required substantial capital investment to pull off, but it was fairly common for ex-servants to invest their money in this way; the most popular role for women was to become the landlady of an inn, lodging house or tavern.[21] There is no evidence that anyone invested any money to aid Elizabeth in her enterprise, but it certainly was not unheard of for ex-employers to invest in their outgoing servants' business ventures.

Elizabeth set herself up to work straight away, her first advertisement in Joseph Harrop's *Manchester Mercury* appearing on 22 November 1763, two months after she and John moved to Manchester. The notice primarily advertised her register office, but tagged at the end was this: '[s]he returns her most cordial Thanks for the Cold Entertainments, Hot French Dinners, Confectionaries, &c.' Her pickled and potted meat and fish, such as Newcastle salmon, were particularly popular.[22]

To pickle Salmon the Newcastle Way

Take a Salmon about twelve Pounds, gut it, then cut off the Head, and cut it a-cross in pieces if you please, but don't split it, scrape the Blood from the Bone, and wash it well out, then tie it a-cross each Way … set on your Fish Pan, with two Quarts of Water, and three of strong Beer, half a Pound of Bay Salt, and one Pound of Common Salt, when it boils scum it well, then put in as much Fish as your Liquor will cover, and when it is enough take it carefully out, lest you strip off the Skin, and lay it on Earthen Dishes … let it stand 'till the next Day, put it into Pots, add to the Liquor three Quarts of strong Beer Alegar [malt vinegar], half an Ounce of Mace [and] of Cloves and Black Pepper, one Ounce of Long Pepper, two Ounces of White Ginger sliced, boil them well together half an Hour, then pour it boiling hot up your fish, when cold cover it well with strong brown paper. – This will keep a whole Year.[23]

This first appearance in the local newspaper also hailed the beginning of a successful professional relationship with publisher Joseph Harrop: she would go on to advertise in the *Mercury* throughout her life, and he would go on to publish the first edition of her cookery book.

Many of the foods she produced for dinner parties were suitable for retail and wholesale too, so her premises doubled as a supplier of her products and good quality ingredients. From her premises, Elizabeth catered for almost every aspect of life: the hungry man on the street requiring a hand-sized pie or pasty for lunch; the lady needing a selection of cakes for an understated yet well-stocked teatime; cold cuts for those smaller homes unable to produce every dish themselves; right up to the opulent tables groaning with food and dotted with spun sugar nests and teetering jelly and flummery creations.

This was difficult work: she had to produce the preserves, relishes and pickles in house. Her first major success was portable soup. Though it had appeared in cookery books from the seventeenth century, Elizabeth seems to have been the first to produce it commercially. She tells us that it 'is a very useful Soup to be kept in Gentlemen's Families, for by pouring a Pint of boiling Water on one Cake, and a little Salt, it will make a good Bason of Broth.' Her recipe for it shows the scales at which she was working:

> To make Portable Soup for travellers
>
> Take three large Legs of Veal, and one of Beef, the lean Part of Half a Ham, cut them into small Pieces, put a Quarter of a Pound of Butter at the Bottom of a large Caldron, then lay in the Meat and Bones, with four Ounces of Anchovies, two Ounces of Mace, cut off the green Leaves of five or six Heads of Celery, wash the Heads quite clean, cut them small, put them in, with three large Carrots cut thin, cover the Caldron close and set it over a moderate Fire; when you find the Gravy begins to draw ... put Water in to cover the Meat, set it on the Fire again, and let it boil slowly for four Hours ... then strain the Gravy ... let it boil gently ... 'till it looks like thick Glew; you must take great Care when it is near enough that it don't burn; put in Chyan [Cayenne] Pepper to your Taste, then pour it on flat Earthen Dishes a Quarter of an Inch thick and let it stand 'till the next Day, and cut it out with round Tins ... and set them in the Sun to dry ... The longer it is kept the better.[24]

With the catering arm of her business, Elizabeth quickly got to know much of the middle classes and Manchester elite and saw how they struggled to find hard-working and reliable staff of their own. No doubt when Elizabeth turned up at their houses with her own staff in tow, she noticed the vacuum of capable staff, and they no doubt quizzed Elizabeth as to whether she knew of any good workers looking for employment, or were thinking of leaving the service of another. Houses needed staffing, and there were plenty of folk – desirous and less so – looking for work. It used to be that anyone moving to an unfamiliar part of the country with few or no connections could find employment at a country fair suitably equipped with a token of their trade (a broom for a chambermaid or a wooden spoon for a cook) or a coloured ribbon (blue for a maid and red for a cook).

Such an approach was impossible in the cramped, swirling maelstrom of citizens in a populous city or large industrial town. Register offices provided 'a place where servants seeking work were introduced to employers seeking servants'[25] and were an early form of a modern temping agency. The concept of the register office was the brainchild of novelist Henry Fielding and his brother in 1751. They noticed that 'in Proportion to the Opulence of any Society, the Wants of its Members will be multiplied; and secondly, the more numerous its Members, the less Likelihood will there be that any of these Wants should remain unsupplied'; and that '[i]n large and populous Cities, and wide extended Communities, it is most profitable that every human Talent is dispersed somewhere or other among the members [but] the Largeness of the Society itself makes finding those people more difficult.'[26]

The system was simple: an annual or monthly fee was paid by both parties. For servants, it was a chance to appear in the register's books, and for employers a chance to gain access to those books. Register offices advertised extensively in local newspapers, a much more efficient and cheaper option than the alternative of advertising in newspapers oneself. Those running the office would vet individuals keen to establish themselves on their books and check they had a testimonial from their previous employer, reducing the risk of gaining a lazy or untrustworthy worker; that was the theory, anyway, but it was an employee's market. 'The number of Masters and Mistresses who are in Want of good Servants in every Capacity, is infinitely superior to the Number of good Servants out of Place'[27] and it was the register offices' job to sort the wheat from the chaff.

Elizabeth realised that Manchester needed a register office and there was enough call to warrant her to sit down and plan out a scheme to create one. Elizabeth's November announcement in the *Mercury* declared:

> By particular Desire of many Ladies and Gentlemen in this Town and Neighbourhood, E. RAFFALD, At her House in Fennel Street, has open'd A Public REGISTER-OFFICE, For supplying Families with Servants of all Denominations, and Servants with Places.

It was a simple set-up that was probably based on Seth Agur's own model: 'any Person may be supply'd with a Servant of Character, for any Place … for one Shilling', and 'any Servant may stand in the Books two Months, and have a chance of what Places are on the List … for one Shilling.' It did come with one important caveat, however:

> No Servant will be entered in the Books without a Character [reference], which must be sign'd by the Master or Mistress of Credit they have served, – and for this Purpose she has printed Characters, which every person will be required to get so signed, on their first Application for a Place.

And if the reader was unsure of Elizabeth's credentials, she provided her own 'character':

> As Mrs. Raffald has many Years had the Direction of all Sorts of Servants in Noblemen's and Gentlemen's Families, and has a Correspondence in most of such Families in this Neighbourhood, she presumes to hope she has many Qualifications for this Business…

One great difficulty register offices had to overcome was the incredibly specific and disparate skills asked for by employers, the reason being that many just wanted just one employee to fulfil the roles the housewife, the young bachelor, or perhaps their other single employee, could not. For example, one household required a 'Livery Servant who has been used to wait at Table, and knows something of Horses, and if he has any Knowledge of Gardening it will be the more agreeable', another 'a woman-servant in a Gentleman's Family that can cook plain Roast and Boil'd, and manage Three Cows'.[28] For those who could only afford one member of staff, the poor maid-of-all-work cooked and shopped, fetched water, and cleaned and titivated the house in a never-ending cycle of work.

With all of its domestic staff, Manchester was becoming more like York every day; indeed, there was enough wealth to warrant a small season with races and various other forms of entertainment including theatre. One company put on a farce by playwright Joseph Reed entitled *The Register Office*. It was lowest common denominator stuff, satirising some of the less desirable register offices, and their managers and clientele. The lead female part was Miss Marjorie Morningside, a stereotyped dour Yorkshire woman, complete with thick accent, who was looking for work as a housekeeper. It turns out that, unbeknownst to her, the register office to which she had signed was an establishment where 'the good Trade of Pimping is carried on with great Success'. In the final moments of the play, the lead male character, Mr Harwood, announces, 'I should be apt to conclude, from the Trick, Villainy, and Chicanery I have seen practised with this Hour, that none but a Fool or a Knave would ever set food within its Walls.'[29] The erroneous connections folk could make to Elizabeth and her register office were palpable, and the crass characterisation of the Yorkshire housekeeper was too close for Elizabeth to bear. This plotline didn't come from nowhere; many register offices had gained a poor reputation and 'did not enjoy the confidence of the public', taking money for non-existent places and forging testimonials, but the 'more flagrant malpractice of which some register offices were undoubtedly guilty [of] was procurement for prostitution.'[30]

Elizabeth was livid and worried in equal measure that mud might stick to her burgeoning reputation and business; many of her clients who made use of both her register office and catering business would have been in attendance, and if not, they would have heard about it soon enough.[31] She was probably worried too about folk making the spurious assumption that she could be the madam at the helm of a prostitution ring because the foods for which she was becoming famous in the region – those jelly and flummery creations – were often served in brothels and seedy jelly houses 'for reasons about which one can only speculate'.[32] Anxious to ensure her reputation remained fully intact, or perhaps because she heard the wagging of tongues, Elizabeth placed an announcement in the *Manchester Mercury* assuring everyone that she was trustworthy and that everything was above board, reminding the good people of Manchester exactly what they *would* get for their shilling. Hesitant to appear she wasn't protesting too much, she made sure it was 'nothing too obvious', placing it below an advertisement more typical of Elizabeth for cold meats and brawn:

> As several of Mrs. Raffald's Friends in the Country have
> mistook her Terms and Designs of her REGISTER OFFICE,

She begs Leave to inform them that she supplies Families with
Servants, for any Place at One shilling each; and Servants with
Places for One Shilling each.[33]

It was extremely canny of Elizabeth to create a register office for
Manchester, and it is testament to her entrepreneurial nature and ability
to form professional relationships quickly and with many types of people.
And both office and shop were most profitable: in August 1766, Elizabeth
travelled to Arley Hall to visit Lady Betty and deliver food and laundry. To
get there, Elizabeth travelled in a new post chaise – a light carriage fitted
with sprung suspension and therefore a much lighter and more comfortable
way to travel – and they did not come cheap. There is an entry in Arley's
granary book from this time that shows Elizabeth's horses had been fed
and kept in the stables, and that she was the only person outside of the
Warburton family to receive the privilege of doing so that year.[34]

Chapter 5

Market Place (1766–1772)

Elizabeth quickly outgrew her premises on Fennel Street, business was booming, and she and John had started a family; she had given birth to Sarah in 1765 and Emma in 1766. The family moved a few streets south to a larger property on Market Place, part of the cramped and claustrophobic Shambles area of Manchester in the August of 1766. There were several benefits to moving: most immediate was the size of the new premises; the streets may have been tighter, but her new shop was larger and it enabled her to offer a greater variety of foodstuffs, still leaving adequate space to keep the register office going and to rent her cellars to other local businesses.

Market Place also offered a prime location: it sat adjacent to the market square and the Shambles, putting her at the very fulcrum of trade in the town where a whole host of stalls and sellers offering local, national and far-flung exotic produce, including the Raffalds brothers' stall, which was now almost on her own doorstep. She was also situated close to the offices and printing house of Joseph Harrop, publisher and editor of the *Manchester Mercury*. She was in the midst of the throng: busy streets filled with all classes and sorts of people, and the main draw was Manchester's principal inn, the Bull's Head. Aside from generating a great deal of passing trade for Elizabeth, the proprietor of the Bull's Head also used Elizabeth's catering services for the frequent high-class dinner parties and functions held there.[1] The move also put her closer to fashionable Deansgate, King Street and St Ann's Square popular with the upper classes, doctors and physicians. Market Place was unfortunately bombed and destroyed during an air raid in the Second World War.

Elizabeth had built a reputation based upon skill, knowledge, hard work and honesty; but now, with more space, she could add several more strings to her bow, managing to cement herself into the very fabric of both Manchester business and society. In the six years she would occupy these premises at Market Place, she would finance two local trade newspapers, set up a cookery and finishing school for young ladies, meticulously produce at great effort Manchester's first trade directory, and write the first edition of her bestselling and influential book *The Experienced English Housekeeper*.

Elizabeth wasted no time advertising the wider range of goods she could now offer; along with established products, there were pickled walnuts, boiled tripe, coffee, tea and chocolate, and a range of 'confectionery goods as good and as cheap as in London' including mangoes, dry and wet sweetmeats, fruit cakes for weddings and christenings and macaroons.[2] Living adjacent to the market square was especially advantageous when she needed expensive ingredients that were high in demand but low in availability like sturgeon. She acquired one and delivered it to the Warburtons at Arley Hall on 29 December 1770; there is a receipt in the Arley Hall archives for 'Mrs. Raffald's Bill for Sturgeon'. It cost them a hefty 14s 2d.[3]

She must have taken full advantage of her proximity to the Raffald brothers' produce too, no doubt receiving good rates from them as family. John's brothers ran two stalls in the marketplace beautifully laid out with an immense range of fruits and vegetables. James was the second eldest brother and George the youngest. They 'kept the only seed shop in Manchester at that day, at the bottom of Smithy Door, on the side next to Deansgate, and nearly opposite the shop of Mr. Brereton the druggist'. Keeping these businesses supplied were their 'very extensive' market gardens, a short walk across the River Irwell in Salford, a journey of mere minutes. 'These gardens are said to have extended from his house near the workhouse and from Garden Lane ... all along the southerly side of Greengate, as far as Gravel Lane.' The area was dubbed Paradise by locals.

James Raffald was quiet and stalwart, a very different character to George, who was 'irascible, "swearing and tearing" [but] much respected for his integrity and hospitality.' George lived a few miles south in Millgate, Stockport, next to its marketplace; Millgate had been home to the Raffalds for 'two centuries' and even more gardens and nurseries were located there.[4]

Elizabeth didn't put all of her eggs in one basket though, and sourced fruit and vegetables from John's ex-employer Perfects of Pontefract, as well as trusted Arley suppliers Caldwell's of Knutsford, and the renowned Pinkerton of Wigan. The choice was staggering: Pinkerton alone proffered a 'magnificent collection of fruit, more than 120 varieties of apples, 14 different apricots, 24 different cherries, 49 different peaches, 68 pears,

38 plums, two quinces and 30 vines.'[5] Horticulturalists like the Perfects and the Raffalds were able to provide towns and cities with just as much variety as countryside manors, offering the same forced fruits and vegetables and hothouse exotics. It was a time of unparalleled variety and choice, for those who could afford it. And not everyone could; there is one story regarding Elizabeth, the Raffald brothers' stall on Market Place, a woman and an expensive cucumber that demonstrates this fact. John Harland recounts the tale:

> one day, when the wife of one of the brothers was attending the stall, she was accosted by a poor woman, who asked the price of a fine cucumber. Satisfied that the woman could not afford to buy such a luxury, she rather curtly named its price, 7s. 6d. [90p]; and the woman went away dejected. About an hour afterwards she was again at the stall, banging about, and at length she again asked the price of the cucumber. Somewhat annoyed at being thus teazed [sic] a second time by the same person, the stallkeeper answered her angrily, 'Why, woman, I told you before.' Again the poor woman was creeping away, when Mrs. Raffald seeing that she was *enceinte* [pregnant], at once understood the matter, called her back, gave her the longed-for dainty, and dismissed her, amidst expressions of the most fervent gratitude.[6]

Similar choice and volume applied to other foods as well, and Elizabeth was able to purchase locally and nationally produced meat such as beef and veal, or lamb and mutton, all year round. The agricultural revolution had been well under way for decades and now vegetables could be grown and stored in such amounts that animals (as well as the poor) could be provided with vegetables such as turnips throughout the winter months. No longer did all but the breeding stock have to be slaughtered in early winter because of a lack of fodder. This arm of the agricultural revolution came out of necessity; the population of England was increasing from a shade under six million individuals in 1700 to over nine million in 1800.

The problem was that there were all of these extra mouths to feed but fewer hands in the countryside to produce it. Such feats required the ingenuity typical of the age: there was Townshead's four-field crop rotation system with its focus on brassicas to feed overwintering livestock; Tull's horse-drawn seed drills that could plant large amounts of seeds quickly and uniformly; and Bakewell's revolutionary ideas surrounding selective breeding. Application of his methods saw the weight of a sheep carcass double, and specialisation of domestic breeds with cattle artificially selected for either milk yield or their meat. Food staples such as wheat, oats and beef were produced in the countryside and sent to towns, initiating the modern world's disconnect with its food, fuelling the stomachs of the people, and therefore fuelling industry itself. Now the working classes could fill up on porridge, bread, bacon and onions, but would have accessed only a tiny proportion of the variety potentially available to them in the market stalls and shops of towns such as Manchester.

Much of Elizabeth's food was high-end and required expensive ingredients, but she could buy in bulk and transform them into anything from mushroom ketchup to fruit cakes, via brawns and potted tongues, all of which could be purchased in any amount, large or small. The goods Elizabeth sold and displayed in her shop are representative of a time when the scale of consumption really cranked up. The long eighteenth century turned the English into a nation of consumers; capitalism had reared its ugly head, and it used the ideas of civility and social betterment (and all of its accompanying anxieties) as a mechanism to propel itself forward. One's civility and therefore one's place in society were directly correlated with the clothes one wore and the possessions one held. It was civility writ large and the beady eye of society decided whether or not one was worthy. We have seen how food was very important in this respect, but why was it so scrutinised? The reason is simple: everybody eats. Everyone needs clothes and shelter too of course, but unlike these necessities, food is fleeting: once consumed, it is gone. Also, having too much of it is wasteful or greedy; and fat, sugar and meat are expensive. It spoiled, and it required a great deal of effort, and therefore staff, to make it. Eating – or rather dining – in an indulgent manner was the ultimate sign, crass as it may seem, of social mobility, and civility.[7]

This concept applied particularly to the products of empire: sugar, tea, tobacco and to a lesser degree, coffee and chocolate. What they lacked in nutritional value, they made up in pep and the social kudos they provided the consumer. Elizabeth was selling these goods, as well as pastries and sweetmeats containing some of them, at a time when some of the working classes were just finding a way to purchase these goods, albeit in very small amounts. In the late seventeenth and early eighteenth centuries, working families struggled to afford sufficient staple foods and any luxuries were sporadic and slight, bought only on the rare occasion there was a small amount of cash left over after the essentials had been paid for. However, with the evermore efficient and upscaled efforts of the colonies reducing the prices of the 'ingestibles' of the empire,[8] a whole new demographic of people, who seemed to choose aspiration over nutrition, appeared to those in the business of food and drink. Now almost everyone consumed at least some tea and sugar, whether it be a five-kilogram sugarloaf, a few ounces of light brown sugar or a pot of treacle, and grocers and merchants began to stratify their offerings and appeal to a range of price points. At the turn of the eighteenth century, for example, there were two types of tea available; by the middle, there were nine.[9]

Being a skilled baker and confectioner, Elizabeth was able to transform small amounts of luxury ingredients, such as refined sugars, dried and candied fruits, and essential oils, that she bought in bulk, mixed with cheaper wheat flour and lard, into affordable cakes and biscuits, as well as more fancy confectionery and desserts. Such goods needed showing off and for the first time, shops such as Elizabeth's created beautiful, opulent and attractive window displays, showing the passing clientele the very best of what the interior had to offer, including her fantastically decorated wedding and christening cakes, whilst inside was a range of prices and quality.[10] One example is the Eccles cake, a sweetmeat of which Elizabeth has been recognised as the inventor, though they were yet to have been given their regional distinction. She called them 'Sweet Patties':

> Take the Meat of a boiled Calf's Foot, two large Apples, and one Ounces of candied Orange, chop them very small, grate half a Nutmeg, mix them with the Yolk of an Egg, a spoonful of French Brandy, and a quarter of a Pound of Currants clean washed and dried, make a good puff Paste, roll it in different Shapes, as the fried ones, and fill them the same Way; you may either fry or bake them.[11]

Calf's feet notwithstanding, all the elements are there: dried and candied fruits mixed with spices and wrapped and rolled in puff pastry. The inclusion of apples and the meat from a calf's feet show it is a kind of mince pie filling.

Elizabeth sold these patties from her shop; she did not make her fortune from selling them, but somebody else did. Apparently,

> [a] worthy female servant leaving her, and going to settle at Eccles, Mrs. Raffald made her a present of the recipe for this dainty, which made the recipient's fortune, and that of her niece, who succeeded her in the business, – many thousands of pounds having, we are told, been realised by this sweet little monopoly.[12]

A rare example of Elizabeth missing a trick.

***

A year after moving into Market Place, Elizabeth opened 'a normal school for young ladies', a place where young women who expected to marry well and become housekeepers, or rather the employers of housekeepers, could be taught a comprehensive set of practical skills. Elizabeth

> was in the habit of receiving as pupils, paying handsome premiums, the daughters of the principal local families; they attended the cuisine of the establishment, and received lessons in cookery, confectionary, &c. They were taught how to pluck poultry, to skin hares, &c. no less than how to cook them afterwards, and to carve them when placed upon the table.[13]

An article in the *Manchester Guardian* in 1927 revealed that Elizabeth was not the only individual in the vicinity 'grounding young ladies' in these important skills. Mrs Raffald was in direct competition with a certain Mrs Blomily, who 'provided accomplishments indispensable to any young lady who wished to make a profitable marriage'.[14] Elizabeth's 1773 directory reveals there was Mr Blomily – a cook – residing at, and working from, premises at 'Fox Entry' which sat perpendicular to Market Place;[15] it is highly likely that this was also the headquarters of his wife's school.

> Mrs. Blomily seems to have challenged Mrs. Raffald's claim to be the arbiter of Manchester cooking. She taught 'the polite

accomplishment of killing turkeys, ducks and sucking pigs, of making mock turtle, apple pasties, mince pies, and fish sauces, as well as the art of keeping steady in their paces, by the help of a short whip, the little bandy-legged dogs who were condemned to the treadmill by the help of which the spits, loaded with beef, mutton, pork, poultry and game, were kept on constant rotary motion.'

She also had the edge over Elizabeth in that she taught the young women to play instruments, such as the harpsichord (such 'were the sorts of accomplishments instilled by the celebrated Mrs. Blomily') and to dance. She employed at least two dancing masters, who, aside from teaching them the subtleties of restrained, ladylike public dancing, regularly took the young women out for walks 'to inure them to the stare so liable to overcome young ladies when they came out, on their first introduction to a crowded assembly.' Eager to match Mrs Blomily, Elizabeth also employed a dance master, and it is highly likely he worked at both schools, there being only two dancing masters, both listed in Elizabeth's 1772 directory – Messrs Francis Cleavin and Peter Fischar – 'doubtless there was some pretty hard staring as the products of the Blomily treatment and the products of the Raffald treatment passed one another on opposite sides of Deansgate.'[16]

It seems to have been Elizabeth's mission to match everything in Mrs Blomily's curriculum and there seems to be an element of self-importance, perhaps even arrogance, to Elizabeth's character displayed here because with her shop, catering business and the register office, she was already head and shoulders above the other businesswomen in the vicinity. She was also compiling her cookery book at this time, which would be published in 1769, so she didn't need to start a school in direct competition with another.

Another success was, of course, *The Experienced English Housekeeper*. The first edition quickly sold out, prompting a second edition to be pressed in 1771. With book, school, shop, catering business and register office, Elizabeth found herself in a very good financial position, and that is reflected in the very fancy luxury items she began and buy and sell in the shop. Her nephew, Joshua Middleton, a talented perfumer, who had none other than King George III, King of England, Scotland and Hanover on his books, supplied her with a whole range of high-class toiletries unmatched in their quality and variety.[17] In one advertisement in the *Manchester*

Mercury on 28 May 1771, Elizabeth 'Begs Leave to acquaint the Publick, and her Friends in particular, That she has just received a large Assortment of PERFUMERIES' with 'PERFUM'D WATERS' like the 'Finest Honey Water' and 'Eau de Bergamot', 'French Soap', 'Tooth Powder', 'Lip Salve' and 'Royal Marble Wash Balls'.[18]

Clashes with Mrs Blomily aside, Elizabeth was now well-regarded amongst almost all parts of society: servants, working families, the middle classes, and the merchants and upper classes residing both within and without the town. It was at this point that Elizabeth began to acquire a reputation as a philanthropist when she invested heavily in the *Manchester Mercury*, which, for reasons that are unclear, was under threat of bankruptcy. The paper was essential to her own and many others' livelihoods, so whilst this was not an act of complete altruism, it was greatly beneficial to Manchester as a whole that it could carry on. The *Mercury* was printed every Tuesday, the day after the London papers arrived, a strategy typical of regional newspapers of the time, and within its four pages was contained a useful mix of local news and trade information from the North-West of England and London. The readership was far-reaching; it was widely distributed throughout the region, finding its way into coffee houses and into the hands of anyone, regardless of their social standing.

Whilst running all of these businesses, Elizabeth and John also found time to grow their family. She gave birth to Grace in 1767 and then Betty in 1769, the same year she published *The Experienced English Housekeeper*. By the time the school opened in 1770 she had had Anna. Around the time Anna was born, Grace died aged three, and then in February 1771, Mary was born. This means that amongst all of her industry, Elizabeth had given birth to six daughters in seven years. How Elizabeth managed to parent children and go through the ordeal of multiple pregnancies during this time of intense work makes her feats all the more impressive and astounding; the word 'indefatigable' doesn't quite seem to do her justice.

Keen to capitalise on the success of the *Mercury*, she also funded the production of a second, competing paper, printed on the other side of the Irwell in Salford called *Prescott's Manchester Journal* in 1771. In funding these publications, she was supporting not just her own, but all of the businesses of Manchester, contributing greatly to the economic success of this most industrious of towns.[19] But then, in 1772, Elizabeth would outdo even herself and bring the business community and commerce even closer together in a way never before seen, by producing Manchester and Salford's first trade directory, a publication that collated all aspects of Manchester industry and commerce, plus useful travel information, all in an inexpensive pamphlet small enough that it 'could be slipped into the pocket'.[20]

***

Battling through the street rabble of the Shambles was Elizabeth's army of delivery boys who transported orders large and small throughout the town. These workers were mostly made up of her nephews, who had been sent to Manchester:

> A sister of Mrs. Raffald married a Mr Middlewood; they were flaxgrowers at Howden, and had twelve children, all sons; so, now and then the Yorkshire sister used to send 'a few of her lads' to be company for her Manchester sister's 'lasses', and Mrs Raffald used to put them apprentice in Manchester as soon as they reached the proper age.[21]

Calculating the most efficient routes required remarkable memory and knowledge of the towns. To aid her, and her nephews, Elizabeth drew and collated great lists and maps which proved to be indispensable. Aside from deliveries, she also needed to know from whom she could buy the best goods and ingredients, keep tabs on her client base for the catering wing of her empire, as well as the scores of houses in and around the town that she helped staff via her register office. Elizabeth had also noticed that people were becoming frustrated with just how difficult it had become to find businesses, individuals and buildings in the two towns: 'The want of a DIRECTORY for the large and commercial Town of MANCHESTER, having been frequently complained, and several useful Regulations being lately made.'[22] She knew the benefits a directory would bring, and that it was something in demand; other cities such as London and Liverpool had developed their own, and no doubt she owned copies of them and recognised that Manchester and Salford were by now complex enough to require one. No doubt she wasn't the first to have the idea, but she was the first to act upon it.

Elizabeth had her fingers in so many pies that she was now the best-connected person in the area, and it was from her vast data set that she would create the skeleton of Manchester and Salford's first trade directory, an A to Z of merchants, families, businesses and people of note in the two towns, a proto-version of the Yellow Pages of the twentieth and early twenty-first centuries. Even though her list of connections was already long and varied, the project was still a huge undertaking, a mammoth task she obviously found both tiring and tiresome, writing in the introduction to her directory: 'I have taken upon me the arduous Task of compiling a Complete Guide, for the easy finding out every Inhabitant of the least Consequence';[23] 'arduous' because she had set the bar high in its comprehensiveness, as her advertisement in the *Manchester Mercury* on 31 March 1772 clearly communicated:

> This Day is Publish'd, Price, 6d, A NEW DIRECTORY, for the Town of MANCHESTER. Containing an Alphabetical List of the Merchants, Tradesmen, and Principal Inhabitants, with the Situation of their respective Warehouses and Places of Abode. Also separate Lists of the Country Tradesmen, with their Warehouses in Manchester – Officers of the Infirmary and Lunatic Hospital – Officers of Excise – Principal Whitsters [people who bleach cloth] – Account of the Stage Coaches and Waggons, with their Days of coming in and going in – Lists of the Vessels to and from Liverpool, upon the Old Navigation, and the Duke of Bridgewater's Canal, with their Agents – Manchester Bank and Insurance Office – Justices of the Peace in and near Manchester, and the Committee for the Detection and Prosecution of Felons, of Receivers of stolen or embezzled Goods.

Due to the complexity of the task, and the fact there was constant immigration and emigration, she knew the directory was imperfect, anticipating the requirement of a second edition in her introduction to the first:

> But as the Difficulty of a private Person's knowing every one, and his Connections, without the Assistance of the People themselves, must be apparent to every one, it cannot be expected but that some Errors and omissions will appear: Any Person's Name, therefore, that may be omitted, shall, on proper Notice, be inserted in the next Edition.[24]

Despite a smattering of mistakes and a few omissions, it was a huge success. Yet another feather in her cap, demonstrating her ability to take developments and innovations that had been unleashed onto other, larger towns and cities and implement them in Manchester herself just as they were most needed, but before anyone else got in there. Perhaps with her connections with almost the entire spectrum of Manchester folk, she was the only citizen who could have realistically put it together. It is astounding that she managed to keep all of her other plates spinning as she gave this new and complex venture momentum and it is another example of her ambition and practicality of mind.

It was so successful that Elizabeth published the second edition the next year, somehow finding time to update it *and* move premises to the King's Head, Salford. It's likely that she was already correcting mistakes and adding new entries as the first edition was being published as they cropped up. However, to be sure she omitted as little as possible in her new edition, she placed a notice in the *Mercury* on 16 March 1773, asking individuals to provide their business credentials:

> A New Edition of the MANCHESTER DIRECTORY being intended to be published with all convenient speed; it is proposed, in order to make such an useful Work as correct as possible, to send proper and intelligent Persons round the Town, to take down every Name, Business and Place of Abode of every Gentlemen, Tradesman, and Shop-keeper, as well as of other whose Business or Employment has any tendency to public Notice; the Proprietor therefore humbly requests, that everyone will please to give the necessary Information to the Persons appointed, that she may be enabled to give an accurate Edition of a Work so advantageous to such a large, populous, and trading Town as this is; in the Completion of which, she can assure the Public, that no Labour or Expence shall be spared to make It worthy of their Approbation, as an easy and sufficient Directory, not only to Strangers, but likewise to the Inhabitants of the Town.

Aside from correcting errors, it was made more user-friendly with the addition of house numbers to the address. It was published on 29 June 1773 and was 50 per cent longer than the 1772 edition. Elizabeth would go on to write a third and final edition in 1781.

Elizabeth's directories offer a unique snapshot of life in Manchester in the latter half of the eighteenth century, and it is interesting to see too that there are various artisan businesses and people of note living in the towns, benefitting indirectly from the textiles industry: clock-makers, attorneys, cabinet makers, physicians and china dealers. Elizabeth also included others in competition with herself and victuallers, bakers and confectioners abound in its pages. Fascinating too is her 'Account of the Stage-Coaches, Waggons and Owners Names; where they inn; Days of coming in and going out', with destinations across the country including to the capital city on the 'London Flying Machine, by Samuel Tennant and Co.', whose speedy service got one there in just 'two Days, from the Royal-oak, Top of Market-street-lane, [it] sets out in the Summer Season on Monday, Wednesday and Friday Mornings, at One o'Clock; and comes in on Tuesday, Thursday and Saturday evenings.' In wintertime, the journey took three days.[25]

Her directories are indispensable to social historians, and they gained a great deal of interest in the mid-nineteenth century. The *Manchester Guardian* ran two articles written by John Harland regarding the benefits and relevance of the directories, one on 2 August 1843 and the other on 8 October 1845: 'The Directory list of the principal inhabitants is full of interest for the sexagenarian inhabitants, and is full of names of the ancestors of our principal merchants and manufacturers many of them in a more humble line of business.' The first article points out oddities and people of interest such as Clare Pete, a female 'clock and patent smoke-jack maker', 'Jones Samuel and Co. bankers and tea dealers' – proof positive of the huge profits that could be made in the tea trade – and 'Phoebe Byrom, milliner, Market Place'. Phoebe was a relative of the great poet John Byrom, who hailed from a family of Manchester milliners and is believed to be the inspiration for the heroine of Byrom's pastoral poem 'Colin and Phoebe'.[26]

In the second article, Harland obviously delights in seeing just how much Manchester and Salford had grown and developed in the sixty-four years since the directories' publication: 'Manchester then boasted of only two architects', he observes, '[t]here were just a score of bakers ... a dozen booksellers, stationers and bookbinders, and letterpress printers ... 4 printers (all in Salford) ... 6 cheesemongers ... 11 chemists and druggists (of whom 6 were apothecaries) ... 2 fishmongers, 59 flour dealers, 2 fruiterers.'

He relishes the inhabitants' niche occupations: the town beadle, sexton, arrow maker, gingerbread maker, coffin furniture maker and postmistress. He also remarks that 'according to the directory of that worthy mistress of the gastronomic art, Elizabeth Raffald, Manchester, contained 223 individuals classed as "nobility, gentry and clergy"' plus a good number of schools, tutors and academies.[27] Harland could see that it was from these foundations that the compact and densely populated town of Manchester had now bloomed into the modern city of trade, culture and commerce in which he worked and lived.

From the second edition of her directory, we can piece together the inhabitants of Market Place when Elizabeth moved from there to the King's Head in Salford. John Cook, 'Chymist Druggist and Seedsman' occupied the Raffalds' old premises at number twelve and her direct neighbours before her move had been linen drapers, Messrs Greenway and Phillips, and Phillip Worral, 'Peruke [wig] maker and Hair-dresser'. The occupants of Market Place are a microcosm of eighteenth-century working life: also living close by was apothecary John Walker, 'Chandler and Tythe-gatherer' Richard Wroe, shoe smith John Mellor, and John Bennet who ran the punch house. Elsewhere on the street were grocers, clock-makers, taverns, wool drapers, a hosier, an ironmonger, the Three Tuns Tavern, which was occupied by Henry Lomax the cooper and – of course – Joseph Harrop owner of the *Manchester Mercury* and publisher of the first edition of *The Experienced English Housekeeper*. The only women listed as living on Market Place in 1773 were Elizabeth Simpson, who was a 'Widow, Cook', and one Mary Berry, grocer.[28]

***

That a large cross-section of society could afford a treat once in a while did not mean that the quality of life of the working poor was in any way catching up with that of the middle and upper classes; there may have been an agricultural revolution, but even it could not buffer six years of poor weather. This made the country dependent upon expensive imports. The 1760s was a time of food riots and food thefts, especially in market towns. But the late eighteenth century is painted as a land of plenty, and indeed it was 'for those with money ... the Georgian larder was always full.'[29] But in these supposedly enlightened and civilised times, the poor were taxed disproportionately to the middle and upper classes, and were without state financial support or housing, unless one counts the dreaded workhouse. The working poor would do anything to avoid such places and many turned to sex work.

So desperate were people to avoid destitution that there was even a trade in teeth. Because the poor ate little sugar, their teeth tended to be in much better condition than the upper classes, whose teeth were rotting in their heads. Many poor individuals had their perfectly healthy teeth excised so that the 'vain and rich' could smile with confidence once again.[30] These stark differences were not born of a passive apathy or ignorance. It was generally accepted that it was God's will for there to be both rich and poor, and everyone who sat in either of these two tiers deserved their place; it was all part of God's plan. The philosophy behind this was simple: 'Poverty encouraged social order – it was believed that people could escape the worst of their condition by sobriety, obedience and constant hard work every day except Sunday. People could be as poor as they could bear, and they were obliged by God to bear it.'[31] But as far as the wealthy were concerned, the poor are inherently lazy, and therefore will only work as hard as they need to make ends meet, such is their lack of drive and ambition, so to get work out of them, employers had no other option but to force them to work long hours for meagre wages. If they chose to spend their pittance on tea and sugar over beer, bread and vegetables, that was their problem.

This was an egregious case of gaslighting on a vast scale: using God and His order as the reason or cause of this gross disparity when it simply suited the wealthy who were very happy with the *status quo*, thank you very much. But, utter tosh though it may be, this belief was the mechanism that drove the ever-increasing gulf between the rich and the poor. The concept was similarly believed by the working classes – at least to some degree – including Manchester where workers often took a stance against the greediness of bosses. The same principle did not apply to royalty, presumably because they were chosen by God, and there is one incident that occurred on Market Place during the Regency of a rather vocal reformer who, offended by the greed displayed by Prince George who lived a life of opulence and greed whilst the people of Manchester had to fork out thruppence just for a loaf of bread, decided there should be a protest. He marched 'to the pillory opposite the Bull's Head gateway in Market Place'. Shocked and offended by what they heard, 'the starving people of Manchester turned on him without mercy' and he had to stand an hour in the pillory 'in order that the working classes might have the pleasure of pelting the poor wretch with mud and all kinds of filth, including rotten eggs, dead cats and rats.'[32] This filth wasn't difficult to find because the streets were full of waste food and vermin, and the area of the town within and around the Shambles was so densely populated that the town struggled to limit the dangers to public health. In 1775, an Act of Parliament was issued by George III to widen the streets, a problem exacerbated by the shop owners' signs which got in the way of the constant march of the multitude.[33] In addition to these trip hazards, the people had also to contend with farm animals which were regularly brought into town for sale or slaughter.

Being the focus of trade in the town, Market Place and the Shambles saw the very best and worst Manchester had to offer and there are several incidents of note to be found that occurred there during the time Elizabeth occupied her premises. Public punishments were common, the public element considered important and a necessity – it was, at the very least, a humiliation to the wrongdoer, but it also doubled as an effective deterrent to anyone considering a life of crime; this is a time of public hanging and the ducking stool. One man was flogged on Market Place for 'misusing' some hatting material.[34] In the *Manchester Mercury* on 19 May 1771, a gentleman placed an advertisement for an African boy he had for sale:

> Any Gentleman, or Lady, wanting to purchase a BLACK BOY, 12 Years of Age, with a good character, has had the Small-Pox and Measles. Whoever this may suit, may, by applying to the Higher Swan and Saracen's Head, in Market Street-lane, Manchester, meet with a proper Person to deal with them on reasonable terms.

A reminder that the enslavement of Africans wasn't just perfectly legal, but also something that did not just happen out of sight and out of mind elsewhere in the sugar colonies of the West Indies.

There is also an account of a man who sold his wife on Market Place. Bizarrely, this was a completely legal exchange, viewed as a kind of divorce: upon selling her, the man was single and free to do whatever he liked with his newfound marital freedom. His wife, on the other hand, being a chattel with no rights, could be exchanged or sold at will. It also meant that a wife didn't own anything either and anything she might have achieved belonged to her husband. Remarkably, not only was he successful in this, but his wife left more than happy with her new spouse. These marital laws applied to Elizabeth too, of course, so '[l]egally he [John Raffald] had complete dominance and control over her and her money.'[35] This is a viewpoint that Elizabeth held, at least publicly: in her directories, the vast majority of named individuals listed are male, with women appearing mainly as widows and only sometimes as midwives, innkeepers and weavers. Elizabeth is conspicuous by her absence from *her own* directory. John Raffald is included in the list, of course, and as both seedman and confectioner.

Putting together her Manchester and Salford directories, saving the local trade paper and financing a second firmly planted Elizabeth in the consciousness of those not just inside the two towns, but also the north-west region of England. However, it was the publication of *The Experienced English Housekeeper*, written and published in 1769 whilst she lived at Market Place, that would put her in 'very comfortable circumstances', elevating her to the position of the most highly regarded woman in Manchester and making her a household name, not just in Britain but also North America.

Chapter 6

The Experienced English Housekeeper

The Experienced English Housekeeper is Elizabeth's greatest achievement, and it was written when she lived at 12 Market Place. It is much more than a cookery book, it is a handbook, guiding one through 'the social and technical mazes of cookery in Britain'. She did this 'by successfully negotiating the pitfalls of frivolity [but] without alienating those who aspired to be fashionable',[1] and she executed it simply, without fuss and with clear instruction, using the dignified voice of a member of the domestic class.

That Elizabeth was of servant class worked in her favour; she was proud of her achievements and her status, and she used her identity to convince the reader that she knew what she was doing. She was not some upper-class gentlewoman with no idea what it was like to work at the coalface, who suggested menus and dishes too opulent, expensive or logistically challenging. No, Elizabeth was of different stock – she was a *housekeeper* and an excellent one at that. She wrote entirely by experience, everything gleaned from her diverse knowledge and the copious written notes and recipes she must have kept with her, both in the shop and in domestic service. 'Her earnest enthusiasm is all-compelling', wrote journalist Doreen Taylor in *The Manchester Guardian* in 1957, '[s]he explains in the preface how she studied the art of cookery herself, a good cook in those days being hard to come by.'[2] The book would be an extension of everything she had already achieved: housekeeper, teacher, confectioner and cook. With her credentials, Elizabeth knew she could garner the trust of a readership and invite herself into strangers' homes to improve their self-esteem, organisation and repertoire with a firm focus upon frugality, but not austerity.

Aside from her own self-assurance, the factor driving her confidence the most was the small flurry of female-written cookery books in the first half of the eighteenth century, the most notable of which were Eliza Smith's *The*

74

Compleat Housewife in 1727 and Hannah Glasse's classic work *The Art of Cookery Made Plain and Easy* in 1747.[3]

Eliza Smith blazed a trail, for it was she who was the first woman to frown upon those books that did 'bear great names, as Cooks to Kings, Princes and Noblemen', finding the recipes 'unpracticable, others whimsical, others unpalatable, except to depraved palates'. Her recipes, though fewer in number compared to these books, were all tried and tested and guaranteed 'wholesome, toothsome [and] all practicable and easy to perform'.[4] Though her book was successful (indeed, it was the first English cookery book to be printed in North America), Eliza sadly died just a few years after the publication of *The Compleat Housewife*, and little is known about her. Much more is known of Hannah Glasse. When Hannah wrote her book, she was already a person with a great deal of experience of both sides of domestic life: she was an illegitimate daughter of Isaac Allgood of Hexham, a member of the minor gentry, and therefore enjoyed being waited upon, but yet secretly married John Glasse, 'a subaltern on half pay'. Upon leaving the family home, she spent a good deal of her adult life in domestic service herself, most significantly to the fourth Earl of Derby. *The Art of Cookery* was 'born of necessity' because John had left military service with a meagre pension and very little business sense of his own. Hannah attempted several ventures, including a high-end haberdasher's and a business selling 'elixirs', before she found success as a cookery book writer.[5]

Before this, cookery books by women were few and tended to be written by members of the upper classes. More typically they were written by men, who assumed it was their place to inform ladies of the best way to run their home. Writers of both genders wrote assuming that the reader was of the higher sort, and the recipes and language reflect that. These were books of high-level aspiration, and fairly useless as a workable text for the inexperienced new middle classes trying to get economical meals on the table.[6] Books such as these only fuelled the fire of anxiety to purchase expensive ingredients and cook rich foods that required a small army of kitchen staff. Eliza and Hannah's objective was to equip the lady of the house or her housekeeper with practical recipes.

Hannah's work was a runaway success. It was different: yes, it contained lavish recipes, but they were tempered with more straightforward ones. She had the edge over Eliza Smith because she wrote with authority, but in a very down-to-earth voice so that anyone could use it. Her plain-speaking was her unique selling point; with 40 per cent of English women now literate, but not necessarily learned, there was a significant, largely untapped audience desperate for information. As Hannah put it:

> If I have not wrote in the high polite Stile, I hope I shall be forgiven; for my Intention is to instruct the lower Sort, and therefore treat them in their own Way. For Example; when I bid them lard a Fowl, if I should bid them lard with large Lardoons, they would not know what I meant: But when I say they must lard with little Pieces of Bacon, they know what I mean.[7]

She demystified many recipes by modernising old-fashioned terms, avoiding French words where possible and 'simplifie[d] flavourings, ingredients and methods'.[8]

The most significant of these is the rejection of what they both perceived as over-the-top French cooking, French chefs and all who tried to emulate them. Hannah took no prisoners:

> A Frenchman, in his own Country, would dress a fine Dinner of twenty Dishes, and all genteel and pretty, for the Expence he will put an English Lord to for dressing one Dish. But then there is the little petty Profit. I have heard of a Cook that used six Pounds of Butter to fry twelve Eggs; when every Body knows, that understands cooking, the Half a Pound is full enough, no more than need to be used: But that would not be French. So much is the blind Folly of this Age, that they would rather be impos'd on by a French Booby, than give Encouragement to a good English cook![9]

And who can blame her, when there were chefs who were inclined to show off about their French credentials and were as patronising to women as they were flashy with their ingredients. A typical example of this approach can be found in *A Complete System of Cookery* (1759) by William Verral, published just before the rise in the popularity of women's food writing. He wastes no time letting the reader know that he was trained by the great French chef Pierre de St Clouet, the 'sometimes cook to his Grace the

Duke of Newcastle',[10] and his two main foci appear to be grandiose French cookery and self-congratulation; there's no false modesty contained within his pages. Every dish is given both a French and an English name, though a large proportion of the so-called English names contain at least one French term in them, 'English' dishes include 'Calves heads, with *ragout melée*', '*Fricasee* of eel with Champagne', '*Fricando* of veal *glassée*' and 'Sheeps tongues *en gratin*'. In his preface, he declares 'The chief end and design of this part of my little volume is to shew ... the whole and simple art of the most modern and best French Cookery.'[11] It is anything but that; his recipes are complex and the preface is used as an opportunity to point out his superior knowledge, especially over female English cooks. He is gossipy in his style, listing incidences where he swished into a kitchen and saved the day after a house's – usually female – cooks had buckled under the pressure.[12]

Hannah rejected this approach completely, and one particular aspect of French cookery really got her goat: the use of cullis or *demiglace*, meat stock boiled down until it became an umami-rich and viscous base for sauces. It required a huge amount of meat: several legs of veal and ham were boiled down to a mere glaze. Her alternatives used more economical ingredients: bread, egg yolks or *beurre manié*. Extravagance is in the eye of the beholder, of course, for she also used morel mushrooms, truffles and spices in her cullis alternative. She didn't like the English habit of adding suet to foods to enrich them either, and instead insisted on butter. She may not have used as much as those French cooks, but still a great deal, and seeing as weight-for-weight butter cost double that of beef, this was certainly not a cookery book for the short of cash.[13]

Hannah's confidence and philosophical approach to cooking and running a household was something others could identify with, and her book was in print for well over a century. Her phraseology even hit the mainstream, with the adage 'Made Plain and Easy' being tagged onto the title of many an instructional manual and 'bec[oming] a stock phrase in everything from political negotiations to printed instructions of all types.'[14]

By taking Hannah's lead of writing in a straightforward way, and taking Eliza's practical approach, Elizabeth produced a book that was the perfect combination of frugality, plain-speaking, clear writing and level-headedness. Food writer and historian Mary-Anne Boermans certainly considers her food 'delicious and unfussy contrasting with the fashionable and over-the-top styles of fashionable French cooks of the time'. Indeed, she goes further, saying 'I absolutely consider her an equal, if not more important, than the rest of the 18th century doyennes of Hannah Glasse ... etc.'[15] But together these three great writers – Raffald, Glasse and Smith – all equally popular in their time, gave generations of inexperienced housewives around the country the skills with which to express themselves in their homes.

For a book to be successful, it had to be a finely balanced mix of standard recipes of the time and unique and fancy ones, as well as a philosophy and approach that stood out against the others. These three women's philosophies could not be bettered, so they became the standard and were therefore perennial favourites for decades, hence their comparisons with modern female cooks and food writers Fanny Cradock, Delia Smith and Nigella Lawson.[16] Elizabeth would buck several trends of the day in several ways: firstly, she avoided recipes for medicines, unlike Smith and Glasse, and stuck to her brief of helping women in the kitchen: 'neither have I meddled with Physical Receipts, leaving them to the Physicians superior Judgement, whose proper Province they are.'[17]

Her 'prodigious energy and unflagging industry'[18] really has to be admired, writing a book so comprehensive whilst simultaneously running several existing businesses and being a mother to her girls. Indeed, given her workload, one has to assume that the majority of her recipes already existed in some form. Even so, one does wonder why she should have felt it was a good idea in the first place to write such a volume, so stretched thin she must already have been with her other responsibilities, but that's Elizabeth for you, and somehow time was made. It did mean that she worked every spare moment, and by her own admittance, writing a book of almost 800 recipes was ruinous to her health.[19] She must have been very confident of its success; either that or she was convinced by another's certainty. Perhaps her respected friend and colleague Joseph Harrop, who would go on to print the first edition, planted the seed.

The first edition is split into three sections that very much reflect her own life. The first is made up of savoury dishes and puddings, soups and fish, from simple 'plain' cooking to more complex 'made dishes' such as 'ragoos', 'fricassees' and more bizarre dishes like 'Rabbits Surprised'. There are also pies, batters and puddings, both sweet and savoury. Most of these recipes originate from her time at Arley Hall. The second part focuses upon 'Receipts of the Confectionary' that she sold every day in her shop. So assured was she of their quality, she urged local ladies to pop into the shop so they could examine them in person at their pleasure.[20] There were 'Creams, Custards and Cheesecakes', cakes and sweet biscuits, her table decorations, as well as a chapter covering the basics of making all manner of candied and preserved fruits and syrups, all constituent parts of delicious sweets – important basic skills for those who wanted to make their own confections from scratch.

To preserve Kentish or Golden Pippins

Boil the Rind of an Orange very tender, then lay it in Water for two or three Days, take a Quart of Golden Pippins, pare, core, quarter, and boil them to a strong Jelly, and run it through a Jelly Bag, then take twelve Pippins, pare them and scrape out the Cores, put two Pounds of Loaf Sugar into a Stew Pan with near a Pint of Water, when it boils skim it, and put in your Pippins with the Orange Rind in thin Slices, let them boil fast 'till the Sugar is very thick and will almost Candy, then put in a Pint of the Pippin Jelly, boil them fast 'till the Jelly is clear, then squeeze in the Juice of a Lemon, give it one boil, and put them into Pots or Glasses with the Orange Peel.[21]

The final part deals with the rather less glamorous, but essential, recipes and seasonal kitchen tasks required of a housekeeper: potting and collaring meats and fish – often made up of leftovers from the previous day's meals – gruels, posset drinks, country wines, 'Catchups' and vinegars, pickling, 'Keeping Garden Stuff' and distillation. She then very helpfully includes 'A Correct list of everything in season', an extensive month by month calendar of all of the available meat, fish, vegetables, herbs and fruits.

Each section is split into several chapters, each of which begins with some 'Observations', short introductions providing general advice. Contained within these, and in many of her recipes, she describes the difficulties one can encounter, the essential pieces of equipment required, or when focus or deftness of touch is needed. Her practical and poetic turns of phrase really help when subtle changes or cues need to be spotted in order to successfully cook a dish. It is a difficult skill: it's one thing demonstrating a technical process, but writing down a clear description of the process and its subtleties is quite another. Elizabeth tells us that poaching fish requires a delicate touch: 'boil all Kinds of Fish very slowly, and when they leave the Bone they are enough.' 'In making Possets, always mix a little of the hot Cream or Milk with your Wine, it will keep the Wine from curdling the rest', or when making wine to make sure that before adding the yeast, the liquid is so clear the 'summer-beams and blinks in the Tub'. When larding meat with bacon and lemon peel, it should be 'cut the Size of Wheat Straw'. She helpfully tells us to rub some extra salt into our bacon as it cures because 'the dry Salt will candy and shine like Diamonds on your Bacon'.[22]

By the time Elizabeth's book was published in 1769, Hannah Glasse's *Art of Cookery* was in its sixth edition.[23] Elizabeth likely owned a copy and seeing Hannah's success, and that she had achieved it using her own voice, Elizabeth did what she did best and leapt on a new phenomenon and made it her own, just as she had with her catering business, register office and normal school, and would do later with her series of Manchester and Salford directories.

Elizabeth, like Hannah Glasse, aimed to ease minds around the pressure to opt for French cuisine, and its inevitable accompanying expense. She was not quite as disparaging as Glasse, and admitted there were several positive, useful and economical aspects to French cookery. Hence the appearance of 'ragoos' and 'florendines':

I have made it my Study to please both the Eye and the Palate, without using pernicious Things for the sake of Beauty … [Al]though I have given some of my Dishes French Names, as they are only known by those Names, yet they will not be found very Expensive, nor add Compositions but as plain as the Nature of the Dish will admit of.[24]

Like Hannah, she also avoids the use of cullis, preferring to use 'Lemon Pickle and Browning [which] answers both for Beauty and Taste (at a trifling Expence)'.[25] Unlike Hannah, she doesn't use churnfuls of butter.

Raffald and Glasse's books, in their criticism of (almost) all things French, really required readers to make a leap of faith. The English had been conditioned by their cooks, their cookery books and their visits to other people's homes that full-on French cookery was the only civilised and socially acceptable way of doing things. The English had been 'haunted' by the disparaging comments and withering looks received from picky French visitors, who had been dismissive of English cookery, looking down even at the roast meat for which the English were so famous.[26] As far as the French were concerned, the English had lost their way culinarily. But Raffald and Glasse were proud of good English cuisine and, in modern parlance, *owned it*, and were not so insecure of their Englishness to not borrow from the French when appropriate. Perhaps their nods to French cuisine made their Anglocentric philosophies more palatable to those who sat on the fence.

Though economy and restraint were high on the priority list, many recipes are ostentatious; a good housekeeper would limit this sort of thing, of course, and stick to lowlier and more plain cooking in the main, but gentlemen and women were expected to entertain, so appropriately fancy dishes had to be represented within the book. One entry describes the process of butchering and cooking a turtle which is so complicated it takes up four pages. One really has to wonder whether her recipe was ever followed by a novice of turtle cookery. Four dishes are made from a single turtle; the first is made from the heart, liver, lungs and head of the animal plus the green fat and meat found under its shell (called the 'Monsieur' and 'Callepash', respectively), four quarts of veal gravy and two bottles of Madeira. The second dish is made from the external parts of the fins ('Pinions') and the reptile's blood. The third was made from 'the vealy Part of your Turtle' as well as 'the chicken part', plus artichokes, another four quarts of veal gravy and 'a score of Oysters'. Finally, the guts are chopped and sauteed with morel mushrooms, a pint of Madeira and two further quarts of veal gravy.[27] It seems more likely that it was only really included to provide the reader with an insight into the techniques and the unique vocabulary and expense associated with turtle cookery.

There is also her example of that grand table for January, made up of a full menu of three substantial courses, with diagrams showing where to place the myriad of beautifully laid out dishes. This was something Hannah Glasse had avoided, saying she would not 'direct a Lady how to set out her Table; for that would be impertinent, and lessening her Judgement'.[28] Elizabeth's menu would be a feat impossible in all but the largest homes. But why not have at least a few aspirations? It is always fascinating to see how the other half lives, and the majority of individual dishes were possible and would have been just as appropriate at other, smaller dinners.

In many cookery books of the time, the aspiration, and the panic of their readership associated with it, was milked for all it was worth – anxiety was, after all, the emotion that was being tapped into to sell those books – but now they added an extra dimension to it because usually making up the frontispiece of the books were illustrations of kitchens and women working in them; women who before had been unseen and invisible. Well, not anymore, and what proud housekeepers, cooks and kitchen maids they seemed! There they were: hard-working, perfectly poised over ovens or selecting perfect produce from a beautifully arranged pantry bounty. They were clean and well turned out, their kitchens were spotless, and their shelves were stacked with a wide range of gleaming iron and copperware. This is what was expected of an eighteenth-century domestic goddess. Elizabeth avoided this trick; she encouraged cleanliness and organisation, of course, but the work of women was difficult enough already without putting on a show in the kitchen as well as the dining room.

As someone who always had an ear to the ground, Elizabeth's book contained many new dishes, including several culinary firsts. As already noted, she was a pioneer of edible table decorations, and many of her creations such as Solomon's Temple, cribbage cards, and bacon and eggs in flummery are all unique to her. And let's not forget the humble Eccles cake. *The Experienced English Housekeeper* also contains the earliest known recipe for macaroni cheese, a dish of British, not American, origin:

> To dress Macaroni with Permasent Cheese
>
> Boil four Ounces of Macaroni 'till it be quite tender, and lay it on a Sieve to drain, then put it in a Tossing Pan, with about a Gill of good Cream, a Lump of Butter rolled in Flour, boil it five Minutes, pour it on a Plate, lay all over it Permesent Cheese toasted; send it to the Table on a Water Plate, for it soon gets cold.[29]

Elizabeth was also a pioneer of modern cake decoration because it seems that she was the first to have the notion of decorating a fruit cake with a double layer of marzipan and icing. This 'Bride's Cake' would soon replace the traditional bride's pie, which was essentially a huge mince pie packed

Above: The Assembly Rooms in York were one of the main attractions for young ladies during the eighteenth century, and the ladies were, in turn, an attraction for young men looking for wives. (Wikimedia Commons: Chabe01)

Right: Frontispiece of the fourteenth edition of *The Compleat Housewife* by Eliza Smith. Notice how pristine and well ordered the kitchen is, and the kitchen maid making sauce directly over the fire. In reality, she would not have been so composed.

Above: Arley Hall, Cheshire as it stands today. There is very little left of the building Elizabeth would have recognised. (Neil Buttery)

Left: Hogarth's *Six Servants* (1750). A rare naturalistic glance at eighteenth-century domestic service.

Below: One of Elizabeth Whitaker's Arley food orders, dated 10 October 1761. (Arley Hall Archives)

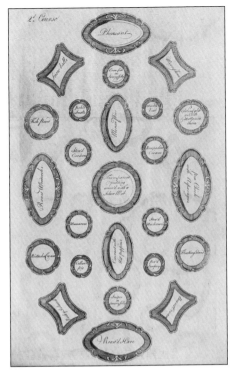

Above left: Elizabeth's second course for 'a Bill of Fayre' in January. No two dishes are the same. Foods now considered desserts were eaten with savoury roasts and vegetable dishes. From *The Experienced English Housekeeper*.

Above right: The last Arley Hall receipt signed by Elizabeth – now Raffald – on the very day she and John left for Manchester. (Arley Hall Archives)

The eighteenth-century walled gardens at Arley Hall as they look today. Several of the walls have cavities in which coal or charcoal was burnt to make 'hot walls' for growing fruit out of season. (Neil Buttery)

A view of the town of Manchester from Kersal Moor, mid-nineteenth century, by William Wyld. (GetArchive)

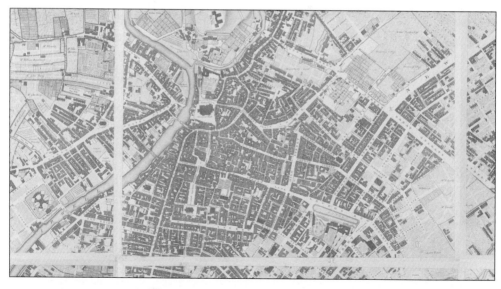

A map of Manchester and Salford, 1819. The two towns are divided by the River Irwell.

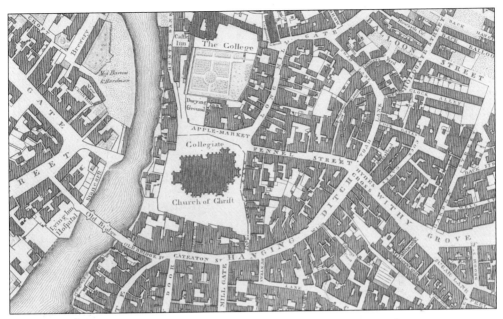

Detail of the 1819 map showing Fennel Street, the Collegiate Church and the Old Bridge over to Salford, where the Raffald brothers' market gardens could be found.

Detail of the 1819 map showing the Old Shambles area of Manchester, including Market Place and upmarket Deansgate.

A watercolour painting of Fennel Street in 1780. The streets were much more broad than in the narrow, enclosed Shambles. (Manchester Libraries, Information and Archives)

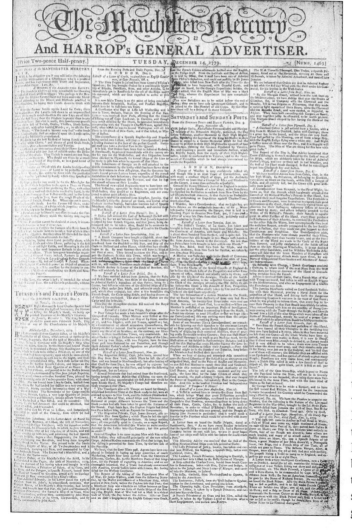

The front page of an issue of the *Manchester Mercury*, dated 14 December 1779. Elizabeth advertised her businesses and books throughout her time in Manchester within its pages. Harrop would publish the first edition of Elizabeth's cookery book. She also gave the paper financial support when it faced going under.

Right: Elizabeth's first notice in the *Manchester Mercury*, 4 December 1764, advertising her shop's wares and the opening of her register office for servants.

Below: A Second World War decontamination squad clean up the junction of Market Place and the Shambles. Many of the area's medieval buildings were razed. The area was then cleared for the Manchester Arndale shopping centre in the 1970s. The Old Wellington Inn, just visible behind the destruction, was relocated to Exchange Square and is still a popular pub. (Manchester Libraries, Information and Archives)

Matters, after *Carla, Maratti, Raphael, Hannibal, Caracbi, Andrea Sacchi, Dominichino, Poussin,* and other Masters.
His Stay will be about twelve Days.

Manchester, December 4, 1764.
Just arriv'd, and now selling Wholesale and Retail, at Mrs. RAFFALD's, in Fennel Street,

Fine *Canterbury* and *Derbyshire* BRAWN,

Whole, Half or Quarter Collars, of the *Canterbury* Brawn at 16d a Pound, and those of the *Derbyshire* at 14d. a Pound. As several of Mrs. Raffald's Friends in the Country have mistook the Terms and Design of her

REGISTER OFFICE,

She begs Leave to inform them, that she supplies Families with Servants, for any Place, at One Shilling for each; and Servants with Places for One Shilling each Masters or Servants therefore, at any Distance, may be supply'd on the shortest Notice, by directing (Post paid) to Mrs. Raffald, at the Register Office, in Fennel Street, Manchester.

She also continues to supply Families with made Dishes, cold Suppers, &c. as usual.

WILLIAM BANCROFT, Upholsterer,
Takes this Method to acquaint his Friends & the Public in general,

THAT he has open'd a Shop in the Upholstery Business, in all its various Branches, at the Lower End of *Smithy Door, Manchester*; those Ladies and Gentlemen who please to favour him with their Commands, may always depend on being

ELIZABETH RAFFALD,

Begs Leave to acquaint the Publick, and
her Friends in particular,

That fhe has juft received a large Affortment of

PERFUMERIES, viz.

PERFUM'D WATERS.	Royal Chymical ditto
French, Hungary, from Montpelier	Italian ditto
Fineft Honey Water	Naples ditto
Double Diftill'd Lavender	Camphire ditto
Arquabufade	Cream ditto
Eau Sans Pareille	French Soap
Eau de Luce	Shaving Powder
Eau de Jafmin	Violet Powder for the Hair, &c.
Eau de Violite	Tooth Powder
Eau de Bergamot, &c.	Powder Boxes, and Swan Down Puffs
Syrup de Capillair, from Montpelier, &c.	Sweet fcented Pomatums
Effence of Lemon	Lip Salve
Effence of Bergamot, &c.	Wafh Ball Boxes
Royal Marble Wafh Balls	Burgamot Boxes, &c. &c

N. B. Several good Cooks are wanted for Gentle-
mens Families.

Genteel Lodgings and a front Cellar to Let.

RUN AWAY

From his Mafter Thomas Stockport, jun. Shoe-maker,
at High Afh, near Afhton,

NICHOLAS BOOTH, an Apprentice, near five
Feet four Inches high, about 15 Years of Age,
born near Mottram; had on when he went away a

Elizabeth advertises the fancy 'perfumeries' in her Market Street shop which were supplied to her by her nephew, who was perfumer to King George III. *Manchester Mercury*, 21 April 1771.

Elizabeth announces her book *The Experienced English Housekeeper* is available to purchase by subscription for five shillings, *Manchester Mercury*, 4 April 1769.

Ready for the Prefs, and fpeedily will be publifhed,
An entire new Work,
Wrote for the Ufe and Eafe of Ladies, Houfe-keep-
ers, Cooks, &c. entitled,

The EXPERIENCED

ENGLISH Houfe-keeeper.

By ELIZABETH RAFFALD.

Wrote purely from Practice, and
Dedicated to the Hon. Lady *Elizabeth Warburton,*
Whom the Author lately ferved as Houfe-keeper.
Confifting of near 800 Original Receipts, moft of
which never appeared in Print.

First Part, Lemon Pickle, Browning for all Sorts of
made Difhes, Soups, Fifh, plain Meat, Game, made
Difhes both hot and cold, Pyes, Puddings, &c.

Second Part, All kind of Confectionary, particularly the Gold and Silver Web for covering of Sweetmeats, and a Defert of Spun Sugar, with Directions
to fet out a Table in the moft elegant Manner, and
in the moft modern Tafte, Floating Iflands, Fifh
Ponds, Tranfparent Puddings, Trifles, Whips, &c.

Third Part, Pickling, Potting, and Collaring,
Wines, Vinegars, Catchups, Diftilling, with two
moft valuable Receipts, one for refining Malt
Liquors, the other for curing Acid Wines, and a
correct Lift of every Thing in Seafon in every Month
of the Year.

N. B. At every Place where the Subfcriptions are
taken in, the Contents of the Book may be feen.

CONDITIONS.

I. The Work fhall be printed with all convenient
fpeed, and a good Paper, and with a new Letter,
in a large Octavo.

II. Price to Subfcribers, Five Shillings, neatly
bound.

III. After the Subfcription is clofed, the Book will
be advanced to Six Shillings.

IV. The Book to be figned by the Author's own
Hand-writing, and to be entered at Stationers Hall.

Subfcriptions to be taken in by Meffrs. *Fletcher* and
Anderfon, Bookfellers, St Paul's Church yard, in London; Mr. *Ager,* Confectioner, in *York;* Mr. *Eaton,*
Silk Mercer, in *Doncafter;* Mr. *John Wefterell,* in
Hull; Mr. *Tindell,* Confectioner, in *Leeds;* Mr. *Ken-
dall,* at the *Peacock, Derbyfhire;* Mr. *Afhburner,* Book-
feller, in *Kendal;* Mr. *Afhburner,* Bookfeller, in Lan-
cafter; Mr. *Stuart,* Bookfeller, in *Prefton;* Mr. *Dun-
bitin,* Printer and Bookfeller, in *Liverpool;* Mr. *Poole,*
Bookfeller, in *Chefter;* Mr. *Leigh,* Bookfeller, in
Northwich, and by the Author, *Elizabeth Raffald,*
Confectioner, near the *Exchange, Manchefter.*

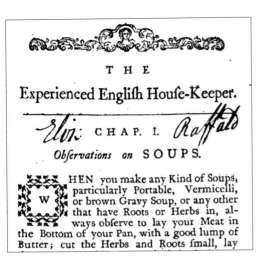

Above left: The first page of the first chapter of every copy of her book was individually signed by Elizabeth as proof of authenticity. After she died, a facsimile of her signature was made by the publisher, Robert Baldwin.

Above right: Samuel Johnson neither approved of, nor rated, female cookery writers. 'Women,' he said, 'can spin very well; but they cannot make a good book of Cookery.'

Above left: The portrait of Elizabeth published in the eighth edition, 1781 – the first to be published posthumously – going against her express wishes. The portrait is the only existing likeness we have of Elizabeth, and it was probably owned by her daughter Emma.

Above right: The 'portrait' of Elizabeth in an unofficial 1803 edition of her book, described by Raffald enthusiast John Harper as 'a plump dairy-maid looking person'.

Sweet Patties.

TAKE the Meat of a boiled Calf's-Foot, two large Apples, and one Ounce of candied Orange, chop them very small, grate half a Nutmeg, mix them with the Yolk of an Egg, a Spoonful of French Brandy, and a quarter of a Pound of Currants clean washed and dried, make a good puff Paste, roll it in different Shapes, as the fried ones, and fill them the same Way; you may either fry or bake them. They are a pretty Side Dish for Supper.

Elizabeth's recipe for 'Sweet Patties', reckoned to be the first Eccles cakes recipe. Elizabeth's book was the first to have a recipe for macaroni cheese, and the first to have a fruit cake (Bride's Cake) decorated with a layer of marzipan and icing.

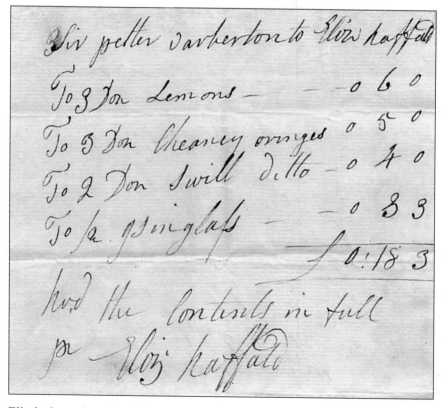

Elizabeth continued to send parcels of food to Arley Hall, usually in person. This one dates from 29 May 1771 and is most likely the ingredients to make a jelly during Lent. (Arley Hall Archives)

A modern recreation of Elizabeth's 'Good Plum Cake'. (Neil Buttery)

Above left: Elizabeth's 'Mulled Ale' is a cross between a drink and a custard. (Neil Buttery)

Above right: 'A Hunting Pudding' from *The Experienced English Housekeeper*, most likely served up in the second course and eaten with roast meat. (Neil Buttery)

Manchester, August 8, 1774.

FLORISTS FEAST.

THE
Annual CARNATION MEETING,

Will be held at

Mr. JOHN RAFFALD's, the KING's-HEAD, in SALFORD, on MONDAY the 22d Inst.

Stewards { Mr. JOSEPH DALE,
{ Mr. JAMES DURY.

Dinner on the Table at Two o'Clock.

To be LETT,

To enter upon at CANDLEMAS next,

John Raffald advertises the 1774 Florists Feast at the King's Head in the *Manchester Mercury*.

Manchester, May 12, 1772.

H. COOPER,

HOSIER, in MARKET-STREET-LANE,

Begs Leave to acquaint the Ladies and Gentlemen of this Town and Neighbourhood,

THAT she has taken up the Business of a RE-GISTER OFFICE, as resigned to her by Mrs. Raffald, and hopes to give Satisfaction to all who will please to favour her with their Commands, as no Servants will be entered but those whose Characters will bear the strictest Scrutiny.

Ladies and Gentlemen may depend upon their Letters being duly answered

WANTED, several Servants of good Character, a second Cook for a Nobleman's Family, and an upper Servant for a single Lady.

The said H. Cooper, hath just laid an elegant and neat Assortment of SILK STOCKINGS, which she sells as cheap as elsewhere.

When the Raffalds moved to the King's Head, they both had to give up their previous businesses. H. Cooper (called Widow Cooper in Elizabeth's directory) took over Elizabeth's register office, as this notice in *Manchester Mercury*, 12 May 1772, demonstrates.

William Hogarth's *A Rake's Progress*, Plate 3 (1734) showing the debauched goings-on in a supposedly high-class tavern. Was this happening in Elizabeth's tavern too? Probably. (Wikimedia Commons)

Above left: William Hogarth's *Gin Lane* (1752) infamously shows a babe in arms falling from a flight of stairs as its drunk mother reaches for some snuff. (New York Public Library)

Above right: The lesser-known accompanying second part to *Gin Lane*, *Beer Street* (1752), showing just how happy the common folk could be if they just stuck to beer or ale. The two pieces are a satire, and neither should be taken literally. (New York Public Library)

Mary Whitaker, Elizabeth's sister, opens a shop and register office in a bid to boost the failing King's Head. *Manchester Mercury*, 25 June 1776.

Elizabeth places notices in the *Mercury* every week throughout December 1770 and January 1771 advertising the third edition of her *Manchester and Salford Directory*. Things seemed to be turning around for her.

Above: Leaving John to run the Exchange Coffee House, Elizabeth runs a stall at 'The LADIES STAND on Kersal Moor', selling strawberries and hot drinks. *Manchester Mercury*, 4 July 1780.

Right: A satirical poster (1787) showing a Chancellor Thurlow visiting a disreputable coffeehouse called Nando's. The priest behind him reminding him 'Thou shall not Commit Adultery'. (Library of Congress)

LAW and EQUITY at most NANDO's

Below: The unfortunate announcement in the *Mercury* letting Manchester know that the entire contents of the Exchange Coffee House are to be auctioned, 31 May and 1 June 1781.

Elizabeth's commemorative blue plaque which sits inconspicuously, hiding in plain sight on the side of Selfridges & Co., Exchange Square, Manchester. (David Dixon)

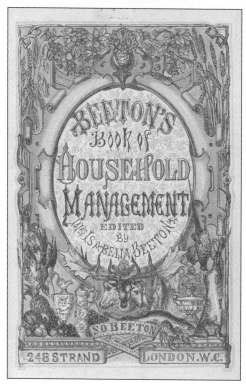

Above left: The behemoth that was *Mrs Beeton's Book of Household Management* (1861) plagiarised many of Elizabeth's – and others' – recipes and caused a huge drop in sales of almost all other cookery books. (Wellcome Images)

Above right: Elizabeth was one of six Manchester women nominated to be immortalised in bronze; she lost out to Emmeline Pankhurst, whose statue was installed in St Peter's Square 2016. (Delusion23/Wikimedia Commons) with meat, grated apples, dried and candied fruit, spices and laced with brandy and (seeing as it is a wedding pie) a glass of champagne. Tradition went that the pie would be broken over the head of the bride to ensure the marriage was a happy and productive one. In a world more civilised, Elizabeth's idea of slicing up a fruit cake was much more sensible and befitting of the time.[30] The cakes were unusual in that the marzipan was set first by baking before applying the icing:

To make Sugar Iceing for the Bride Cake

Beat two Pounds of double refined Sugar, with two Ounces of
fine Starch, sift it through a Gawze Sieve, then beat the Whites
of five Eggs with a Knife upon a Pewter Dish half an Hour,
beat in your Sugar a little at a Time, or it will make your Eggs
fall, and will not be so good a colour, when you have put in
all your Sugar, beat it half an Hour longer, then lay it on your
Almond Iceing, and spread it even with a Knife; if it be put on
as soon as the Cake comes out of the Oven, it will be hard by
that Time the Cake is cold.[31]

As she makes the point that the icing should remain a bright white so the oven had to be very cool to ensure no brown discolouration, exactly as meringues are prepared today. Elizabeth's cake has been made for centuries, essentially unchanged.

She was the first to make and popularise the aforementioned portable soup, and although she has few recipes inspired by the East Indies, her recipe for piccalilli ('Indian Pickle, or Piccalillo'), that great preserve, a favourite of allotment owners around the world, is one of the first,[32] and is a wonderful collision of Britain's productive market gardens and the fruits of its empire: a medley of fresh vegetables – cucumbers, radishes, beans, beetroot and garlic combined with the spices turmeric, mace, white pepper, cloves, long pepper and nutmeg, all boiled up in malt vinegar.[33] This is not to say Elizabeth was stealing these recipes just because she wasn't the first to write it. Recipes were still being swapped between housekeepers, housewives and kitchen maids, so they will have been doing the rounds for years before they were printed in a book.[34]

Elizabeth included many foods that were fashionable at the time and that we would identify as modern cuisine like omelettes, ice creams and sherbets, but there are others that appear 'positively medieval'[35] or barbaric. There are recipes for gruesome fayre such as a sparrow dumpling:

> Mix half a Pint of good Milk, with three Eggs, a little Salt, and as much Flour as will make it a thick Batter, put a Lump of Butter rolled in Pepper and Salt in every Sparrow, mix them in the Batter, and tie them in a Cloth, boil them one Hour and a half, pour melted Butter over them, and serve it up.[36]

And let's not forget her 'Rabbits Surprised'.

The book is liberally scattered with dishes that would certainly make many of us rather queasy today: potted lamprey, fricasseed ox palates, broiled calves' heads, giblet pies and chitterlings. There are also instructions on how to 'To dress a Dish of Lambs Bits' (testes) or 'To Collar a Swine's Face'.

Just because she was on the cutting edge of food fashion, it did not mean she was unafraid to point out when traditional methods were more appropriate. She was, for example, in favour of using old-fashioned wooden garths rather than modern metal tins when baking fruit cakes or larger cakes that take a long time to bake; a problem bakers have today, and one can buy insulated cake strips that wrap around tins, dampening the harshness of the oven's heat, just like Elizabeth's garths.

***

However confident Elizabeth was in her ability to produce an excellent cookery book, success was not guaranteed, and new authors had two options open to them. The first was to sell the copyright of the work to a publisher for a single lump sum. The benefit to this is that one can essentially wash one's hands of it and leave the production, marketing and promotion associated with it to the publisher. The downside, at least for first-time authors, was that the copyright might be purchased at too low a price; it must have been terribly galling to have sold the copyright to one's first book, only to see the volume become a bestseller.

Many authors, particularly women, chose this method because the alternative was to raise the cash themselves via patronages and subscriptions, which required a great deal of legwork. Hannah Glasse financed the first edition of *The Art of Cookery* in this way. It will come as no surprise that Elizabeth, like Hannah, chose to keep in full control of her work and raised the funds by subscription, thus remaining in control of her intellectual property. The subscription system worked very simply and was essentially a form of crowdfunding. Advertisements were posted in shops and newspapers, asking individuals to purchase a copy of the book before it was published, usually at a reduced rate. If anyone was unsure of the quality of the book, sample pages were distributed to various booksellers and other shop owners for inspection. Elizabeth placed an advertisement in the *Manchester Mercury* on 4 April 1769, letting everyone know the terms of the subscription offer, and of course, the quality of the recipes:

CONDITIONS
   I. The Work shall be printed with all convenient speed, and
      a good Paper, and with a new Letter, in a large Octavo.
   II. Price to Subscribers, Five Shillings, neatly bound.
   III. After the Subscription is closed, the Book will be advanced
      to Six Shillings.
   IV. The Book to be signed by the Author's own Hand-writing,
      and to be entered at Stationers Hall.

She then lists the places 'Subscriptions may be taken in', letting us see just how far and wide her connections spread about the country: London, York (including Seth Agur's shop), Doncaster, Hull, Leeds, Derbyshire, Kendal, Lancaster, Preston, Liverpool, Chester, Northwich, 'and by the Author, Elizabeth Raffald, Confectioner, near the Exchange, Manchester'. Finally adding: 'At every Place where the Subscriptions are taken in, the Contents of the Book may be seen.'

The subscription offer was a resounding success, raising a total of £800 (remember her annual wage as housekeeper at Arley was a mere £16).[37] When authors were financed by subscriptions, it was the done thing to list and thank the supporters at the beginning of the book, but Elizabeth found she was unable to reproduce her list because there were just too many.

However, there was one supporter who could not be omitted, and that was Lady Betty, whom Elizabeth visited to ask her to patronise the book and for her permission to publish it, presumably because so many of the recipes and meal plans originated from Elizabeth's days at Arley. It wasn't just that, of course; Elizabeth also knew that to receive Lady Warburton's patronage would be a stamp of approval, reassuring anyone who might be in two minds as to how experienced this English housekeeper really was.

Elizabeth was very keen to highlight the fact that the work contained within her volume was hers and hers alone, declaring, 'I can faithfully assume my friends that [my receipts] are truly written from my own Experience, and not borrowed from any other Author.'[38] This assurance was important, as it was not uncommon to find cookery books with entire swathes of material copied from other sources, especially for standard recipes such as pound cake, where the same ingredients are used in the same amounts and prepared in the same way wherever in the country you may be. As Roy Shipperbottom put it: 'the writers were all drawing from the same well of culinary knowledge and used the same bucket.'[39] But recipes, by their very nature, are passed around, so to have the odd one repeated might be expected, and the first to publish it may not have been the first to write it. Today, this would be regarded as plagiarism, and sources would be expected to be credited.

Eighteenth-century cookery writer Mary Cole held the same opinion: 'I soon perceived that every subsequent writer had borrowed very largely from those who had preceded.'[40] Cole's 1788 book, *The Lady's Complete Guide*, was heavily supplemented by other writers' recipes, including Glasse and Raffald. She was unusual in that she fully credited her sources right down to the page numbers, citing that she lacked the 'Vanity to pass herself as an Author'. Amongst the individuals in her rogues' gallery were both Raffald and Glasse, though it was the latter she had it in for ('She steals from ev'ry author'),[41] and not without good reason; indeed, it has been shown that 35 per cent of the recipes in Hannah's book were plagiarised.[42] That said, Cole was heavily biased and avoided telling off male writers who had also done a great deal of blatant copying, such as John Farley, who stole amply from Hannah Glasse, including the first known recipe for a Yorkshire Christmas Pye. However, the number of recipes inside Elizabeth's first edition that have been based on others' work are very few are plagiarised, so *The Experienced English Housekeeper* can very much be considered her own work. Much more worrying for Elizabeth was the blatant pirating of entire works. So concerned was she that, to prove every copy of her book was indeed genuine, she signed her name on the first page of the first chapter on every single copy.

***

After the success of the first edition, Elizabeth quickly produced an expanded second edition just two years later in 1771. Within that time, she had become acquainted with the London publisher Robert Baldwin, and it was he, not Joseph Harrop, who published it.[43] Whether he had seen the success of the first edition and approached Elizabeth, or if they had an existing connection, we do not know. Either way, she continued to work with Baldwin over Harrop for all future publications. The frontispiece of the second edition announced two new elements: 'The Second Edition with an Appendix, containing 102 additional Receipts, and the Plan of a Fire Stove, wherein any common fuel [i.e. coal] may be burnt instead of Charcoal.'[44] Realising that publishing a second edition with over 100 additional recipes could potentially annoy her existing readers and supporters who had bought the first edition two years previously, she saw it

> necessary to apologize to my subscribers for making an addition to my work so soon after the speedy sale of the first edition, and for which my sincere thanks are due to my friends and the public, and especially to some worthy ladies who had not the least knowledge of me; but by trying my receipts, and finding it answer their expectations, and useful to their families, generously offered me the aid in making the second edition still more valuable.[45]

She was also keen to let owners of the first edition 'who are desirous of having the additions, may be supplied with the appendix separately' and wouldn't have to shell out for an entirely new book.[46]

Oddly, the additional recipes are not her own; she was probably far too busy to come up with another 100 recipes, especially if her entire repertoire had been poured into the first edition. It seems that including recipes written by another's hand had not been part of her plan for the next edition, but according to Elizabeth,

> a noble generous-minded lady, whose domestic qualifications do honour her sex presented me with her receipts to try their value, and take out of her fine collection what I thought would be acceptable to the public. Those I have tried, I really found valuable; and those which I have not yet had such an opportunity of proving the goodness of, I have weighted them the best I could, and carefully examined their probable goodness, before I ventured to publish them.

For anyone who may have suspected this to be a cynical cash-in or that the recipes would be inferior or out-of-step with Elizabeth's existing canon, she reassured the reader:

> These are given genuine as they were purchased at a considerable expense from the inventors, so hope, as they are found new, they will prove serviceable; and, as my first edition has met with a favourable reception from the public, I flatter myself these additions will meet with the same approbation, being the fruits of a good intention, and presented to the curious with sincerity.

Recipes include 'artifical Chickens or Pidgeons', 'A receipt to Pot Lobsters, which cost ten Guineas' and 'To stew a Rump of Beef', a recipe that uses a great deal of garlic, demonstrating that the English hating it is a myth.

The second run of 400 copies quickly sold out, and as a result, sometime between 1772 and 1773. When she was living at the King's Head, Baldwin made an offer Elizabeth could not refuse: £1,200 for the copyright to her book. The moment the full cash amount was delivered to her house was recounted by her nephew, the perfumer Joshua Middleton, to John Harland. The story goes that Joshua, upon seeing Baldwin enter her room, stood up to leave, 'when Mrs Raffald called him back, saying: "My dear, don't go; it is only Mr Baldwin, from London, who is come about the copyright of my book."' And so he remained, and watched agog as 'Mr Baldwin hand[ed] over to Raffald a large roll of bank notes, which Mrs Raffald received for the copyright of her work on cookery.'[47]

As it turned out, Baldwin wanted to make some changes to the book too; he wasn't happy about the use of northern English colloquialisms, which he thought many southern readers would not understand, those wooden garths used to bake cakes being a case in point. But even at the point of handing Baldwin the copyright, Elizabeth was still in full control of her work and its contents, and according to John Harland, told him exactly what she thought of his editorial suggestion:

> Mrs Raffald, who is described as a fine, dignified, lady-like woman, of high bearing and carriage, and with a considerable spice of pride, drew herself up, as was her wont when her dignity was ruffled, and said with a marked emphasis: 'What I have written I proposed to write at the time; it was written deliberately, and I cannot admit of any alteration.'[48]

The changes were not made and, one presumes, Baldwin left the Raffald residence with a flea in his ear.

Baldwin would go on to publish a further five editions within Elizabeth's lifetime, and although she had handed him the rights to the book and its contents, she continued to keep a close eye on them and even edited some of them; perhaps, as the author, she still received some royalties. Most importantly, she made sure the book remained exactly how she wanted. The only obvious further change in her lifetime was made in the third edition when the appendix of recipes from the second edition was integrated into the book, so from the third edition onwards, one could not be sure which recipes are genuine Raffalds, and which are simply Raffald-approved.

Elizabeth was the first woman in England to benefit from selling her copyright *after* the first edition was a success. The idea of copyright emerged at the beginning of the eighteenth century and the roots of copyright law can be found in the 1710 *Act for the Encouragement of Learning*, also known as *The Statute of Anne* (that is Queen Anne, the last of the Stuart monarchs), the aim of which being to end the unregulated printing and distribution of works. There would be over a century's worth of debate as to how this might be achieved in practice. It was settled that new authors would enjoy fourteen years of protective ownership of their intellectual property, and if the author was still alive, it would be extended a further fourteen years. After that, the work could become part of the public domain.[49]

Importantly for Elizabeth, these early copyright laws didn't exclude women. Actually, to put it more accurately, they did not explicitly state the exclusion of them, possibly because the writers of the laws never considered them in the first place, but in doing so unwittingly made the new world of regulated publishing rather progressive, and a handful of women took advantage of this loophole. Suddenly women's voices were being heard, at least in the gendered realms of romantic fiction, cookery, self-help manuals and other works of betterment. Men largely kept away from these topics, as they considered such diminutive literary areas not worth their attention. They were readily snapped up by male publishers, who cared less about literary merit and more about the number of copies they could sell. It is not an overstatement to say that 'Elizabeth Raffald serves as an example of how women used the written word as a way to take part in their society and economy like female novelists, poets, and playwrights.'[50]

This phenomenon happened outside of London much more frequently because women could take a more prominent and visible role in business and the common marketplace, especially in the north of England.[51] Elizabeth may have owned her copyright, but John, as her husband, owned Elizabeth. This created the curious situation where 'women writers of cookbooks produced textual property that [on one hand] they could manage and sell; [but] on the other, their ability to own any sort of property was strictly controlled by the laws of England.'[52] Despite this, shrewd Elizabeth used copyright to successfully establish a brand and to protect her intellectual property.

***

Aside from the quality of the recipes and writing, *The Experienced English Housekeeper* was successful because it is a book written by a woman for women, and it was not looking for the approval of men. Dr Samuel Johnson, though he approved of the contents of Hannah Glasse's book, was disparaging against women cookery book writers in general. There was a piece of gossip going around that the reason *The Art of Cookery* was so good was because it was really written by a man called Dr Hill, using a pseudonym. Johnson disagreed, his evidence being her use of nitrates saltpetre and salt prunella for curing meat: 'I doubt if the book be written by Dr Hill', he said 'for, in Mrs Glasse's Cookery, which I have looked into, salt-petre and sal-prunella are spoken of as different substances, whereas sal-prunella is only salt-petre burnt on charcoal; and Hill could not be ignorant of this … Women,' he continued, 'can spin very well; but they cannot make a good book of Cookery.'[53] However, Johnson failed to see the point: it was not scholarly, nor was it meant to be. Neither Hannah nor Elizabeth were trying to astound learned men with some great unifying theory of gastronomy; they were helping women successfully manage their household and kitchen in a practical language that anyone could understand.

Elizabeth did not hide her class or name; a full name and the title Mrs 'was not associated with class, but with respectability and confidence' – exactly what the out-of-her-depth gentlewoman, housekeeper, cook or maid-of-all-work was in desperate need of. This comes in contrast to the first half of the century, when names were often not given, and when they were, it was because the writer was a member of the gentry. Even plain-speaking Hannah Glasse wrote anonymously; her book was written simply by 'A Lady', which she was not. Anyone buying the book would have assumed it was written by a member of the upper classes and so she told her little white lie.[54] In the latter half of the eighteenth century, forty-five cookery books written by women were published and, of these, twenty-six published under their first and last names, sixteen used the prefix 'Mrs', two didn't use their first names, and just four used pseudonyms.[55]

Although Elizabeth's book was extremely successful, and her influence upon the genre never in doubt, when it comes to celebration and recognition of female literary talent, she is excluded. Unsurprisingly, it is the prose and poetry written by women that have received the attention, but cookery writers like Elizabeth should be recognised and celebrated too. Whilst it is safe to say cookery or instructional books do not count as high art or creative writing, they did function as a way for women writers to find their way into the home in a non-threatening, gender-appropriate manner by 'remain[ing] within an acceptable space and subject'.[56] Writers like Elizabeth, then, provided a gateway for female writers of fiction to find their way into the libraries of Britain.

Just because female cookery book writers had become popular, the genre had in no way become an exclusively female one; there were plenty of male cooks writing bestsellers too, but after the successes of Elizabeth *et al.*, the masculine writing style and approach to cookery changed markedly, becoming less elitist. The inclusive approach became the order of the day, and in a post-Raffald world, the tone completely changed. Now there was a focus on economy and a range of recipes for a range of tastes, classes and budgets. John Farley, chief cook at the exclusive gentleman's club the London Tavern, rather than using his book to show off his superior knowledge and the expensive elitist foods he made, instead wrote *The London Art of Cookery* (1783) for the 'Use of all Ranks in general, not only for those who have attained a tolerable Knowledge of Cookery, but also for those who are but young in Experience … and thereby directed them how properly to decorate the Table of either the Peer or the Mechanic.'[57]

In William Augustus Henderson's *Housekeeper's Instructor*, he assured the reader that '[t]he receipts for each article are formed on so easy and cheap a plan, as to be within the purchase of all ranks of people.'[58] Well-respected restaurateurs Collingwood and Woollams of the Crown & Anchor tavern on The Strand would go one step further in their book *The Universal Cook* (1806) and namedrop them as influences. For instance, when introducing their approach to cooking 'made dishes' of meat, 'it may not be amiss to give some general observations thereon, as we find them in Raffald, Glasse … and other modern books of cookery', so at least they are crediting their sources.[59] But this change in tack only served to drive the genre forwards, and Raffald, Glasse and Smith created the momentum, shifting the cookery book from its upper-class niche into quite possibly the most progressive genre, aimed at and appealing to all classes and genders.

FALL

Chapter 7

The King's Head (1772–1779)

By the close of 1771, Elizabeth had accrued quite the portfolio, with her shop, a normal school for young gentlewomen, a register office, two editions of *The Experienced English Housekeeper* as well as the first edition of *The Directory of Manchester and Salford* under her belt. The other major arm of her empire was the catering businesses, the lion's share of which occurred in the Bull's Head, which sat adjacent to Market Place, preparing upmarket dinners for its clientele. Indeed, she spent so much time there that some biographers of Elizabeth have assumed she ran the place. She didn't, but perhaps it felt like it at times. According to her directory of 1772, Richard Allsopp was the owner. It was a profitable partnership, and it put to work her skills in designing, cooking and pulling off impressive dinners similar to those at Arley Hall. Indeed, there was probably no one else in Manchester with the requisite experience, skill and professional connections than she. But in 1772, the Raffalds decided to open her own premises and, in April 1772, Elizabeth and John placed a notice in the *Manchester Mercury*, announcing they were to cease trading at Market Place:

> To be Let, and entered on immediately, A Good and well-accustomed Seed and Confectioners SHOP, situate in the Market-Place, Manchester, now in the Possession of John Raffald, Seedsman, and Elizabeth Raffald, Confectioner, who are declining those Branches, and entering a different One.

The new business was obviously to be very different to her shop on Market Place, because in the same notice she declares that 'The Stock in Trade [is] to be disposed of, consisting of a large Quantity of … Olives, Catchup … &c. now selling at Prime Cost and will continue till all are sold.' The notice was repeated in the *Mercury* a further nine times.[1] Then, in May, another notice in the *Mercury* cropped up from H. Cooper, 'Hosier in Market-street-lane' announcing that she had 'taken up the Business of a REGISTER OFFICE, as resigned to her by Mrs. Raffald.'[2]

The Raffalds settled on the King's Head as their new premises and it sat just on the other side of the bridge over the Irwell in Salford. This was not the case of just needing a larger property because they had outgrown their current one; what Elizabeth and John had taken on was complex and very different. King's Head Yard[3] was the largest tavern inn in Salford at the time and consisted of 'extensive ranges of stabling, coach-houses, and other outbuildings … Under her régime the King's Head was less an ordinary inn than a sort of superior hotel'[4] with 'a 40-foot room suitable for events' and a daily afternoon dinner. She used her connections to maximum effect, purchasing the best quality food and wine, filling the stables with horses, and fitting out the hotel with new beds and fresh linen.[5]

Elizabeth and John both knew that such an undertaking would require all of their time, energy and focus, and there would be no time for her to run a shop, register office and school, and for John to carry on working and trading as a seedsman. All efforts and, as it would play out, all profits from their previous businesses and the two editions of the book were poured into this new venture. By summer, they had readied themselves enough to place another notice in the *Mercury* on 12 August 1772, this time on the front page, announcing their exciting plans:

> John and Elizabeth Raffald, Desire to acquaint their Friends and the Public, That they have taken and entered upon the Old, Accustomed and Commodious Inn, known by the sign of the KING's HEAD in SALFORD, MANCHESTER, which they have fitted up in the neatest and most elegant Manner for the Reception and accommodation of the Nobility, Gentry, Merchants, and Tradesmen who shall be pleased to honour them with their Company where they may be assured of the utmost Civility and good Treatment, they being determined to make it their Study as it will always be their Interest and Inclination, to merit the Approbation of their Friends.

According to John Harland, the clientele was made up of those who had previously frequented the Bull's Head. Elizabeth was certainly keen to let 'her new house to her old customers and their foreign friends on their arrival in Manchester.'[6] Had Elizabeth poached them? There is certainly potential for that to be true; we have already seen that she could be ruthless when it came to business, especially when it came to those in direct competition with her. The events at the tavern may simply have been discontinued by the owner of the Bull's Head, of course, or perhaps Elizabeth had had a row with the owner. Whatever the reason, it is obvious that her reputation preceded her, and where she went, her customers went with her.

The King's Head quickly became *the* place for visiting merchants and businesspeople to stay and for Manchester residents to entertain – or show off to – new and potential business partners, especially the French; not only could they trust Elizabeth to provide them with first-rate victuals, but because she spoke the language she was able to chitchat with her French guests and help them feel at ease. This was an exception for Elizabeth because front of house was not her natural domain; she much preferred working in the kitchens, back of house.[7] The meeting and greeting of guests would be John's domain. In all of the notices regarding the King's Head, it is John who is named as business owner, not Elizabeth.

It wouldn't just be Elizabeth's connections who would create business for them, for John organised several events held at the tavern. One of which was a 'Florist's Feast', a celebration and gardening and flower show for professional and semi-professional nurserymen, which had become very popular across the whole country. Of course, they used the *Mercury* to make the event known. It must have been a great success, for the next year it had become known as 'The Annual Carnation Meeting'.[8] It seemed as though they had both found their perfect niche: the charismatic John charming the guests on full show as Elizabeth worked diligently behind the scenes, delighting all with her impressive banquet food.

When she wasn't working in the kitchen, Elizabeth sat in her specially built 'sanctum', 'a comfortable little bar, enclosed by glass on three sides, where she sat to give her orders, and to receive applications, and where she compiled her books.' It was from here that 'servants came for instructions, especially as to dinner [where she] always gave them neatly written orders; and if she wished to give them directions, she put them in writing, and sent a messenger with them up or downstairs, as the case may be.'[9] It was within her sanctum in 1772 and 1773 that she prepared the second edition of her

Manchester and Salford directory, and received her windfall of £1,200 from Robert Baldwin for the copyright to *The Experienced English Housekeeper*. In November and December 1773, she heavily advertised the third edition of the book in the *Mercury*, listing the various establishments where one could purchase a copy.

This division of labour suited their unique personalities worked, and they were presumably happy with this set-up. In 1774, they even managed to have another child, so they were able to find at least a modicum of intimate time together. The baby was a daughter, named Harriot, who sadly did not survive infancy. Harriot was Elizabeth and John's last recorded child.[10] Things were going well and in these initial years at the King's Head, Elizabeth's almsgiving became legendary: '[i]n Salford, as in Manchester, she became a sort of Lady Bountiful to the poor, giving them food, clothing, and occasionally simple medicines, or nourishing broth, wine &c.'[11] Being charitable had become a social necessity because '[m]any eighteenth-century states were not well equipped to deal with large-scale poverty nor was there a strong sense that [it] was the state's responsibility.'[12] Instead, a great number and range of charitable organisations popped up, essentially an extension of the popular clubs and societies of the time. Anyone who could afford to spend a good deal of cash, or better, a good deal of time with charitable organisations was expected to do so, and they made sure they were seen to be taking part. One has to wonder how much of this was real care and feeling of duty, and how much is keeping up appearances. For Elizabeth, of course, business and standing came first, and whilst the quality of her moral fibre is not in doubt, her showy almsgiving would only have continued to promote her status as community pillar, which, in turn, would have a positive effect on her business. No act of Elizabeth's seems to be truly altruistic.

At the end of 1774, just before Christmas, the Raffalds obviously felt they weren't doing enough and announced yet another new venture. Unusually, it was done in partnership with someone else, and it seems only John was involved. The advertisement in the *Mercury* ran:

> Messrs. SWAIN and RAFFALD, Beg Leave to acquaint their Friends and the Public, That they have fitted up in the genteelist manner, a new MOURNING COACH and HEARSE, with handsome Furniture, able Horses, and careful Drivers.[13]

Their stables and yard were extensive and the idea to fully utilise them seems like a sound idea. That neither John nor Elizabeth seem to have had much experience working with horses was an issue, hence why Mr Swain lent his skills. According to her 1772 directory, John Swain ran the 'Liverpool Stage-Coach' from outside a tavern called the 'Spread-eagle', also in Salford. It's difficult to ascertain from the advertisement, and there are no mentions in the sources, just why Elizabeth's name was not included. It could, of course, be because it would have been unseemly to have a woman's name – no matter how well-respected – on the signage. On the other hand, it may have been John's (and perhaps Mr Swain's) brainchild, and Elizabeth, sufficiently swamped with her own work, left them to it. The endeavour did not succeed, so if she was closely involved, it would be the first time her magic touch had failed her. Mr Swain may have been the guilty party; had he moved to King's Head Yard because his previous business had gone under? He does disappear from the directories, so he either left town or stopped trading. It may have all been down to bad luck or mistiming, of course. As Elizabeth was such a canny businessperson, it is generally concluded that it must have been run by John. Whoever or whatever was to blame, it made a huge dent in their finances, but there was no time to dwell because they had to deal with everything else life at the King's Head threw at them.

***

In the eighteenth century, there were broadly two tiers to the great British institution that is the public house: the upper tier was made up of inns and taverns, both of which were 'well respected' and very much considered high-end; then there were the establishments frequented by the lower sort, the alehouses and gin houses. Of course, within these two groups there would have been 'different grades of care',[14] but the Raffalds were sure they would fit nicely into the upper end of that upper tier, running one of the premier inns of North-West England. Now that they were in the business of catering for the upper classes, Elizabeth's cooking was more lavish, and the drink on offer more select. As a result, Elizabeth oversaw more and more often the cooking of beasts such as turtle and sturgeon. Diet of the well-to-do by now had become so rich and heavy with a focus on beef, puddings and rich sauces that many of these people suffered greatly for 'the common complaints of the time: heartburn, colic, bleeding piles and gout'.[15] Take, for example, Elizabeth's recipe for 'Ducks a-la-mode':

> Slit two Ducks down the Back, and Bone them carefully, make Force-meat of the Crumbs of a Penny Loaf, four Ounces of fat Bacon scraped, a little Parsley, Thyme, Lemon Peel, two Shallots or Onions shread very fine, with Pepper, Salt and Nutmeg to your Taste, and two Eggs, stuff your Ducks with it and sew them up, lard them down each Side of the Breast with Bacon, dredge them well with Flour, and put them in a Dutch Oven to Brown, then put them into a Stew Pan with Three Pints of Gravy, a Glass of Red Wine, a Tea Spoonful of Lemon Pickle, a large one of Walnut and Mushroom Catchup, one of Browning, and one Anchovy, with Chyan Pepper to your Taste, stew them gently over a slow Fire for an Hour, when enough, thicken your Gravy and put in a few Truffles and Morels, strain your Gravy and pour it upon them. – You may a-la-mode a Goose the same way.[16]

One group of people the Raffalds entertained regularly was the officers of regiments stationed in and around Manchester, which 'possessed neither infantry nor cavalry barracks' and therefore needed somewhere to host their mess tables. This was a service that had been offered at the Bull's Head, but with 'her removal to the King's Head, Salford, the "mess" removed thither also.'[17]

Much of John and Elizabeth's entertaining surrounded society meetings; there had been formal and informal groups in the past – indeed, florists' feasts originated in or around the Civil War – but by the eighteenth century, the idea of a society or club 'became one of the most distinctive social and cultural institutions of Georgian Britain'.[18] The main philosophy of these clubs was to always strive toward 'the improvement of learning and keeping up good humour and wit'.[19] One of the earliest of these is the renowned Royal Society, set up in the previous century. One hundred years later, there were over 130 types of club; around the country, there were doctor's clubs, poker clubs, as well as medical, musical and debating clubs, all of which, irrespective of their apparent speciality, 'conformed to a stereotype of male camaraderie, with a regime of eating, gambling and heavy drinking.'[20]

Excessive drinking was particularly encouraged, as it was associated with masculinity and facilitated discussion and sociability. At Edinburgh's Poker Club, the six-hour drinking sessions were legendary, as were its members, with men such as Adam Smith and David Hume in attendance.[21]

In the same issue of the *Mercury* in which the Raffalds had announced their move to the King's Head, they published another notice declaring 'THAT THE CARD ASSEMBLY Will be Opened At JOHN RAFFALD's, The King's-Head, in Salford, On Thursday the 24th of September next, And to be continued every Tuesday Fortnight during the Winter Season.'[22] Again, John's name and not Elizabeth's is attached to these events, and he was pushed to the fore even more so than usual for such meetings because not only was he the public, smiling face of the King's Head, but the members were made up of men, and men only. The only women who entered only did so to bring in food and drinks, before promptly leaving.

The initial core values of mirth, good humour and improvement often descended into depravity. In fact, for some, it became *the* reason to attend: the Beggar's Benison in Fife was an upper-class sex club that operated between the 1730s and 1830s, with events revolving around sex, obscene songs and stories.[23] But this was not an isolated incident, and was perhaps an inevitable consequence of a climate of heavy drinking in a male-only environment. It was in these meetings that female servants were most vulnerable to sexual abuse, much more so than those working as servants in private homes.[24] This social acceptance of drunken behaviour was not extended to the poor, of course; if they got drunk at their local gin or alehouse, it was uncivil and shocking, and whilst the great efforts of the well-to-do tried (in vain) to stop the working poor from drinking themselves to death, it never seemed to apply to them. Funny that.

One of the most famous of these clubs was the Beefsteak Club. Established in 1735, William Hogarth (of Gin Alley etching fame) was a co-founder, its full name being the Sublime Society of Beefsteaks. The great diarist and lawyer James Boswell joined one in 1762 and wrote: '[w]e had nothing to eat but beefsteaks & had wine & Punch in plenty & freedom.'[25] Beefsteaks may have been eaten, and the gridiron may have been their emblem, but central to the group's identity was drinking 'and especially the practice of toasting'. The club had toasting rituals that were baffling to any new members, who 'were introduced blindfolded, led by a member wearing a mitre who was known as the bishop'.[26] Once the penny had dropped as to how the toasting system worked, one was very drunk, and a member of the club. These self-indulgent behaviours combined with alcohol to allow male bonding.[27] Beefsteak Clubs were both popular and select, and it would have been a great coup to the Raffalds when the Manchester wing of the sublime society decided to hold their meeting at the King's Head in 1775 and again in 1776.[28] They dined every Wednesday and the 'Hour of Dining [was] three o'clock'. The drinks of choice, in the first half of the eighteenth century, were punch, which was served from a huge central bowl, and claret.

> To Make a rich Acid for Punch
>
> Bake Red Currants and strain them as you do for Jellies, take a Gallon of the Juice, put to it two Quarts of new Milk, crush Pearl Gooseberries when full ripe, and strain them through a coarse Cloth, add two Quarts of the Juice and three Pounds of double refined Sugar, three Quarts of Rum and two of Brandy, one Ounce of Isinglass dissolved in Part of the Liquor, mix it all up together, and put it in a little Cask, and let it stand six Weeks, and Bottle it for Use. It will keep many Years and save much Fruit.[29]

In the 1760s, however, claret – delicious and distinguished it may be – fell out of favour. The issue was that although it was appropriately expensive, it was also French, and was therefore deemed unpatriotic to consume, so the switch to port was made. Port was much cheaper than French wine, and it was already being drunk with aplomb by the middle classes, but upon finding it delicious, it was quickly adopted by the upper classes to fill the gap that claret had left – a rare case of a trickle-up effect of a commodity. It was enjoyed so much that this Portuguese 'blend of wine and spirit' became 'the national wine of England'.[30]

There was another contributing factor to the English taking up port as their favourite tipple, and that was because they had developed a taste for stronger liquor after gin had entered the public houses and imagination. Gin may have become associated with the poor, but it had, like so many other commodities, been originally a drink of the middle and upper classes. The upwardly mobile must have been most relieved when port came along, because – although it was cheaper than French wines – it was still reassuringly expensive compared to gin, the poison of the poor, and therefore had no stigma associated with it.

Because much of the drinking done by those who patronised the better taverns went on behind closed doors, gambling and debauchery were commonplace. This is illustrated in William Hogarth's sequence of paintings called *The Rake's Progress* (1734), which follows the protagonist Tom Rakewell stumbling through life over a sequence of eight plates. In the third, Tom has squandered his money, is drinking heavily and cavorting with some equally inebriated ladies; it is unclear whether the gentlewomen depicted are fellow patrons or sex workers, but one is led to assume the latter. Such behaviour, if kept behind closed doors, was socially acceptable, but drinking to inebriation in public certainly was not, and this is exemplified in another work by Hogarth, his two drawings *Gin Lane* and *Beer Street* (1751). *Gin Lane* infamously depicts a suckling babe falling from its drunk, toothless mother's breast atop a flight of stairs as she tries to grab a pinch of snuff. On Gin Lane, there is, of course, a gin house, and above it is the legend: 'Drunk for a Penny; Dead drunk for twopence; straw for nothing.' At the bottom of the work, the artist opines:

> Gin cursed Fiend, with Fury frought,
> Makes human Race a Prey.
> It enters by a deadly Draught,
> And steals our Life Away.

However, on Beer Street, everyone is happily chugging away on frothy ale and small beer, rosy-cheeked, chatting, smiling and getting on with their day, be it talking to friends, running errands, or working hard with a great big smile on their face. The poetry in this piece is rather more upbeat and romantic:

> Beer, happy Produce of our Isle
> Can sinewy Strength impart,
> And wearied with Fatigue and Toil
> Can chear manly Heart.

What has perhaps been lost over time regarding Hogarth's work is that it is meant as a satire reflecting the opinions of the upper classes, rather than the reality of daily life in the streets of Georgian London. The trouble is, satire only works when it is distinguishable from reality; gin addiction was a huge issue, not only because of issues surrounding addiction, but also because much of the gin that was sold was adulterated, sometimes wholly, with sulphuric acid made palatable with lime juice.[31] Part of the failure of the satire is that all focus was placed on Gin Lane, rather than both pieces together, and without the sickeningly idyllic Beer Street to compare it to, the point was lost, and the weak-willed and decrepit poor were looked down upon even more. All of this is rich, of course, seeing as most of the upper classes were routinely sozzled. The reason for these double standards is that apparently the poor were drinking to get drunk; it was the sole purpose, which was entirely different to the upper classes, who were drinking to promote sociability and bonhomie. As far as they were concerned, their behaviour was not only acceptable but proof of their civility; inebriation was a mere side effect. Getting blottoed in public was no way to behave, and this fact alone was reason enough not to help them. Sadly, it is likely that the poorest individuals in dire need of help were not driving the gin craze – their poverty, hunger and thirst were so extreme that any money spent or possessions traded were focused wholly on acquiring food. It was those one or two rungs up the ladder from rock bottom who became addicted to the cheap spirit.[32] They could afford just enough of it to destroy their and their families' lives but, of course, that was their fault and their problem. Alcoholism was far from being acknowledged as a disease.

John Raffald, in particular, was exposed to this heavy drinking by the patrons of the King's Head, and then – just as now – anyone running a restaurant, bar, inn or tavern, just by virtue of being around alcohol, found themselves consuming it more often and in larger amounts, his masculinity obliging him to keep up with the gentlemen. There is pressure to drink, too: it was in the business's best interest for him to drink with his guests, perhaps giving them a drink or two on the house so that they would, in the long run, spend more at the bar and frequent it more often.

The long hours and constant hangovers began to get the better of John. Alcohol, a depressant, affected his mood to the point he felt suicidal. John Harland recounts the events; describing John Raffald in rather disparaging terms, he wrote:

> During her compilation of the *Housekeeper*, and her admirable
> discharge of the duties of one in the best-frequented house in

Manchester of that day, [Elizabeth] was much annoyed and harassed by her husband, who, after yielding to intemperance, was frequently 'hypped', and … would talk of doing away with himself. One day, after keeping to his bed till noon, he came downstairs into the glass bar querulously complained of being tired of his life, and said he would go and drown himself. Roused by his unmanly conduct, Mrs. Raffald replied: 'Well, I'll tell you what, John Raffald; I do think it would be the best step you could take; for then you would be relieved from all your troubles and anxieties, and you really do harass me very much.' From that time Mr. Raffald never repeated his determination to commit suicide.[33]

It is obvious that the opinion of Harland – and, it seems, Elizabeth too – was that John had become a rather pathetic figure, and maybe deserved short shrift from his wife; and one can see how Elizabeth would have no time for anyone in that state of mind. It's highly probable he was a serial offender, and frequently hungover and clingy. Perhaps Elizabeth became frustrated because her workload was so great and unrelenting, when, from her point of view, he had the easy and fun side of the bargain, which was not the case. However, it is easy to be too hard on John: surely another contributing factor to John's habitual drinking was that he felt emasculated by his wife's successes, a point brought up by journalist Doreen Taylor, who may have hit the nail right on the head:

Perhaps the Raffald marriage was one of those in which a weaker man attaches himself to a stronger and more capable woman. At any rate, John Raffald, who was said to be a first class gardener, but a rather improvident man, soon fades from the picture; the rest of his glory is entirely his wife's.[34]

The management of her husband in this way is generally considered just '[a]nother manifestation of her shrewdness and tact'.[35] But this is perhaps unfair: one factor has been left out in the assessment of John and his behaviour, and that is that he was a great talent in his own right, and gave up a career in cutting-edge horticulture when he left Arley and moved with Elizabeth to work alongside James, the brother to whom he had deferred his inheritance. Judging him by his future behaviours, it seems he regretted the choices he had made, his own career scaled down through his years in Manchester as his wife went from strength to strength. Now he was entertaining guests – the vast majority being heavy-drinking upper-class men – so he had the chance to claw back some of his masculinity, even if was happening in a tavern purchased from the profits of his wife's talent and hard work. It is not difficult to see how playing second fiddle to his wife whilst entertaining with alcohol could begin as social drinking and, in time, become a compulsion and then addiction. That people use alcohol as a way to self-medicate their mental health issues was just as obvious a concept in the eighteenth century as it is today. Where opinion differed, however, is that in the eighteenth century, a 'drunkard was fully responsible for his sorry condition'.[36]

With John's heavy drinking, things began to unravel: Elizabeth was now unsupported, and the King's Head was no longer the tight ship it had been at the beginning of the venture. Without John at the helm front of house, and no longer the charismatic male presence he was, things started to go wrong. Being unable to attend to guests properly led to a series of major thefts from the hotel rooms.[37] John was unable to keep order and Elizabeth was pushed from pillar to post to compensate, but with John drinking a good deal of the stock, the tavern soon stopped turning a profit. This storm should have been weathered, but with the failure of the expensive coaching and hearse service, and the money from the copyright of her book from Robert Baldwin gone, Elizabeth had lost her cash flow. Suddenly, Elizabeth was living hand to mouth, and she could not afford to let anything else go wrong.

How obvious these troubles were to their clientele or the locals is not clear; the first indication in the sources that things were going awry is in a notice in the *Manchester Mercury* on 25 June 1776, stating 'at the request of many friends … [t]he Register Office for Servants' would be reinstated. The notice asked interested readers to apply

> to her Shop, opposite the King's Head, in Salford, where all SORTS OF CONFECTIONARY may be had, and every decoration for a Table, such as Jellies, Creams, Flummery, Fish Ponds, Transparent Puddings, Almond Cheese-Cakes, Sweet-Meats, Tarts, Crawcrans, Paste Baskets, Silver and Gold webs &c. Likewise, all kinds of Catchup, Lemon Pickles, Brownings for made Dishes; also all kinds of Wet and Dry Sweetmeats, Preserved or Bottled Fruits.[38]

It looks exactly like something Elizabeth would write, but this advert comes not from her, but her older sister, Mary Whitaker. What was this? Her sister setting up a rival business, exploiting Elizabeth's earlier success? No, this was not a cynical cash-in or some kind of sibling rivalry, but Elizabeth's family coming in to support her in bringing back elements of her business that were tried and tested and – most importantly – could turn a profit. Remember, Mary was a talented confectioner in her own right, and it was her foray into pastry that had inspired Elizabeth to follow a similar career path. That Mary was running the register office means that Mrs Cooper must have handed it back to Elizabeth for Mary to manage. It must have been galling for proud Elizabeth to admit she was unable to cope and required help, but she was left with no choice; she needed to turn a profit from the shop and the register office to save the King's Head from going under completely. From this point, notices in the *Mercury* get fewer and fewer. In 1777, there was just one for a single club event.[39] In May the next year, Elizabeth tried to increase footfall by making the King's Head the picking up and dropping off point for the coach and postal service, the 'LIVERPOOL and MANCHESTER Neat and Easy DILIGENCE'.[40]

Despite all efforts, the creditors called. As was typical of the day, bankrupted individuals were listed in the local newspaper for all to see. The announcement in the *Mercury* on 14 December 1779 read: 'JOHN RAFFALD of SALFORD, MANCHESTER, Innkeeper, hath this Day assigned over all his personal Estate and Effects ... on or before the 14th Day of February next.' It continued: 'all Persons indebted to the Estate of the said John Raffald, are required forthwith to pay their respective Debts to the ... Trustees ... or to Mr. Milne [the attorney], otherwise they will be sued without further notice.'[41]

And so, in February 1779, the Raffalds left Salford and the King's Head with few belongings. Everything Elizabeth had worked for had gone, evaporated from her hands. It wasn't just the money either, it was the loss of status: she was a pillar of the community and a prominent woman who was rubbing shoulders with, and respected by, the highest ranking in Manchester. The Raffalds disappear from the records until October 1779, when John and Elizabeth announce their return to Manchester and the Shambles to occupy the Exchange Coffee-House on Exchange Square, now the site of a Selfridge's & Co. department store and the Wellington Inn, the only surviving building of the old Shambles area.

Quite where they dwelled in the nine months between February and October is not clear; perhaps they lived with John's brother James in Salford, or with George Raffald in Stockport. Some of their daughters may have lived with Elizabeth's sister Mary, who by this point had decided to live permanently in Manchester. She had certainly grown very close to Elizabeth's daughters, especially the youngest, Anna. We also don't know how the Raffalds raised the capital for their coffee house venture: perhaps they used equipment from the confectioner's shop Mary was running, assuming it hadn't also been confiscated by the creditors, or borrowed money from family. Elizabeth may too have received a few royalties from her book; it is unclear just what the terms of agreement were between her and Baldwin, but that that she continued to advertise new editions in the *Mercury* suggests she may have. That they were in this sorry mess suggests it was not enough.

Going from a glitzy tavern to a relatively simple and ramshackle coffee house must have been disheartening in the extreme. But a coffee house had the potential to suit Elizabeth well at this time – it was less complex and fewer staff were needed to run it, and it wasn't dependent upon attracting those who lived the high life and all the excesses that came with it. It was in a prominent spot too and had the potential to be a modest money-spinner. A less stressful life could be tonic to both of them, at least once the dust had settled after adjusting to their new place in Manchester and Manchester society.

Chapter 8

The Exorcist and the Midwife

There are a few tales of Elizabeth that appear somewhat far-fetched or even fantastical and whether or not they are rooted in fact; compared to the things we do know about her – the tangible books, directories and businesses – they seem almost plausible. If the sources are to be believed, she successfully exorcised a house, ridding it of the evil entity that resided within it; co-wrote a long-lost book on midwifery with one of the country's leading surgeons; and, perhaps the best known of these stories, she gave birth to sixteen daughters.

Elizabeth's ghostly encounter occurred during her time at the King's Head, and the story is recounted by John Harland first in the *Manchester Guardian* on 5 May 1852, and then later in his *Collectanea* in 1867. Like much of his material, it was proffered by Elizabeth's granddaughter 'Mrs Hodgkinson', whose mother was Elizabeth's youngest surviving daughter, Anna ('Mrs Munday'), neither of whom were present at the incident in question. It all began when the tenants of a Doncaster property left abruptly due to harassment from some kind of spectre. 'The story was that "at the witching hour of night" a female apparition rushed into one of the chambers, drew the bed curtains, and shook some parchments in the face of the scared occupant of the bed.' The property in question had been left to Elizabeth and her sister Sarah ('Mrs Middlewood') by their father, Joshua. But this wasn't the first time something like this had happened, and the property had gained a reputation as a haunted building. So widely believed was this that the sisters couldn't rent the property. Something had to be done.

> As the sisters were deprived of a considerable yearly sum by this evil reputation of the house, and as they had been told that if any one could muster courage enough to address the ghostly visitant, with certain scriptural adjuration, it would disappear,

and no more trouble this sublunary sphere, they determined to pass a night together, without any male protector, in the haunted house. Accordingly they awaited the hour in the haunted chamber, and as recorded by the testimony of Mrs. Munday ... there was some apparition, suddenly visible to both, with its crackling of parchment deeds and rolls, and flashing, glancing motion. Mrs. Raffald managed to stammer out, 'In the name of the Father, and of the Son, and of the Holy Ghost, who art thou? Whence comest thou? What wantest thou?'; but they could not finish the adjuration from fright; and the ghost disappeared with an extra crackling of parchments, but without answering their inquiries. The sisters always believed that if they could have proceeded to the end of the formulary, they should have extorted some utterance from the ghost. But their purpose was answered; the ghost was laid; the property was let; and the matter was almost forgotten in the enlightenment of another generation, when it became necessary to take down the house, and then, near the foundations, some human bones were found; which it is conjectured may have been the remains of the poor murdered ghost, and thus have caused the restless spirit to revisit 'the pale glimpses of the moon'.[1]

This account contains several tropes typical of eighteenth-century ghost sightings: wailing and shouting; the presentation of parchment deeds or wills; a phantasm expelled by the power of words; and a rather conveniently discovered pile of human remains to conclude the whole affair. These are familiar tropes today, but they were created in the eighteenth century. Ghosts have always been seen, but in the more enlightened times of the long eighteenth century, what ghosts were and did changed significantly now that the country was now a Protestant one.

The medieval viewpoint had been simple, straightforward and perfectly reasonable given the religious beliefs of the time: ghosts were simply the souls of the dead stuck in Purgatory, tormented, bound and only making an appearance in the plane of the living so they could right some misdeed they were guilty of and win passage to Paradise. Problems arose with the doing away with Catholicism, because adopting Protestantism meant saying goodbye to the concept of Purgatory, and if Purgatory couldn't exist, *ergo*, neither could ghosts.[2] Then, the rise of natural philosophy – modern scientific thought and reasoning – a discipline that demanded real data and rigorous testing if the existence of ghosts were to be approved created more doubt.

The cases for and against were discussed in clubs, societies and coffee houses across the country. That's not to say all of these 'learned men' rejected the idea of spirits; pioneering physicist Robert Hooke, Royal Society fellow, was very interested in the paranormal and sought accounts of the supernatural. As usual, Samuel Johnson had something to say on the subject, keeping surprisingly open-minded, saying: '[i]t is wonderful that five thousand years have now elapsed since the creation of the world, and still it is undecided whether or not there has ever been an instance of the spirit of any person appearing after death. All argument is against it, but all belief is for it.' He also admitted that if the appropriate evidence were presented, he would be compelled to believe.[3]

The trouble for the Protestant church was that they suddenly found themselves on the same side of the argument as the intelligentsia, whom the Church viewed as dangerous atheists who wanted to debunk Christian and biblical doctrine. So the clergy was rather relieved when – even though it went against their new beliefs – people carried on seeing plenty of ghosts. After all, ghost sightings did remind people of 'the omnipotence of God and of fragility of the human condition'. But what were they seeing if not spirits of the dead? After some liturgical soul-searching, it was concluded that these entities must in fact be angels, sent by the Almighty Himself to right wrongs or to warn wrongdoers of the consequences of their actions; hence the waving or conjuring of important documents such as deeds. This came with the caveat that some of these presences might be satanic minions sent by the Devil to tempt or torment unsuspecting individuals.[4]

Eighteenth-century ghosts were different to the ghosts of the Victorian era and the spiritualism movement: there was certainly no ectoplasm, they appeared just as often in the daytime as at night, and they were not transparent.[5] They only became see-through when Victorian photographic images 'captured' them *in situ*, showing them as translucent doubly-exposed forms. Nor were they swaddled or covered by white sheets, that's another nineteenth-century trope derived from the practice of wrapping corpses in burial garb of white woollen swaddling.[6] They did, however, communicate by tapping, making loud noises – banging, screeching and wailing – and there are scores of cases. The two briefly presented here contain elements common to Elizabeth's supposed encounter, and more importantly, neither were intended for publication and were therefore not written with sensationalism in mind.

The first comes from the unpublished writings of Yorkshireman Ralph Thoresby in the early eighteenth century. Ralph had retired early, at the age of forty; a religious man, he spent his time collecting witness accounts of ghostly encounters from the inhabitants of Leeds. His most complete account concerns the behaviour of the ghost of a Mrs Savage who was tormenting her grandson-in-law, John Fawcett. He had determined that she was the source of the strange goings-on, after Thoresby suggested he communicate with the spirit by tapping. It turned out that Mrs Savage was displeased because she had left money to her two granddaughters in her will, but it had not been passed on to them, and she firmly pointed the finger of blame at John Fawcett as the reason for this oversight. Once she had made her reasons for the haunting clear, she became more active, 'taking bed staves and throwing them about' and pulling off bedclothes. She even took physical form in front of the chambermaid, who described her as 'an ancient Gentlewoman grey-headed'. John liaised with a clergyman to work out the best way of ridding the house of the spectre (he obviously wasn't going to entertain giving Savage's granddaughters their inheritance). The clergyman should have pooh-poohed the whole affair as either a hoax or the work of tricksters – he could at least have said it was an angel taking Savage's form and that Fawcett should take heed – but no. Instead, he suggested finding the local wiseman. Wise or cunning folk were often hired to dispel ghosts; interacting with spectres was not seen as devilish, dangerous or subversive in its nature like witchcraft, and this sort of wise folk were not generally stigmatised. Rather anticlimactically, all he said was 'I charge thee by the holy and blessed Trinity to depart this house,'[7] but this is remarkably similar to the method by which Elizabeth dispatched her troublesome spectre.

The second account concerns Mary Ricketts, the wife of Jamaican plantation owner William Henry Ricketts, who purchased a house in 1765 for his young family to reside in while he worked on his plantation in the West Indies. The house was originally Tudor but had recently been refurbished in the eighteenth century a similar way to Arley Hall. Six years later, the family and servants would leave, 'exhausted by inexplicable terrors' and the place was declared by Mary's brother as 'unfit for habitation for any human being'.[8] It began with bangs and moans that escalated to 'the most loud, deep tremendous noise' and 'shrill and dreadful' shrieks. Not only that, but inside the children's room was often seen the apparition of a tall, lean man wearing the dark grey clothes of a servant. Many people came to help or scoff and left terrified. One naysayer, who suspected trickery by someone in the village, placed an advertisement in a local paper offering fifty guineas to anyone who could explain how the noises were being made, assuming that anyone who would torment the household was sufficiently morally corrupt to own up and collect the money. It was increased to 100 guineas – around three times the annual salary of a semi-skilled worker – but there were no takers.

The building was never exorcised; a member of the clergy did visit, but the ghostly goings-on were waved away as servants playing tricks in a 'villainous attempt to make [them] feel uneasy'. This story concludes instead with demolition; when the house was knocked down to make way for a new hunting lodge, a box was found, supposedly under the children's rooms – '[i]n it was found a small skull rather ape-like, but perhaps a human baby. Also found were a great deal of papers, concealed.' The story goes that a previous owner, Lord Stawall, had an illicit affair with his sister-in-law. She fell pregnant, and when the child was born, his steward, a tall, thin man named Isaac Mackrell, smothered the infant and hid the corpse.

The account of these events was written by Mary Ricketts herself, but she hid them; only decades later would it come to light, after they were discovered by family members who read the startling story out to friends. They obviously had some highbrow friends, because certain elements of Mary's account would eventually form the basis of M. R. James's classic gothic ghost story *The Turn of the Screw*.[9]

These stories, including the one involving Elizabeth, are important because they tell us a lot about belief of the afterlife and conceptions surrounding how God Himself interacted with His flock. It also shows that base fears of spirits of evil, and the superstitions surrounding them, do not simply disappear. Elizabeth's story is almost a checklist of gothic ghost story tropes, but perhaps that is not so surprising, bearing in mind that the incident is recounted three-quarters of a century after the supposed event, a time by which gothic ghost lore had become well established. John Garland gilded the lily too, one assumes, but these points are perhaps unimportant. More significant is that the protagonist in the terrific tale is Elizabeth, a woman who needed no male chaperone, who could stand her ground against even the spirits of the dead and successfully (though suspiciously easily) exorcise a building of them. That the story exists is evidence of her real fearlessness, resolve and determination in getting any task done, whether it be a bestselling cookery book or getting her rental income back.

Harland's biography also claims that Elizabeth was a midwife, or at least, someone with knowledge and skill enough to team up with one of the country's most talented surgeons to write a book on the subject. Like her ghost exorcism, written evidence of this only appears in John Harland's writings seventy-five years after Elizabeth's death. He tells us:

> She also wrote a book on midwifery, under the able guidance and superintendence of Mr. Charles White, the celebrated surgeon, who resided in King Street, on the site of the Present Town Hall. This, we believe was her latest literary labour; it was nearly completed, but it was left unfinished at her death. It is believed that the MS. was subsequently disposed of by her widower, when he went to London, where he spent all that she accumulated. We have been unable to ascertain whether it was ever printed; but if so, we believe it did not appear as her work, but would probably have some other name attached to it, perhaps of some celebrated and deceased accoucheur [man-midwife].[10]

At the turn of the eighteenth century, midwifery had 'seemed fairly secure' in the realm of women. There was a simple system; a woman who wanted to become a midwife approached her local bishop, who then issued her with a licence. Such a permit would be granted not on her abilities as a midwife, but on her good character. Then, one assumes, the bishop left the details of the process to the women.[11] Her job was learned by experience, and their medical approach was 'still firmly rooted in superstition',[12] but elsewhere medicine was being treated scientifically by natural philosophers. Female midwives could keep up with modern developments if they desired, and some did, but they were few in number. In Elizabeth's 1772 directory, six man-midwives and two women midwives are listed; for the middle and upper classes at least, the world of midwifery was becoming very masculine.[13]

Charles White was one such innovator, a very talented physician, surgeon and man-midwife, who hailed from, and practised in, Manchester after learning his craft in London. He lived on King Street and worked at his father's practice and as a visiting surgeon to Manchester Infirmary, a post he would occupy for thirty-six years. In 1762, he received the Grand Diploma of the Corporation of Surgeons and was elected a member of the Royal Society, but it would be for his work as an obstetrician that he would be most lauded, writing several texts on the subject, the book garnering most praise being *A Treatise on the Management of Pregnant Women and Lying-in Women, and the Means of Curing, but More Especially Preventing, the Principle Disorders to Which They are Liable*, which focused primarily upon the treatment and prevention of puerperal fever, a disease caused by the infection of the uterus in postnatal mothers which was rampaging through maternity and 'lying-in' hospitals, killing one mother in twenty-five. Lying-in was the period of one month that a mother and baby spent together, isolated except for interactions with female servants or female members of the family.

At the turn of the eighteenth century, there was little or no provision for delivery in hospitals and only in the second quarter of the century did lying-in hospitals and wards begin to be established in London, primarily for poor but respectable (i.e., married) women.[14] White's works on the subject were comprised of his ideas, theories and detailed case studies, the vast majority involving women from Manchester and Salford. His recommendations read like modern public health mantras: as far as he was concerned, cleanliness was paramount because he had surmised that the fever is spread by contact, and insisted that patients' beds, clothing and surroundings were cleaned and disinfected, and the rooms ventilated. He was also adamant that puerperal fever was not caused by a unique pathogen, but that it was a manifestation of diseases already known to be associated with overcrowding.[15]

He was prolific and worked well into his seventies, apparently with great stamina, and he travelled to work on horseback until his retirement. Retiring did not equate to rest: the same year, he founded the Manchester and Salford Lying-In Charity, which would later become St Mary's Hospital. Although a great talent, he became rather a forgotten hero; like Elizabeth, he received a great deal of praise and recognition in his lifetime and the years following his death. He was described as 'the most eminent surgeon by much in the North of England'. The great surgeon Thomas Henry said he had 'a long life of unremitting exertion of great and extensive usefulness'.[16] But he and his work would not experience the longevity they deserved, almost making him and Elizabeth posthumous kindred spirits, so it would be appropriate they should work together, at least from a serendipitous, retrospective point of view. Writing such a book with the talented 'man-midwife' Charles White would have been a very important text: first, White was a visionary, and second, because midwifery had diverged – with women treating the working class and men treating the middle and upper classes – a text written by a man and a woman, both highly regarded in their own time, would have been remarkable in its content, outlook and inclusivity.

In reality, it seems a little too good to be true. How could Elizabeth have become a practising midwife with knowledge enough to write a book on the subject? No doubt she had the potential, but how on earth could she have had the time? Suze Appleton suggests that she may have been aiding Charles on the third (1785) edition of *A Treatise...* or another future title entitled *An Inquiry Into the Nature and Cause of that Swelling, in One Or Both of the Lower Extremities, which Sometimes Happens to Lying-in Women*, published in 1784. If she was a skilled midwife, one might expect mentions of food or drink that were good for expectant mothers or weaning babes in her book, and if it were an important part of her life, one might assume it would be mentioned somewhere. In *The Experienced English Housekeeper*, Elizabeth purposefully avoided medicine, leaving it to physicians to advise upon such things. If she was a skilled midwife, wouldn't she believe it absolutely *was* her place to give advice on the subject? Another explanation, according to Appleton, is that she may have been helping with the case studies, or may have been a case study herself.[17]

However, if we take Harland's account as broadly true (and that is a big *if*), it seems as though it was he advising her.[18] Working close to King Street, and with her connections, it would be no surprise at all if she and White knew each other, but to be working alongside each other as colleagues and peers seems far-fetched. The only real scenario that makes sense – if there is any truth in this tale at all – is that Elizabeth was writing a discourse on midwifery and postnatal care from a personal point of view and that Charles White was fact-checking or advising her on the medical side of things.

Elizabeth's thoughts, knowledge and philosophical approach to midwifery may have been useful to expectant or new mothers: she had made a name for herself now, so putting together a self-help book in this area could have sold well. There is a family story that Elizabeth had sixteen daughters. This number of children appears in many potted biographies of Elizabeth such as that by Jane Grigson in *English Food*, who, like many others, found the 'fact' in *The Dictionary of National Biography* by Charles Sutton.[19] This remarkable 'fact' was picked up from John Harland's interview with Mrs Hopkinson, Elizabeth's granddaughter, who never met Elizabeth, but stated 'that she [had] often heard her mother say that she was the youngest survivor of a family of sixteen daughters, all born to Mrs. Raffald in eighteen years.'[20] The Raffald family bible did not agree. It mentioned the birth of six daughters: Sarah in 1765 and Emma in 1766 at Fennel Street; Grace in 1767, Betty in 1769 and Anna in 1770 at Market Place; and finally, Harriot in 1774 at the King's Head. In some accounts, the bible contained nine names.

The myth has perpetuated firstly because having sixteen children was certainly not unheard of, and judged alongside her other achievements, it seems compelling. Only three daughters, Sarah, Emma and Anna, survived their mother. Betty and Harriot died in infancy, and Grace died at the age of three. There may have been stillbirths and miscarriages that were not recorded.[21] Hannah Glasse too had several children and miscarriages: 'she had eleven live births, though six did not survive beyond the age of five. There were also miscarriages, though these are perhaps not talked about. Once she wrote "I am not well myself. I miscarried two Children last Sunday and have hardly recover'd yet."'[22]

Infant mortality was high in the eighteenth century, and had increased markedly compared to previous centuries. Elizabeth's experience of a 50 per cent infant mortality rate (assuming she had six daughters) is representative of the time.[23] The century is viewed typically as an 'urban graveyard', with infant and child death driving these rates to such a level that the population was only maintained because of immigration. There are a variety of reasons why this might be, but the determining factor was population growth itself. As workers immigrated into the industrialising towns and cities of Britain, commensal diseases spread directly, and Manchester, having a denser population than most, was hit particularly badly. In the latter half of the century and the opening decade of the next, smallpox tore through the town and was responsible for 40 per cent of infant deaths.[24]

Infant deaths hit wealthier families more than the poor, something that perhaps seems unintuitive, but driving this phenomenon was not disease, but changing cultures and fashions surrounding motherhood: the women of wealthy households traditionally used wet nurses so that the mother could regain her strength as quickly as possible and have another child; the families needed male heirs, so there was pressure to become pregnant again as soon as possible. It was this short interval between pregnancies that took its toll on mothers' bodies, and consequently on their babies. For those unable to afford wet nurses, early weaning was implemented instead, worsening things further.[25] For working women, miscarriages and premature birth were common too, brought on by overwork, a phenomenon that probably applies to Elizabeth.

There is a misconception that families were less attached to their children because of the high mortality rates. This is untrue; each death was deeply felt and mothers mourned every child. Elizabeth loved her children, though one has to wonder what type of mother she was. She was certainly very close to Anna, but is impossible to elucidate how much time she spent with them whilst running her businesses. We do know that she used her children to proudly advertise her wealth when about town:

> When her three eldest children were little girls, they attracted no small attention at that time in walking out, each child in a clean white frock, with a nurse walking behind – for there was a nurse to each girl.[26]

This behaviour appears rather crass, and smacks of self-importance, and shows that she may have been affected by the snobbery so commonly observed in ex-upper servants. We must assume that these nurses were wet nurses, simply because it is inconceivable that Elizabeth could have been working so hard and being a nursing mother to – at times – more than one sucking child. She would go on to send them to a nearby boarding school, so she considered education of girls an important and positive thing. She had certainly benefitted from her father's tutelage. But it is very difficult to see where Elizabeth's priorities did lie. Was she working so hard (at least in part) to pay for their school places, or were the children living away so that Elizabeth could focus fully on her work?

Chapter 9

The Exchange Coffee-House
(1779–1781)

Morale had to be low; a coffee house in the Shambles was no comparison to a grand inn and tavern serving gentry and nobility. What a step down it must have felt – though not a small property by any means, it was simple and basic, and therefore so was the fayre that was on offer. On 12 October 1779, the following notice was placed in the *Manchester Mercury*: 'JOHN RAFFALD, Begs Leave to acquaint the Gentlemen of Manchester, and the Public in general, THAT he has Entered on the EXCHANGE COFFEE-HOUSE, in the Market-place.' Aside from coffee, John 'laid in a Stock of the best WINES, and other LIQUORS': it was typical for coffee houses to open until the late evening and exchange coffee for alcohol. Just like the King's Head, John's name, not Elizabeth's, was used in newspaper notices, but Elizabeth worked diligently behind the scenes, cooking up and offering 'Soups of all kinds … from Ten in the Morning, till Two o'Clock in the Afternoon for Town and Country Gentlemen' such as 'Tureens of Vermicelly, brown, white, Sagoe Peas, Cellery and Transparent Soups'. She also provided a service making tureens of soup for families 'on the shortest Notice'.

> To make a Transparent Soup
>
> Take a Leg of Veal, and cut off the meat as thin as you can, when you have cut off all meat clean from the Bone, brake the Bone in small Pieces, put the Meat in a large Jug, and the Bones at the Top, with a bunch of Sweet Herbs, a quarter of an Ounce of Mace, half a Pound of Jordan Almonds blanched and beat fine, pour on it four Quarts of boiling Water, let it stand all Night by the Fire covered close, then the next Day put it into a well tinned Sauce Pan, and let it boil slowly till it is reduced to two Quarts; be sure you take the scum and fat off as it rises

118

all the Time it is boiling; strain it into a Punch Bowl, let it
settle for two Hours, pour it into a clean Sauce Pan clear from
the Sediment, if any at the Bottom; have ready three Ounces
of Rice boiled in Water; if you like Vermicelli better, boil two
Ounces, when enough, put it in and serve it up.[1]

The Exchange Coffee-House sat on Market Place, adjacent to fashionable
St Ann's Square where the streets were particularly closed in, 'gloomy
and dismal, even at noonday'. The narrow streets were wide enough only
for carriages, yet it was a popular thoroughfare for pedestrians because it
served as a handy shortcut. But with no pavement to walk on, accidents
were common enough for the street to be called Dangerous Corner by
locals.[2] 'The streets, which were improved by acts of 1776 and 1777, had
long been felt to be a disgrace to the town'[3] but remained closed in and
dangerous regardless. Could the Raffalds make the place work? Surely with
Elizabeth's business head they could, as long as John could rein himself in.
Coffee houses may not have been as popular as they once were, but they
were still common in towns and cities right across the country.

Elizabeth will have been pragmatic about their situation, at least from
the point of view of business: the Raffalds had fallen on hard times, but
it was essential that this endeavour, whether they liked it or not, worked
for them. Their chances looked slim: by now, John had become 'an
improvident spendthrift'[4] and could not, or would not, cut down on his
drinking. Perhaps she thought she could support him and get them out of
their rut, or perhaps she looked at him with disdain; a drunk and a shadow
of his former self, who had ruined her business and shaken her from her
place in Manchester society.

***

Tea may be Britain's national beverage now, but from the seventeenth
century onwards, coffee was king, and coffee houses sprang up in London,
then Bath and York, before popping up all over the country. Before long,
every place of note had at least one and by the turn of the eighteenth century,
there were around 500 coffee houses in England and '[v]isitors to London
… were often struck by the extraordinary number'.[5] Coffee houses were not
just about the drink, but also the culture. They were vibrant, social places

'frequented by men who came, not to idly talk, but to read; the smaller tradesmen and the better class of mechanic now came to the coffeehouse, called for a cup of coffee, and with it the daily paper, which they could not [otherwise] afford to take in.'[6]

John's notice makes clear that newspapers – being a necessity for any coffee house – were available, and that 'every Paper that may be thought useful, shall duly be taken in.' People of all classes mixed and mingled, ideas were exchanged and issues were debated as papers were read aloud. As William Tullett puts it in *Smell in Eighteenth-Century England*: 'coffeehouses were not simply civil, scentless, and sober places, but full of pungent words, acts, and people.'[7] Says Anthony Hilliar in his *Brief and Merry History of Great-Britain* (1730): '[t]hey smoak Tobacco, game, and read Papers of Intelligence: Here they treat of Matters of State, make Leagues with Foreign Princes, break them again, and transact Affairs of the least Consequence to the whole World.'[8] It was for these very reasons the English establishment did not approve of them, viewing them with fear and contempt in equal measure; in 1675, King Charles II had published a *Proclamation of the Suppression of Coffee-Houses*, claiming

> that many Tradesmen and others, do therein misspend much of their time, which might and probably would otherwise be employed in and about their Lawful Callings and Affairs; but also … by occasion of the meetings of such persons therein, divers false, malitious and scandalous reports are devised and spread abroad, to the Defamation of His Majesties Government, and to the disturbance of the Peace and Quiet of the Realm.[9]

From the punters' point of view, there were mixed feelings; according to Anthony Hilliar, on one hand they were 'the most agreeable things in London … very proper Places to find People that a Man has Business with, or to pass away the Time a little more agreeably than he can do at home'. On the other hand, however, he thought so many of them 'loathsome, full of smoak, like a Guard-Room, and as much crowded. I believe 'tis these Places that furnish the Inhabitants with Slander, for there one hears exact Account of everything done in Town, as if it were but a Village.'[10]

Their popularity began to wane in the first quarter of the eighteenth century, losing out to competition from new upmarket Parisian-style cafes and to tea, which was being consumed more and more at home,[11] its success driven by falling prices and the fact it requires little paraphernalia to make it well. They also began to lose their vibrancy as the upper classes began to be drawn away to the popular gentlemen's clubs and societies, recreating class segregation.[12] By the time the Raffalds took on the Exchange, coffee houses were not the exciting places they once were, and many became drinking and gambling dens that 'bred dishonourable behaviour'.[13] And matching up to this description was the Exchange Coffee-House; it was not a vibrant crucible of heated discussion and philosophical rhetoric, but 'a den of iniquity, filled with dark, unhygienic places for the listless and lacklustre to loiter'.[14]

Elizabeth must have been relieved that it was John's name and not hers attached to the venture. Perhaps if it had been, it might have become a more reputable place, but having John playing that role made sense: the public relationship was maintained and besides, coffee houses were usually the domain of men, not women. Though the only real exception to this was the proprietor, which was a role often filled by women. It wasn't uncommon either for coffee houses to be fronts for brothels. The most famous case involved Elizabeth Adkins, a coffee house owner, who, after being found guilty of theft, was sent to the colonies for seven years' indentured labour. Upon her return, she opened another coffee house in Covent Garden, from which she ran an 'elite prostitution ring and illegal money-lending enterprise' for which, in 1721, she was jailed. Adkins was better known as Moll King and she was the inspiration for the anti-heroine in the novel *Moll Flanders* by Daniel Defoe.[15] Elizabeth had been associated with sex work once before, and would not want a repeat of such a thing; anyway, she had business ideas of her own, beyond soup-making, to bring in some revenue.

***

Elizabeth made sure that not all of their eggs would end up in one basket with the coffee house and earned extra money where she could; the *Manchester Mercury* notice regarding the coffee house also highlighted that the sixth edition of *The Experienced English Housekeeper* was available and that they had some 'WAREHOUSES, suitable for Country Manufactures … to be LETT'. Though, with the undependable John always drinking and haemorrhaging money, one has to imagine whether this was merely a way to tread water, like the Queen of Hearts of *Alice in Wonderland* running as fast as possible just to remain in the same spot. One successful venture was the acquisition of a stand at the popular racecourse at Kersal Moor for which she placed a notice in the *Mercury* on 4 July 1780:

> The LADIES STAND on KERSAL MOOR, WILL be Opened on Wednesday next, for the Accommodation of LADIES and GENTLEMEN of the Town and Neighbourhood of Manchester, where Coffee, Tea, Chocolate, Strawberries, Cream &c. will be provided every Wednesday and Friday during the Strawberry Season. By the Public's, Most obliged humble servant, ELIZABETH RAFFALD.[16]

Now this was something she *could* attach her name to, selling a limited selection of high-quality food and drink to the ladies of Manchester, something no doubt they had missed since the closure of the King's Head. She did a roaring trade, aided by the popular fashionable dish of the time: strawberries and cream. Strawberries were in vogue; they had been a firm favourite for centuries, of course, but they had not been successfully cultivated on a large scale until the 1750s, with commercial strains created only through happenstance rather than via the scientific process or agricultural knowhow. Before this, the fruit of the strawberry plant – the wild, or alpine, variety – was fragrant and sweet but they were also tiny, and therefore a fruit for the gardens of the better off. Varieties of strawberries with large fruits had been discovered in the Americas and brought back to Europe in the previous century. One of which was a variety discovered by French spy Amédée-François Frézier, who had been sent by the King of France to Chile to spy on the Spanish. Visiting markets, he spotted a variety of strawberry commonly for sale that was delicious and '[a]s big as a walnut, and sometimes as a Hen's egg and white in colour'. Frézier was a botanist as much as he was a spy and brought back a specimen. The plant miraculously survived its transatlantic voyage to France and there it was handed to the King's gardeners, who easily got it growing and flowering, but it refused to fruit. What they didn't know is that the strawberry is dioecious – the plants' flowers are either male or female and therefore cannot self-pollinate.

Fifteen years later, another interesting species of strawberry made its transatlantic journey to France, this time from Virginia. This one had large red fruits that were most delicious, but it also refused to fruit.[17] However, in 1750, cuttings from the two plants found themselves in the same greenhouse and, lo and behold, the two plants were of opposite sexes and a new hybrid species was born, producing large, brilliantly red, juicy, sweet and fragrant fruits. It was the descendants of these plants that became the first to produce commercially viable crops like those on Elizabeth's stall.

The races had been held at Kersal Moor since 1730 and would continue well into the next century.[18] Horse racing had become a popular sport and social event since the early eighteenth century, after equine-loving aristocrats formed sports clubs and societies where their members applied the new principles of selective breeding to horses, creating highly sought-after thoroughbreds. Over the initial couple of decades, the complex system of gambling was devised.[19] The races were initially just for the upper classes, but by the 1730s, the races were open to all; the society members saw it as their responsibility to entertain everyone, and the events and goings-on at Kersal were reported weekly on the front page of the *Manchester Mercury*. These races were held in the late spring until the summer, but it was the galas held in August that were the highlight of the town's social calendar.

It wasn't just horses that raced at Kersal either; between 1777 and 1811, a popular part of the entertainment were 'male nude races'. In 2017, a manuscript was auctioned which was 'an Autograph Manuscript, being a catalogue ... of 35 nude male races at Kersal Moor' and it contains details of the names of the runners, with details of times, distances and wagers won. It is reckoned that these races have their root in the naked fell-running that had been popular since the sixteenth century. The runners were naked for two reasons: in homage to the Greek Olympians of the ancient world; and 'so that the lasses can way up [sic] form'. One such lass was Barbara Minshull, the 65-year-old widow of the esteemed apothecary Thomas Minshull, who attended the races in 1769. Watching the races, and 'relish[ing] the view', her eye was drawn to one runner in particular; a strapping, towering 6ft 4in (193 cm) tall Scot named Roger Aytoun, better known to the people of Manchester as 'Spanking Roger', so named because of his skill in the ring as a bare-knuckle fighter. Roger was hard-living and drank heavily, but had once been a major-general and war hero, taking a leading role in the Great Siege of Gibraltar. Now he was stationed in Manchester with the Scottish Dragoons. Bucking tradition, Barbara asked for his hand in marriage, which he accepted. A ceremony quickly followed in which Roger was so drunk that he had to be held upright by two ushers as he slurred his vows. It seems that Barbara quickly realised her error and they lived separately almost immediately. She owned several properties and gave him Hough Hall in Manchester to reside in. Left to his own devices, he drank so much that the hall had to be sold to pay off the debts he'd accrued. Their marriage lasted twelve years until Barbara passed away in 1783.[20] Roger went on to marry again and died in 1810.

At the time Elizabeth was working at the races, she heard of the death of Lady Betty on 24 August 1870. The news 'would have [been] felt deeply';[21] Elizabeth might have left her service seventeen years before, but she and Lady Betty had maintained a positive and affectionate relationship. Elizabeth held a deep respect for her too and was indebted to her for her support when compiling and funding *The Experienced English Housekeeper*. Receiving her patronage helped the book become the success it was. The news must have forced Elizabeth to think introspectively: Lady Betty, a link to a previous existence, a charming woman who had helped put her on an upward trajectory to heights greater, and more dizzying, than she ever expected. Heights from which she had now fallen. But all was not lost, and they could turn it around: the coffee shop wasn't ideal, but if managed well, it should be able to tick over, and she had made a tidy profit from her stint at the races.

Never one to rest on her laurels, Elizabeth got to work on the third edition of her Manchester and Salford directory, placing an announcement in the *Manchester Mercury* on 12 September 1780, calling all businesses to nominate themselves, the last edition now years out of date and requiring 'Alterations and Great Additions'. She begged 'the Favor of the Country Gentlemen to send the Firms, of their Houses, and where their Warehouses are to be found', and asked the same of 'the Town in general'. They were instructed to visit the Exchange Coffee-House, where 'a proper person will constantly attend' and receive such changes. She likely charged a nominal fee to be included in the new edition, which was not atypical. She placed notices almost every week on the run-up to its publication in January 1781 and several weeks thereafter: this edition obviously *had* to sell well. Her advertisements do not fail to mention that the third edition would be available to buy at the Exchange, along with copies of the seventh edition of *The Experienced English Housekeeper*. It is around this time that she worked on her book on midwifery (if it is to be believed). It seemed like things were beginning to turn around.

Chapter 10

Suddenly Gone

On 19 April 1781, Elizabeth's three daughters Sarah, Emma and Anna were 'taking exercise' with friends in the sports fields of their school three miles away in Barton-upon-Irwell, Salford. Everyone was enjoying a good run around, except for Anna, the youngest, who was rather less boisterous than the others, preferring to sit daydreaming under

> a bright April moon, and exclaiming: 'Oh, what a beautiful moon! see how it runs through the clouds! now it's dark, and now it's light again. I wonder whether dear mamma sees that beautiful moon.' Just then a man servant from the school ran hastily into the field, and called repeatedly, 'Miss Raffalds, you're to come in directly.' Anna wondered whether she had done anything amiss to cause her recall, and having satisfied herself that she had duly put on her bonnet and shawl, she thought all was right, and disregarded the summons which her sisters obeyed. On seeing this the man came to her and said, 'Miss Anna, the vehicle's come to take you to Manchester; your mamma's poorly.' They went to Manchester; found that their mother had expired some hours before; and they returned no more to school.[1]

Elizabeth had died suddenly 'of spasms', most likely a stroke or aneurism, within an hour of taking ill. She was 47 years of age. The *Manchester Mercury* announced her death four days later:

> Died, lamented by a numerous Acquaintance, Mrs. Raffald, Wife of Mr. John Raffald, Master of the Exchange Coffee-House in this Town, Authoress of The Experienced English House-keeper which has rapidly passed thro' no less than 7 Editions, and Compiler of the Manchester Directory.[2]

She was buried in the Raffald family plot in Stockport Old Church, now St Mary's, and her gravestone still sits there, somewhere: her name was never carved upon it (presumably because John couldn't afford it). At some point, it was relocated to an area of the grounds now inaccessible.[3] Writing in 1866, the poet Richard Wright Proctor said: '[i]t is not poetically just that the grave of Elizabeth Raffald should be thus lost. Whosoever renders to the state some service – whether that state be Denmark or England – has a proportionate claim to public gratitude. Surely a name kept visible on a gravestone cannot be too great a requital.'[4]

Hannah Glasse has a life story that parallels Elizabeth's in several ways. Hannah's husband, also called John, was an alcoholic and spendthrift who accrued a great deal of debt. But it was he who died early, where upon his death, his debt was passed on to Hannah. Unable to pay, Hannah was sent to Marshalsea debtors' prison, the institution so evocatively described in Charles Dickens's *Little Dorrit*. She might have been able to avoid prison had she not sold her copyright to her book. Upon her release, she wrote a second called *The Compleat Confectioner* (1760), and she made sure she kept the copyright, but it wasn't anywhere near as successful as *The Art of Cookery*. She died in 1770, aged 62, 'still fairly destitute'.[5]

The coffee house folded almost immediately and on 1 May 1781 – just twelve days after Elizabeth's death – a notice appeared in the *Manchester Mercury* announcing,

> To be LETT, Enter'd on immediately, The Exchange Coffee-House, Now in full trade, and situated in the Market-Place, Manchester. For further Particulars Enquire of Mr. Raffald, the present Tenant, who is decling [sic] the public business.[6]

'[C]reditors now lacking in the security of Elizabeth's industry' swooped in[7] and on 12 May, another notice was printed informing the citizens of Manchester of John's bankruptcy and that he had 'assigned over all of his estate and effects' to the creditors: James Fitchett, liquor merchant; a brewer named Hugh Adamson; John Jones, a merchant dealing in porcelain; and Richard Tunnadine, a 'Gentleman'. The notice went on: 'ALSO will be SOLD, All the Household Goods and Furniture belonging to said John Raffald.' A third notice on 22 May announced to the town that 'ALL the Household Goods, Furniture, &c. and the entire Stock in Trade of the said

John Raffald, consisting of Old Hock, Burgundy, Red Port, Mountain, Lisbon Wines and Spiritous Liquors' would be sold at auction on 31 May and 1 June, 'the Sale to begin at Nine o'Clock each morning'.

John left Manchester abruptly and, according to Raffald family legend, he absconded to London and lived 'a very gay life', returning several years later with a new wife, a 'poor, illiterate creature' named Molly. He was a changed man:

> From his return to Manchester he became reformed in conduct and joined the Wesleyan Methodists, and attended their chapels for the last thirty years; but strangely enough, combined with other pursuits the study of astrology for the last twenty years of his life, and even 'ruled the planets,' not publicly or for gain, but solely for his own private amusement.[8]

There may be more myth than truth at work here, for it seems that after Elizabeth's death, John returned to a life of horticulture in Salford and Stockport, working and living with his younger brothers. This brings us to another reason (though not a mutually exclusive one) as to why the coffee house folded so swiftly, and that is because John simply desired it. He saw a way out and took it. According to Elizabeth Raffald biographers Charles Foster and Roy Shipperbottom, the idea that he legged it to London because he couldn't handle things is simply a convenient story.[9] He's the perfect scapegoat, the one who caused the collapse of Elizabeth's empire, hurrying her death as she exhausted herself, scrabbling to get a purchase on some of her previous successes. But the truth is Elizabeth was working too hard before the coffee house, indeed even before the King's Head; working too hard was her natural state and something was going to give eventually – the work she undertook was never going to be sustainable neither to her physical nor mental health.[10]

When the Raffalds moved to the King's Head, John had to say goodbye to his career – or what remained of it – and he was put to use with his good looks and charm by Elizabeth, who utilised him well, front of house. During the early days at the King's Head, at least, he was part of the vibrant inn that attracted so many different and interesting people from across Britain and continental Europe. When the King's Head closed, it must have been miserable running a dilapidated and dodgy coffee house in the Shambles area of town (it would be demolished in 1792[11]), something we can be very sure he did not want to do. Beggars can't be choosers, of course, and they hadn't been cast out onto the streets, and if run properly, perhaps the coffee house could have become just as vibrant in its own way, but John had no desire to run a coffee house; he was only working in hospitality to support his wife. The coffee house was not what he had signed up for at all. Elizabeth's untimely death released him from the life choices he had regretted, a life that led him into a depression he self-medicated with alcohol, a life that took away his wife. Returning to his beloved brothers and working in the family gardens was the only sensible thing to do.

John Raffald lived to a fine old age, and John Harland swaps his usual curtness for kindness when describing John's autumn years:

> After he was eighty he wrote a beautiful small hand; and as he advanced in years he received much substantial aid and kindness from gentlemen of the town, who had known him in his earlier and palmier days … He continued to live in Salford, being for the last seven years of his life confined to his room, where he amused himself by writing much, but on what subjects we could not learn. He died at the age of 89 years, and was interred in the grave-yard of Trinity Chapel, Salford.[12]

However John spent the first few years following Elizabeth's death, he did not live with his children.[13] Elizabeth's sister, Mary, took on the task of looking after them. She also opened a shop on Hanging Ditch Lane by the gates of the Collegiate Church, offering an array of foods and ingredients very similar to those Elizabeth had sold at Market Place. The two eldest sisters, it seems, left home to pursue careers of their own, but the youngest, Anna, stayed with Mary, who taught her the arts of the confectioner, 'and brought her up to the business, and she was very useful in assisting her aunt'.[14]

The shop was a success and 'the resort of many respectable persons including the [great eccentric] Rev. Joshua Brookes, then chaplain of the Collegiate Church [who] used frequently to drop in and take his jelly there. He was very friendly with Mrs. Whitaker, and used to call her niece, Anna Raffald, his child.' Eventually, Mary and Anna began to accept young women as 'apprentice-pupils for three years, receiving with each a premium of £50 … and they generally had three such apprenticed pupils.' Mary Whitaker died in June 1785, leaving 'her property, goods and chattels, to "[her] niece Anna Raffald, daughter of John Raffald."' Ten years later, Anna met Thomas Munday, a successful textile manufacturer, whom, after a brief courtship, she married in Eccles in August 1796.[15] The Mundays remained in the Manchester area, but because of the change in her circumstances, she didn't carry on with the shop. Rather bizarrely, Rev. Brooks insisted the couple be married again because their first marriage was outside of her parish, and so

> [t]o satisfy him Mr. Munday reluctantly consented to be re-married, observing that he thought once was quite enough; and they were re-married by Joshua Brookes at the Old Church, on the 16th October, 1796, just two months and four days after they were married at Eccles.[16]

***

The eighth edition of Elizabeth's cookery book was the first to be printed posthumously. Without the beady, controlling eye of Elizabeth watching over him, Robert Baldwin was now able to make changes freely. This edition was the first to contain her portrait, something she would never have approved. Her portrait is the only likeness we have of her. It sits in a 'large oval medallion, surmounted by a bow of ribbon' and was acquired from Elizabeth's second daughter, Emma. Elizabeth was unable to sign these books as proof of authenticity, of course, and from the eighth edition, Baldwin used instead 'a metal stamp fac-simile ... at the head of the first chapter of the book'.[17]

Baldwin continued to publish further editions, adding extra appendices and continually updating her portrait. The portraits became poorer in quality and were probably made because he no longer had access to the original work. The 1798 edition contains a 'treatise on brewing' that, according to John Harland, contains one recipe with ingredients 'contain[ing] various articles prohibited by law', adding that he hoped 'no one will be disposed to try this pernicious concoction'.[18] In the twelfth edition (1799), he added a section of 'family receipts for the cure of ague, consumption, asthma and some other complaints [something] greatly at variance with the author's wishes as expressed in the preface to the first edition.'[19] Elizabeth would have been horrified by these huge alterations to her work. But Baldwin treated her, her image and her writing as a brand, more so than she ever did, and without that treatment, she wouldn't have become quite as well-known as she was. Hannah Glasse received similar treatment from her publisher who, ignoring her request to remain anonymous, revealed her name. Hannah had always wanted to remain 'A Lady'.

In 1786, Baldwin sold the copyright to publishers Millar, Law and Cater, who changed the text even more: many Raffald biographers consider them to be pirated, which suggests illegality, which is not the case; a better word, perhaps, would be *unofficial*. Her book was diluted further with more recipes, and some of her own were even removed to save on printing costs, even though these editions still faithfully reproduced her preface that declared all of the work to be her own. None of these publishers had access to Elizabeth's portrait, and they didn't worry about reproducing it faithfully.[20] Harland describes the original portrait: 'The features are good, the character ladylike, with marks of decision and firmness about the lips; the forehead high and broad.' The woman in the unofficial portrait of the 1803 edition was simply 'a plump, dairy-maid looking person'.[21] These changes were all intentional – a younger, more voluptuous woman with softer features sold more copies – and sales won over authenticity. Elizabeth achieved celebrity in a way she would have found shocking and offensive, and it could only have happened without her control. She would have been mortified by the brazen disregard of her image, pride and words. The number of borrowed recipes was 'staggering', and by 1800, Elizabeth's book had become a 'curated collection of borrowed recipes'.[22]

All in all, *The Experienced English Housekeeper* ran to thirteen editions and at least twenty unofficial editions, and coquettish dairymaids and treatises on fermentation aside, it goes to show just how trusted her name, recipes and approach to housekeeping had become. It was upon this foundation of trust that all future editions depended, however dissimilar they may have been to her original works.

Into the nineteenth century, Elizabeth remained popular enough for John Harland to write his meticulously researched biography of Elizabeth for the *Manchester Guardian* in 1852. His timing was perfect, managing to catch all that remained of the Raffalds' family history that concerned Elizabeth and John from their granddaughter and nephew. He wrote several other articles about Elizabeth, and as part of his research into *The Experienced English*

Housekeeper itself, he requested from the readership of the *Manchester Guardian* that they post him their copies of the book, so he could compile a list of differences between the editions. He was inundated, receiving almost forty different versions, the only edition eluding him being the second. He wrote up his findings in great detail. That he received so much from the *Manchester Guardian*'s readers demonstrates just how relevant Elizabeth's work was to Victorian households. That his findings are written in such depth – and almost tiresome detail – in a daily newspaper, along with his other articles, shows just how interested people of Manchester still were.[23]

In William Axon's *Annals of Manchester* (1886), published just over a century after her death, there is an obituary to Elizabeth. It describes the circumstances surrounding her death and lists her many achievements including, of course, *The Experienced English Housekeeper*, as well as her directories, school and her support 'in the continuance of Harrop's newspaper and the commencement of Prescott's'. It concludes that Manchester would have been less of a town, and therefore less of a city, without her hard graft and forward-thinking.[24] No other man or woman in the book gets a longer obituary in the *Annals*; no other person in eighteenth-century Manchester had achieved so much and in such variety. One hundred and five years after her death, the people of Manchester knew who she was, and although the place had changed much since her death, her cookery book was in use and she was still a known figure. But that was Manchester; in the rest of Britain, her star quickly faded, and in time even the people of Manchester would come to forget her.

Chapter 11

Legacy

Mrs. Raffald was an extraordinary person and deserves to have her name rescued, however imperfectly, from oblivion, and to be recorded as one of our Manchester authors and worthies of the eighteenth century ... The influence she exercised in her own day ... is scarcely possible to overrate. (John Harland)[1]

Elizabeth's legacy is a cultural one and her contribution in creating what we think of now as traditional British cuisine is perhaps the most significant compared to any other single individual. It was Elizabeth who struck the right balance between economy, existing traditions, modern fashions and authenticity, which her peers, who certainly achieved, and even pioneered, some of those elements, never quite achieved all.

But what is English cooking? An impossible question to answer? Not really; its roots are in the eighteenth century, at a time of rapid imperial expansion and conflicts when Britain gained access to new territories with new indigenous peoples with new foods and novel cooking traditions. British food became 'at once a mix of foreign ingredients and techniques and a widely proclaimed, unique style'.[2] Elizabeth took the produce of the market gardens and orchards of the country and these new and exciting exotic goods of the empire and passed it all through a prism of *Englishness*. Even foods created decades and centuries after her death have been borne of this approach: kedgeree, spaghetti Bolognese and chicken tikka masala are all examples of this.

The English way of cooking was adapted in Scotland and Wales, making a cohesive, identifiable national cuisine. It became a wonderful assimilation of Britain and its empire with the odd cherry-picked ingredient from Western Europe. British cooks took inspiration from these foods and places to create a new food culture that was unique. The identity of Great British cuisine, created by Elizabeth (and Hannah Glasse and Eliza Smith), passed on to others in their kitchens, inspiring others to write (or copy) recipes for their own cookbooks, all with the underlying Raffald principles of exciting, economical, homely and achievable cooking that didn't exclude a bit of showiness, as long as it was in moderation. The clever part was showing people when these elements were appropriate and when they certainly were not. As Elizabeth said in the introduction to *The Experienced English Housekeeper*:

> I have made it my Study to please both the Eye and the Palate, without using pernicious Things for the sake of Beauty … [Al]though I have given some of my Dishes French Names, as they are only known by those Names, yet they will not be found very Expensive, nor add Compositions but as plain as the Nature of the Dish will admit of.[3]

The key to her success was that she aimed to ease minds around the pressure to opt for French cuisine and its inevitable accompanying expense and tendency toward frivolity. She was not quite as disparaging as Glasse, establishing that there were some positive, useful and economical aspects to French cookery.

Elizabeth's approach managed to appeal to those disillusioned with what British cuisine had become: complicated dishes smothered in sauces too rich for the constitution of many. The fashionable sorts put up with it, but many were very vocal about their dissatisfaction and yearned for proper, old-fashioned British food cooked simply and cooked well. The British had lost their way, a feeling made very clear by R. Campbell in *The London Tradesman* in 1747:

> In the Days of good Queen Elizabeth, when mighty Roast Beef was the Englishman's food; our Cookery was [as] plain and simple as our Manners; it was not then a Science or Mistery, and required no Conjuration to please the Palates of our greatest Men. But we have of late Years refined ourselves out of the simple Taste, and conformed our Palates to Meats and Drinks dressed after the French Fashion: The natural taste of Fish or Flesh is become nauseous to our fashionable Stomach.

Not only that, home-grown British produce was losing out to exotics imported from 'all the Earth, from both the Poles, the most different Climates [which are] ransacked for Spices, Pickles and Sauces, not to relish but to disguise our Food'. As far as Campbell was concerned, a fish cooked by 'a French Cook, is no more a Fish; it has neither the Taste, Smell, nor Appearance of Fish.'[4] An 'Old Fellow' wrote a letter to *The Perth Magazine of Knowledge and Pleasure* in January 1773 complaining that 'instead of that firm roast beef, that fragrant pudding, our tables groan with the luxuries of France and India. Here a lean fricassee rises in the room of our majestic ribs; and there a scoundrel syllabub occupies the place of our well-beloved home-brewed.'

Folk like Campbell were legion, and tough nuts to crack, but rather than trying to crack them, or trying to be all things to all men (and women), Elizabeth provided options and simple instructions, so that the lady of the house and her housekeeper could select dishes appropriate to the day and its guests. With time, the mix of plain and simple and more fashionable cooking became one whole, and the syllabub would come to sit a little easier with the roast ox on the dining table.

***

And all of this positive change was achieved by women writing books for other women from their own knowledge of the domestic realm. But as the decades passed and we tick into the nineteenth century, Elizabeth's book began to appeal to more than aspirational middle-class women who had grown 'to rely on working women to provide services enjoyed by the upper classes in their households' and instead to all women.[5] It spoke to the servants, of course, because it was written in an unpatronising way (unlike Hannah Glasse); after all, Elizabeth was a part of the working class and, as books became cheaper, members of the aspirational working class were able to purchase them. Her book contained many recipes suitable for poorer pockets, but it was also a spyglass for looking into a different world; the world where 'the other half live'. Elizabeth's book 'became a way to learn about the manners and customs of the elite'. Elizabeth became an 'advisor to all women, regardless of class standing'.[6] Some of these books may have been pirated editions with additional recipes from unreferenced writers, so home cooks may have been influenced by Elizabeth without even knowing it. For example, a pirated copy of Hannah Glasse's *The Art of Cookery* contained several Raffald recipes, including her recipe for apricot ice cream.

The popularity of Elizabeth's book, and the two other members of the trinity, Hannah Glasse's *The Art of Cookery* and Eliza Smith's *The Compleat Housewife*, and their more practical approach, meant the culinary literacy of cooks around England increased significantly and inspired a newfound pride in the cookery of England. Most significantly, it meant that all of a sudden, homes all around the country could sit down to exactly the same meal. Though not necessarily their intention, their popularity 'promoted conformity': food was becoming standardised and less diverse as handwritten family cookbooks were replaced by a Raffald, Glasse, Smith or any number of the other books derivative of their work.[7] The use of notebooks did not die out, of course, but their contents changed, becoming filled with recipes copied from Elizabeth's book, rather than from a neighbour's collection or passed down from families' matriarchs. Elizabeth's recipes even ended up in the handwritten notebook of Princess Victoria before she was crowned queen. Her recipes of choice? The smart table decorations, including Solomon's Temple in Flummery.[8] As Troy Bickham puts it '[f]ood has always bound people together, creating regional foods and dishes, but with books such as Elizabeth's, the community became countrywide.'[9]

Another curious effect of this unification of the national cuisine was the sudden proliferation of regional names for dishes, the most famous perhaps being the Yorkshire pudding, a type of batter pudding that was cooked in the dripping tray that sat beneath the meat as it roasted on the spit, and was hardly local to Yorkshire; it had been eaten with gusto by people all around the country, probably for centuries. However, in her book, Hannah Glasse calls this generic pudding Yorkshire pudding for the first time. Perhaps it was the Yorkshire habit of serving the pudding before dinner so that diners would consume less meat that made her associate the batter pudding with Yorkshire. When Elizabeth wrote her book, her batter pudding was also called a Yorkshire pudding, so that name obviously caught on quickly. Pork pies – a food eaten all over the country for centuries – became forever associated with Melton Mowbray. And then, of course, there is the Eccles cake – just a simple 'sweet patty' when apparently invented by Elizabeth. In a generation, it had gained its regional moniker, but there were other baked goods made up of dried fruit, pastry and sugar pretty much everywhere, so they had to come up ways of distinguishing themselves, such as those made in Chorley and Banbury. Steamed and boiled suet puddings made up of a limited number of similar ingredients and cooked in a similar way across whole swathes of the country appeared with unspecific names in recipe collections as 'a good pudding', 'another good pudding', or 'a good pudding another way', and so on. Now they had names like Oxford pudding or Sussex pond pudding.[10] This often false perception of regionality, and therefore of tradition, only aided the cementing of the idea of a great unified British cuisine.

The notion of a true British cuisine was immediately leapt upon by Isabella Beeton with the publication of *Mrs Beeton's Book of Household Management* in 1861. The weighty volume contained over a thousand recipes covering every perceivable aspect of cookery, as well as detailed advice regarding every aspect of housekeeping from rearing children to home medicine, doing the laundry to legal advice. Its success was dependent upon branding, something that Elizabeth knew all about, but this was of a new kind that would make the *Book of Household Management* the massive success it was, pushing out Raffald, Glasse *et al.* 'However,' says Clarissa Dickson Wright, who was vocally anti-Beeton in her time, 'it is not hard to see why the book should have been such a success. For the aspiring Victorian housekeeper with an inexperienced cook it seemed to cover everything.'[11]

Isabella Beeton died at the age of just 28 in 1865, four years after the publication of her book. She did not write the entirety of the tome herself; like many self-help books of the time, it was written by several anonymous contributors. In the year following her death, her husband was forced to sell the copyright, and once modified in successive editions, Mrs Beeton became more brand name than real person. Contrary to popular perceptions, Beeton is less the Nigella Lawson or Delia Smith of her day, and more the Colonel Sanders.

Writing a book by committee means less culpability and in the production of Beeton's book, there was much copying of recipes. This is not something new; even today, recipes cannot be copyrighted, but the wording used in the methods can, and for Beeton, they were copied extensively. She took recipes not just from Elizabeth Raffald, but also Alexis Soyer, Charles Francatelli and Eliza Acton.[12] Because the *Book of Household Management* was liberally peppered with recipes from Elizabeth's and other writers' books, there was less of a need to purchase a selection. Beeton had mined them of their gold and covered all bases, and there was now little practical sense in owning a copy of a Beeton *and* a Raffald *and* a Glasse.

Many of the writers' recipes she took are full of good advice, but with Isabella not being much of a cook, they became mixed up with poor ones from pirated books. Beeton is a proponent of cooking vegetables to a mushy pap (something we still have to suffer today). She has been called out recently for her lack of attention to detail, but this is no surprise from a person who was apparently 'more interested in what she was wearing than what she was eating'. Dickson Wright really had it in for her, though, saying '[i]t would be unfair to blame any one person or one book for the decline of English cookery, but Isabella Beeton and her ubiquitous book do have quite a lot to answer for.'[13] What is particularly depressing is that by the mid-twentieth century, those who did rediscover Elizabeth Raffald often talked of her in terms of Beeton's success. Take this article from the *Manchester Guardian* in August 1951: 'Mrs Elizabeth Raffald, whose recipe for gooseberry paste was quoted … recently, was the writer of an eighteenth century cookery book which might entitle her to the tribute of Manchester's Mrs Beeton.'[14]

Not everyone forgot Elizabeth Raffald: her descendants are most proud of their ancestor. The Arden Arms in Stockport, the public house built by John Raffald's nephew George, is adorned with a commemorative plaque recognising Elizabeth and all that she achieved. The local Women's Institute recognise her contribution to Manchester and to British food culture, and rather endearingly hold a get-together every year on the anniversary of Elizabeth and John's wedding. After a long campaign by her family, a blue plaque was installed on the Manchester City Centre branch of Marks and Spencer in 1986, which backed onto Exchange Square and the old site of the Shambles. Unfortunately it was destroyed in the IRA bomb in 1996. A replacement was eventually installed but only after eight more years of campaigning by relatives and Roy Shipperbottom's widow, Olga.[15] It sits high up on the side of the Selfridges & Co. building on Exchange Square, unassuming, unnoticed. One particularly inspired descendant of Elizabeth, Winifred Shircliff, researched and wrote a detailed biography of Elizabeth Raffald with accompanying family trees, using photographs and other resources the family had kept or acquired over the two and a half centuries since Elizabeth's death.[16] Arley Hall are proud of their housekeeper too and regularly hold talks and tours about Elizabeth and her food, and John and his green fingers.

But these people have an invested interest and pride in all that Elizabeth achieved: a story like Elizabeth's is bound to be retold down the generations of a family. Outside, however, very few recognise the name Elizabeth Raffald, and she is now an obscure figure. There are others who, after delving into British food heritage, discover her anew, become enthused and wonder why or how she has become so unknown. She crops up sporadically in newspaper articles in the twentieth century. In a 1981 *Guardian* article regarding the restaurant scene in Manchester, the writers of the piece, Christopher Driver and John Arlott, commented how 'sad that there is, as far as we know, no restaurant called Elizabeth Raffald's'. They couldn't understand how a person who had done so much for Manchester could be so forgotten.[17]

There was a period of interest in the 1930s when yet another wave of fancy French food fashions dominated food culture, threatening traditional British cooking once more. Traditionalists found themselves in the midst of an existential crisis similar to that of the eighteenth century. Florence White wrote *Good Things in England* in 1932 in 'an attempt to capture the charm of England's cookery before it is completely crushed out of existence'.[18] She trawled though classic works of English cookery, as well as housewives' own recipe collections. Elizabeth Raffald is a dominant presence in her book, and – of course – Florence could not resist including a potted biography of Elizabeth, highlighting her extraordinary achievements.

Elizabeth's biggest fan has to be the great food writer Elizabeth David, who used Elizabeth Raffald as her touchstone for excellent British cooking. David had become despondent about the state of British food in the decades following the Second World War, and encouraged people to look toward the Mediterranean and to France to see the quality of ingredients available and the care given to cook them well and wholesomely. But her agenda was not to forget about British food, because she was well aware that British cookery could be excellent. Her thesis was, essentially, that in order to find examples of good food, one must travel both spatially and temporally. And to illustrate how good the food was, she almost always used Elizabeth Raffald as the exemplar. In David's eyes, Elizabeth is the poster girl for cookery excellence. David takes care to mention her recipes not just as a source of practical advice, but also for their 'charm'.

She uses many Raffald recipes in her classic work *English Bread and Yeast Cookery* (1977) and is particularly impressed by her fancy bread recipes; of her recipe for Bath buns, David comments: 'Mrs Raffald's proportions and method work perfectly, and produce an excellent dough', and of her recipe for wigs, she notes that 'Mrs Raffald's recipe needs little adaptation'.[19]

For those in the know, Elizabeth is a go-to for anyone interested in the eighteenth century or in Britain's culinary roots. In 2018, food historian Sam Bilton was asked to bake a traditional and historical wedding cake for English Heritage.[20] She had never made one, but she knew exactly who to ask: our Elizabeth. The bride cake that appears in *The Experienced English Housekeeper* is huge, so Sam had to change proportions, but otherwise it remained the same. And it worked. Sam, like anyone else who knows how important Elizabeth is to British cuisine, is also of the opinion that she should be better known. For Sam, the main draws aren't those fancy banqueting dishes like turtle soup but the everyday ones, and a good deal of those recipes could be reprinted today.[21] Mary-Anne Boermans, *Great British Bake Off* contestant and food historian, agrees, though she recognises that 'not all of her recipes are suitable for modern tastes, but the majority are and deserve a much more prominent place in our culinary repertoire'. When it comes to updating Elizabeth's recipes, the majority of the work is in the updating of weights, measures, timings and oven temperatures.[22] But for anyone who can cook, and knows approximately how hot a 'quick fire' or a 'slow oven' is, the majority of her recipes can be cooked with success. See the appendix for more details on the updating of recipes to modern kitchens and tastes.

Jane Grigson cites Elizabeth David as a great influence on her, so it is not surprising then that she also grew to appreciate Elizabeth Raffald's recipes and achievements. Writing in 1974, Jane highlighted the importance of remembering cookery writers who preceded Mrs Beeton:

> We need to renew and develop the old traditions of Hannah Glasse, Elizabeth Raffald ... and Eliza Acton as far as we can in our changed circumstances. It is no accident, I hope, that these early writers are being reprinted ... and that their dishes appear on the menus of some of our best restaurants as well as in an increasing number of homes.[23]

Elizabeth Raffald got her reprint in 1997 when *The Experienced English Housekeeper* was printed by Southover Press, updated by Roy Shipperbottom. Roy sadly passed away before the reprint was published, and with the deaths of both Elizabeth David in 1992 and Jane Grigson in 1990, it seemed that there were no prominent food writers left who might shout about Elizabeth Raffald. In the twenty-first century, historical cookery books became popular again, with many reprinted lavishly.[24] Elizabeth, alas, was left out.

Despite this, Elizabeth and her way of cookery had a boost in the twenty-first century in other ways, most significantly from a subset of British chefs once again interested in traditional British food, but this time it was not a case of rediscovering the odd forgotten or unfashionable recipe, but a case of rediscovering the lost philosophy and economy of the eighteenth-century cookery writers. Best known of these is the infamous, charismatic and eccentric 'nose-to-tail' chef Fergus Henderson, who opened his restaurant, St John's, in the mid-1990s, which became very popular and influential in its own right in the 2000s. But his style of cookery is no gimmick, and he certainly is not cooking the so-called lesser cuts and offal in an attempt to be sensationalist. Quite the opposite, in fact; in the introduction to his book *The Complete Nose to Tail: A Kind of British Cooking* (2012), he says 'it would be disingenuous to the animals not to make the most of the whole beast, there is a set of delights, textural and flavoursome, which lie beyond the fillet'.[25] This is good home economics, respectful to the butchered animal, and, most importantly, *good food*.[26] When chef Norman Miller looked over 'chef Anton Mosimann's extraordinary library of antiquarian cookbooks' for a *Guardian* article in 2007, he picked up *The Experienced English Housekeeper* and found that '[l]eafing through Elizabeth Raffald's 1769 book ... a dish like "Ragoo of Pig's Ears" might not look out of place today on the menu at St John, Fergus Henderson's acclaimed Smithfield temple to "nose-to-tail eating" in London.'[27] Henderson's dishes, whether he realises it or not (and I suggest he does), are direct descendants of Elizabeth's recipes. Another with this philosophy is acclaimed Canadian-Australian chef Jennifer McLagan, who namechecks Elizabeth in her 2011 cookery book *Odd Bits*. Jennifer particularly praises Elizabeth for jellies and flummeries, and she even revisits Elizabeth's methodology for making calf's foot jelly.[28]

These are not the only chefs taking this approach and offal seems to be creeping back onto menus, usually in a fine dining setting, so the message that odd bits are good bits is obviously out there, but not everyone is hearing it.[29] One chef in Manchester stands out; Rob Owen Brown, head chef at the Mark Addy, specifically lauds Elizabeth as an influence and muse. In 2013, he cooked a menu in her honour and memory. Talking to the *Manchester Evening News*, he said of her: 'This woman was an absolute powerhouse with more drive than most men of her time.' The menu was served in the style of one of her Beefsteak Club dinners, and it was comprised 'of rich vermicelli soup, followed by fried sole with egg sauce, Elizabeth Raffald's original beef steak pie and whipped syllabubs'.[30]

But the person who has done most in recent years to raise the profile of Elizabeth is Suze Appleton. Suze became obsessed with Elizabeth and her legacy after spotting a tweet concerning Elizabeth, asking if anyone had heard of her. She hadn't, and she'd lived in Manchester most of her life. After a cursory look into Elizabeth's story, she was hooked. So obsessed was she that throughout the 2010s, she gave talks on Elizabeth and compiled several books of primary and secondary sources about Elizabeth and John, Manchester and Arley Hall. She also transcribed a first edition of *The Experienced English Housekeeper* and all three of her Manchester and Salford directories (which is no mean feat).[31] The zenith of Suze's achievements in improving Raffald public relations was her 2015 campaign to have a statue honouring Elizabeth erected in Manchester City Centre. The WoManchester project was initiated to fund a new £200,000 memorial recognising a prominent woman in Manchester's history, and Suze gave a one-minute pitch to the organisers, outlining why it should be Elizabeth. With Elizabeth's life being so complex and varied, Suze thought a one-minute pitch would be 'well nigh impossible'.[32]

Suze's argument was compelling enough to get Elizabeth shortlisted in the final six, rubbing shoulders with Margaret Ashton, Manchester's first female councillor; anti-racism campaigner Louise Da-Cocodia; author Elizabeth Gaskell; suffragette and women's rights campaigner Emmeline Pankhurst; and nineteenth-century Labour MP Ellen Wilkinson. The winner would be decided by public vote, and there was a flurry of local and national media attention surrounding the project. In a bid to improve Elizabeth's chances, Arley Hall got involved, cooking up food from *The Experienced English Housekeeper* in their restaurant.[33]

The winner was announced in 2016 and Elizabeth lost out to Emmeline Pankhurst in a landslide win, with Emmeline receiving over 50 per cent of the votes. The statue was erected in 2018 in St Peter's Square, adjacent to Manchester Central Library.[34] It's a shame Elizabeth missed out, but to be included in a shortlist with five other worthy women is still a fantastic achievement (for both Elizabeth and Suze), especially in a campaign taking place 250 years after Elizabeth's heyday.

But why weren't Elizabeth's many achievements enough to secure her spot on the pedestal? She helped transform Manchester for all walks of life: from servants to shopkeepers, merchants to the gentry. She wrote a ground-breaking cookery book that contributed greatly to the creation of a modern British cuisine. She was an ex-servant, helping women deal with housekeeping and home economy, and more importantly, empowering them to express themselves in the cut-throat world of keeping up with the Joneses. So, what is missing? The likely answer is that Elizabeth was working strictly within what was expected of her class and her gender; she respected the authority of her 'betters', and remember she did not include herself in her own Manchester and Salford directories. Her successes were made entirely within the confines of society's expectations of her as a servant, businesswoman and wife. Pankhurst wanted to change things for all women, making them more equal to each other and to men, especially with respect to education. Elizabeth educated women to work within the boundaries of what women could and could not do. When it comes to women's rights, Raffald was conservative, Pankhurst progressive and active. Elizabeth may have held similar views, of course; she did send her own daughters to school, and she was taught well by her own father in Doncaster, so she obviously appreciated the importance of a good education. But these views were never expressed in her writing, and her daughters only got their education because she could afford to pay for it. Elizabeth was remarkable in her – or indeed any – time with respect to her list of achievements, and even though her book did empower women, it did not extend much farther than the kitchen and dining room.

Another reason, perhaps, is down to the type of person she was, something which in the writing of this book has been difficult to pin down. It's not difficult to put together a list of adjectives: inspiring, feisty, strong-willed, tenacious, indefatigable, shrewd, fearless, determined, resolute, and so on. She was an entrepreneur, a visionary, an overachiever. These are all good things, but it is more difficult to ascertain how much compassion she had for others, and she seems rather utilitarian in her attitude; her altruistic acts always seemed to benefit her socially or financially. This is not a bad thing *per se*, but compared to passionate and compassionate women like Pankhurst, Da-Cocodia and Gaskell, one can't help but think she is lacking. If you met her, would she be friendly, easy to get on with? One imagines receiving short shrift because she has something much more important to do somewhere else. But perhaps this is a little unkind and possibly incorrect; and an absence of evidence is not evidence of absence. If only the family bible still existed, full of her thoughts, feelings and memories, we could get a clearer idea of what made her tick.

Deciding whether she was compassionate, or if she was a nice person or not, is a moot point, really; her achievements speak for themselves, and eclipse any character traits that may be considered negative when picking them apart and analysing them with twenty-first century values.

Being frustrated by the fact that – and listing the reasons by which – she became unremembered is also moot: Elizabeth transformed the town of Manchester, revolutionised British cuisine, giving it an identity that has endured across four centuries. Yes, most people don't know Elizabeth or her achievements, but her legacy isn't lost, in fact, it is writ large and experienced every day because it runs deep through Britain's food culture. She is an elementary part of it. Like the web of veins in a truckle of blue cheese, Elizabeth is intrinsic. Elizabeth is ubiquitous.

Appendix

Cook Like It's 1769

There is only so much one can learn from reading about the food and drink of the eighteenth century. I believe one has to cook and eat it to get an idea of what it's really about; for me, there is nothing more evocative than eating food from the past. It's the closest we can get to time travel. To eat is to experience, and therefore it wins over battle re-enactments, castle tours and museums any day.

I have cooked several of Elizabeth's recipes from *The Experienced English Housekeeper* and I have always been pleased with how well the recipes translate to modern kitchens and methods, and I hope that after reading about her and her cookery, you will try at least one of the recipes I have updated here. You can find more Raffald (and other eighteenth-century) recipes on my blogs too.[1] This appendix also gives me the chance to look into the ingredients and methods of cookery which would have interrupted the flow of things had I included them in the main text.

Seven of Elizabeth's recipes are presented here. I have kept them simple, and, I hope, achievable. Of course, they cover just a fraction of Elizabeth's repertoire. I have selected recipes from throughout the book and no two are taken from the same chapter. It's a whistle-stop tour, but hopefully or one or two will appeal. And if they do not appeal, or if you want to find and try more recipes, her book is available to view online. I have only used recipes from the first edition of *The Experienced English Housekeeper*.

There are several things one needs to consider when using a recipe from an eighteenth-century cookery book, and I mention specifics as they come up, but there are some essential things one needs to know to interpret Elizabeth's recipes correctly:

1. Pints were smaller. I wish I had known this when I first started cooking historical recipes. The British pint changed from 16 fl oz (473 ml) to 20 fl oz (568 ml) in 1824. Therefore, in the eighteenth century, half a

pint was 8 fl oz and the old 'gill', a quarter of a pint, is was 4 fl oz, not 5 fl oz as it is today. Thank goodness for the metric system.

2. Beware the teaspoon. In 1769, there wasn't the system of standard teaspoon and tablespoon measures we use today, yet Elizabeth mentions teaspoons all the time. These teaspoons were the ones used to spoon tea into teapots, not to stir one's tea.[2] I use a generous dessertspoon whenever Elizabeth asks for teaspoon of anything. She also uses 'spoonfuls' as another measure. These are larger spoons for serving or cooking; a generous tablespoon is a good approximation.[3]

3. Eggs were smaller. Poor old chickens weren't bred to lay huge eggs like they are today, and they were at least a third smaller than a modern egg. I typically use two-thirds of the number given in one of Elizabeth's recipes, and round up to the nearest whole egg. I use medium-sized eggs.

4. Dairy produce was unpasteurised. If you can, use raw dairy ingredients. Of course, I realise it is not usually possible to do this and regular milk, butter and cheese will still produce good results. Cream, however, would turn 'ripe' rather quickly, and this was no bad thing. A great tip I learned from Jane Grigson is to substitute up to half of the cream in a recipe with soured cream or crème fraiche.[4] It works very well in the egg and bacon pye, below.

5. Beer and wine tasted much sweeter. They were not the refined, bitter or dry drinks like today; they were sweet and a major source of calories. To replicate this, I add one or two tablespoons of malt syrup to every 500 ml of ale or beer, depending upon bitterness. Try to use ales with few, or no, hops. Use sweet dessert wines, or sweeten them yourself with three or four tablespoons of sugar per 500 ml.

6. White sugar was too expensive for everyday cooking. Unless triple-refined white sugar is specially called for (in, for example, icing for a bride cake), unrefined or light brown sugar should be used.

7. White flour wasn't that white. We are used to brilliantly white flour these days, but 250 years ago, millers, or their mills, were not quite as efficient as they are today. I swap around 10 per cent of the white flour with wholemeal.

There are many things we can't control, such as the inherent smokiness of the food. All food was cooked with wood, charcoal or coal, which imparted a flavour that modern gas hobs or electrical plates cannot. This is a bad thing for roasts (we, of course, bake our 'roast' meat in ovens these days), but a great thing for delicately flavoured confectionery, sauces and custards. Great pains were made to reduce the smoky flavour of these foodstuffs: Elizabeth would have approved of modern cookers, at least when it came to desserts.

There are some ingredients that are no longer appropriate or even legal today: there are several game birds, such as ruffs, sparrows and larks, that are no longer legal game.[5] In the UK, meat and offal taken from the heads or spinal cords of cattle has been illegal since the BSE ('Mad Cow') crisis of the 1990s. The heads and brains of calves – which crop up a lot in the book – are almost impossible to source from UK farms. Legally they have to be organic and under eighteen months old; what is more, the farmer also needs a specialist licence to do it, making it prohibitively expensive. This is a shame because UK veal is high welfare, unlike the veal in continental Europe, which can still be 'farmed' in cruel crates. This means that if you want to cook calves' heads and sweetbreads and ox palates, you'll have to go to mainland Europe, or ask your butcher to order them for you.[6]

Brisket of Beef a-la-Royale

This recipe comes from Chapter IV, 'Made Dishes', pp. 104–105 of the first edition of *The Experienced English Housekeeper*.

There is nothing more eighteenth-century than the combination of beef and oysters, and this dish uses them both very well. I didn't want to include a roast meat dish, because of the difficulty replicating the methods at home, but this one bakes the beef instead. It also uses an economic cut – brisket – and, economic at the time – oysters. Don't worry about the expense, though, my recipe uses only six, so it won't break the bank. If you fear the oyster, you could swap it for anchovy fillets, and if seafood of any kind isn't your thing, may I suggest using halved, stoned prunes.

Elizabeth's original recipe uses a whole beef brisket, which is huge, so I've scaled it back a little to a piece weighing two kilos; still substantial and enough to feed eight people. It makes a great alternative to a Sunday roast, and goes very well with mashed potatoes.

Ingredients
2–2.25 kg rolled brisket
6 oysters
100 g dry-cured streaky bacon cut into lardons
Small bunch parsley, roughly chopped
1 dsp plain flour
250 ml red wine, warmed
1 tbs sugar
Black pepper

Method
Preheat your oven to 140°C.

Prepare the brisket by first making regular holes in rows around an inch apart using a pointed utility knife. Shuck the oysters and make sure there is no shell or grit on them, before chopping roughly. Reserve the oyster liquor.

Stuff the holes alternately with oyster, bacon and parsley.

Place the beef in a close-fitting casserole with the reserved oyster liquor. Sprinkle the beef with the flour. Dissolve the sugar in the wine before tossing it over the beef. Season with black pepper, put on the lid and braise in the oven for four hours.

When the time is up, remove the lid and turn up the heat to 180°C to allow the cooking juices to thicken and the top to crisp up slightly.

Remove the beef from the casserole and keep warm. Strain the juices and reduce to a thicker, richer consistency.

Slice the brisket in thick slices, arrange on a large serving dish and pour the sauce over.

Egg and Bacon Pye

This recipe comes from Chapter V 'Pies', p. 132 of the first edition of *The Experienced English Housekeeper*.

This excellent recipe for a bacon and egg pie reminds me of the square slices of pie that used to be regularly served at dinnertime at my junior school in Pudsey, West Yorkshire, so I was very pleased to see it has a good heritage. In the original recipe, Elizabeth suggests soaking the bacon overnight in water. This is no longer required because with modern refrigeration, bacon doesn't need to be anywhere near as salty as it was in the eighteenth century.

Elizabeth's pie is supposed to be eaten cold, but I think it is best just warm. If you are worried about making your own pastry, don't be; shop-bought is absolutely fine to use in this recipe.

Ingredients
For the filling:
4 eggs
300 ml double cream, or 150 ml each double cream and soured cream
Salt and pepper
150 g dry-cured smoked back bacon, chopped
For the shortcrust pastry:
100 g butter, diced (or 50g each butter and lard)
200 g plain flour
½ tsp salt
Around 50 ml of water or milk

Method
First make your pastry by rubbing the fat(s) into the flour and salt. When the mixture resembles breadcrumbs, add the water by degrees until you have a soft, but not sticky, dough. Knead briefly, cover and refrigerate for at least 20 minutes.

Now make the filling: Beat the eggs with the cream(s) and season with salt and pepper. Remember the bacon will also contribute a good amount of salt to the mix, so season with less salt than you would usually.

Roll two-thirds of the pastry and use it to line a 20 cm tart tin. Roll out the remainder of the pastry for the lid and set aside. Sprinkle the bacon over the pastry base and pour almost all of the egg mixture over the bacon pieces.

Cut a steam hole in your lid before using the rest of the egg mixture to glue the pastry lid onto the pie. Brush with the egg mixture. Leave the pie to rest in the refrigerator for 20 minutes.

Preheat your oven to 220°C and place a baking tray on the centre shelf.

Slide the pie onto the hot baking tray to bake for 40 minutes, turning the heat down to 180°C after the pastry has started to brown.

Allow to cool on a rack.

A Hunting Pudding

This recipe comes from Chapter VI 'Puddings', p. 145 of the first edition of *The Experienced English Housekeeper.*

I had to include a good old British pudding, and this is an excellent and simple one. This hunting pudding is essentially a type of plum pudding, the kind which would have been served with roast or poached beef. Perhaps this pudding was meant to be served with venison, seeing as it is a hunting pudding. This pudding would usually be found in the second course, though today we would prefer to eat it for dessert with custard. These puddings are great with beef, so if you are curious about this combination, I would certainly encourage you to try it. If there is any left over, it is delicious sliced, fried in butter and eaten with bacon for breakfast.

This is an excellent, simple pudding. I only made three small changes to Elizabeth's recipe: I halved the ingredients to make it a sensible size, I reduced the amount of suet to match modern tastes, and I steamed it in a bowl as opposed to boiling it in a pudding cloth.[7] Boiled puddings are delicious, but because the mixture is quite runny, I decided to go with a pudding basin, reducing the chances of spillage. If you like, you can use self-raising instead of plain flour to give a lighter pudding.

Like many puddings of the boiled or steamed variety, it contains beef suet, which you can buy fresh from your butcher for very little. It is flaky and very easy to chop or grate. Fresh suet produces a much superior pud, but shop bought suet – whether beef or vegetable – works very well.

Makes one 1.5 litre pudding, enough for six to eight people (plus second helpings).

Ingredients
Butter for greasing
220 g flour
3 eggs

240 ml cream or 200 ml milk
110 g suet
220 g currants
100 g sultanas
60 g sugar
60 g candied chopped peel
½ a nutmeg, freshly grated
2 tbs brandy

Method

Grease a 1.5 litre pudding basin liberally with butter and set aside.

Place the flour in a mixing bowl and make a well in the centre. Beat the eggs and cream or milk, pour into the well and beat until smooth. Add the remaining ingredients and stir well. Pour into the basin and cover with a lid of foil, secured with some string or twine. Steam for two hours. Turn out onto a plate and serve.

Ice Cream

This recipe comes from Chapter X, 'Creams, Custards and Cheese-cakes', p. 228 of the first edition of *The Experienced English Housekeeper*.

Elizabeth's ice cream recipe is by no means the first; ice cream had been enjoyed amongst the upper echelons of society for the best part of a century and it was expensive to make; especially if the ice cream was wanted in August. For that, you needed an ice house, and they did not come cheap.

Elizabeth uses apricots in her recipe, but tells us that any fruit can be used. Strawberries, pineapple or mango would all be good, in-keeping substitutes. Unusually, Elizabeth uses raw fruit; she just scalds the apricots, presumably to make the removal of their skins easier. Then they were pounded in a mortar and passed through a sieve. Today we can use a liquidiser. She also heats the cream and mixes in the sugar to dissolve it: this is the opposite way around to modern methods; we prefer the flavour of cooked fruits, so it is best to make a sweet fruit purée and add that to cold cream.

The ice cream was frozen thusly: 'put it into a Tin with close Cover, set it in a Tub of Ice broken small, and a large Quantity of Salt put amongst it, when you see your Cream grow thick around the Edges of your Tin, stir it, and set it again 'till it is all Froze up, take it out of your Tin, and put it in your Mould in the Middle, and lay your Ice under and over it, let it stand four or five hours.' I have tried making ice cream using this method, and I can confirm that it works very well. These days, I use an ice cream maker. If you don't own one, you can try the ice-salt method, or you can pop the mixture in the freezer and give it a good beating with a whisk every half hour. The ice cream would be turned out of its hinged mould and sent up as part of the dessert course.

This is the simplest of ice creams: just fruit, sugar and cream. May I suggest adding 50 ml of alcohol to this mixture; I made pineapple ice cream and flavoured it with rum, and very good it was too. Brandy or orange liqueur would go very well with apricots. I'm sure Elizabeth would have approved.

Makes 1 litre.

Ingredients
450 g double cream
180 g caster sugar
450 g seasonal fruit

Method
Heat the cream and stir in the sugar. Once dissolved, remove from the heat. Prepare your chosen fruit by removing skins, stones, pips, cores, etc. and liquidise until smooth and stir into the sweet cream. Taste and add more sugar if necessary – my advice here is to get the mixture perfectly sweet to your taste and then add a good-sized tablespoon of sugar on top of that: this will make up for the fact that cold food tastes less sweet compared with warm food. If you prefer, cook the fruit with the sugar and blend before stirring in cold cream.

Cover and cool your mixture and freeze in an ice cream machine. If you don't have one, place in the freezer and beat the mixture with a whisk, making sure you work the frozen bits in well. Do this every half hour until the mixture has set. If you have a mould, spoon the mixture in, packing it down well, lest you get air bubbles. Otherwise, freeze in its tub.

When it's time to serve the ice cream, remove it from the freezer half an hour before you want to serve it, then remove the mould, or scoop it using an ice cream scoop dipped in very hot water.

A Good Plum Cake

This recipe comes from Chapter X, 'Cakes', pp. 244–245 of the first edition of *The Experienced English Housekeeper*.

If you are going to cook just one recipe from this appendix, please let it be this one. This cake is deliciously moist and surprisingly light, bearing in mind no chemical raising agents are used. Air was introduced via two methods: leavening with yeast or by folding in whisked eggs. This one uses the latter. No one makes cakes in this way anymore, which is a shame because I really like the final texture: moist and close-textured, but not stodgy. It is flavoured by a good glug of brandy and orange flower water, the latter being a very popular ingredient at the time. Some might find it too scented, but I think it is delicious. You could add less than the recipe indicates, or leave it out altogether, if you suspect it isn't your thing.

This 'plum' cake contains no plums; 'plum' in this case refers to the dried stone fruits. It's not as packed with dried fruits as a typical fruit cake, mainly because these ingredients are expensive, and seedless grapes were yet to be bred, meaning that the pips had to be removed by hand by you or your kitchen staff.

This recipe required a vast amount of elbow grease – the creaming of the butter was literally done by hand, the warmth of one's hand helping to soften it, and the eggs beaten without a balloon whisk; instead, the eggs were beaten with the ribs of long feathers bound together. Jane Grigson said of Elizabeth: '[m]any of her recipes can be adapted to modern kitchen machinery, which she would have thoroughly approved of.'[8] This is particularly true for cakes such as these: modern electric mixers make tasks that would have taken hours in the eighteenth century the work of mere minutes today; her original recipe says 'It will take an Hour and a half beating.'

Ingredients
220 g salted butter, softened
170 g caster sugar
2 whole eggs
2 egg yolks
220 g plain flour
½ tsp salt

¼ tsp each ground nutmeg and mace
120 g currants
80 g raisins
Grated zest of half a lemon
60 g candied peel
60 ml brandy or white wine
2 tbs orange flower water

Method

Preheat your oven to 150°C and line a 16 cm (or thereabouts) tin with greaseproof paper.

In a mixing bowl, cream the softened butter with approximately four-fifths of the sugar. Then, in another bowl, beat the whole eggs and yolks with the remaining sugar until pale and foamy. If you are using the same set of beaters, make sure you wash them after you've creamed the butter – fat prevents eggs aerating properly.

Using a metal spoon, mix half of the eggs into the butter and sugar along with the brandy or wine and orange flower water.

Next, add the flour, salt, spices and lemon zest, fold into the mixture, then fold in the rest of the eggs. Do this carefully, for it's the air captured in these eggs that will make the cake rise.

Finally, fold in the dried and candied fruit. Pour into the cake tin and bake for 2 ¼ to 2 ½ hours. Test to see if it is cooked using a wooden kebab or cocktail stick; if it comes out clean, the cake is ready. Allow to cool on a rack, removing it from the tin when it is still warm.

Stewed Cheese

This recipe comes from Chapter XII, 'Little Savoury Dishes', p. 261 of the first edition of *The Experienced English Housekeeper*.

A simple yet effective recipe, not dissimilar to a fondue. Make sure you use a good hard cheese that melts without splitting. A Cheddar, double Gloucester or red Leicester would work very well. I used a dark ale, sweetened with a little malt syrup to replicate the slightly sweet flavour of eighteenth-century beer. If beer isn't your thing, substitute it wholly or partially with milk. There is a similar recipe in Elizabeth's book that uses red wine instead of ale. I found this combination of flavours absolutely disgusting, but don't let that stop you from trying it!

Feel free to add other flavours to this simple affair: freshly-ground black pepper or a pinch of Cayenne pepper would be very in keeping with Elizabeth's approach to seasoning. She probably wouldn't have been against a tablespoon or two of double cream, either.

Elizabeth recommends pouring it over toast or 'light Wigs' before serving. Wigs were a type of enriched bread, slightly sweetened and subtly flavoured with caraway seeds. They used to come in wedge-shaped pieces, like cheese scones sometimes do today.

This would make an excellent first course or replacement to a cheese course. Don't eat it too close to bedtime, lest you have nightmares.

Serves 6.

Ingredients
250 g thinly sliced or grated cheese
75 ml ale or milk, or a mixture of the two
½ tsp malt syrup
6 slices of toast cut into fingers

Method
Warm the ale or milk and malt syrup in small saucepan, but don't let it boil. Add the cheese and beat with a small whisk. Keep beating until the cheese melts into the ale. It's important not to let the mixture boil because the cheese may split, releasing the oils. Be patient.

When smooth, pour into individual ramekins or leave the stewed cheese in the pan it was cooked in.

Rather than pouring it over toast, dip fingers of toast into the cheese.

Mulled Ale

This recipe comes from Chapter XIV, 'Possets, Gruel &c.', p. 289 of the first edition of *The Experienced English Housekeeper*.

This is an unusual recipe by modern tastes in that the ale is thickened slightly with egg yolks. It doesn't become thick like custard, but it does go deliciously silky and smooth. Try to use an ale on the pale side that isn't too hoppy: too many hops can be a flavour clash with this recipe.

Elizabeth uses nutmeg and cloves to mull her ale, but use whatever you like: a cinnamon stick, a couple of bay leaves or a few cracked black peppercorns would be good alternatives. Toast is traditionally served with mulled ale, but I think some ratafia or shortbread biscuits would suit modern tastes better.

Serves 4.

Ingredients
500 ml ale
1 ½ tbs malt syrup
4 cloves
A quarter of a nutmeg, cracked in a pestle and mortar or the side of a kitchen knife
80–120 g light brown or unrefined white sugar
5 egg yolks
Extra nutmeg for grating

Method
Place ale, syrup, cloves and nutmeg in a saucepan, bring to a bare simmer, turn the heat low and allow the spices to infuse for five minutes. Add sugar to taste.

Beat the yolks and whisk in a couple of ladles of hot ale. Take the ale off the heat and whisk in the yolk mixture. Place over a low heat and stir well with a wooden spoon until the mixture barely simmers and becomes a little more viscous.

Pass through a sieve into a warmed jug. Pour into small cups and grate a little nutmeg over them before serving immediately.

Notes

The full citation of a source is given the first time it is used in a chapter; thereafter only the author's name and publishing date are provided.

Introduction

1. I have written a blog post for each recipe: the blog is called *Neil Cooks Grigson* (neilcooksgrigson.com), and at the time of writing, there are just a few recipes that remain uncooked.
2. She didn't, but she spent so much of her working life in the Bull's Head, many have assumed she must have owned it. Either that, or they got it confused with the King's Head, the Salford tavern she ran with John.
3. Grigson, J. (1992). *English Food*. 3rd edn. Penguin, p. 251.
4. Shipperbottom, R. (1996). 'Elizabeth Raffald', in Walker, H. (ed.), *Cooks & Other People: Proceedings of the Oxford Symposium on Food and Cookery, 1995*. Oxford Symposium, p. 233.
5. Borsay, P. (2003). 'Politeness and elegance: the cultural re-fashioning of eighteenth-century York', in Hallett, M. and Rendall, J. (eds), *Eighteenth-century York Culture, Space and Society*. Borthwick Publications, University of York, p. 1.
6. Dickson Wright, C. (2011). *A History of English Food*. Random House, p. 256.
7. Hecht, J. J. (1956). *The Domestic Servant Class in Eighteenth Century England*. Routledge & Kegan Paul, p. 197.
8. Raffald, E. (1769). *The Experienced English Housekeeper*. J. Harrop, p. i.

Chapter 1: Foundations (1733–1760)

1. This is according to Winifred Shircliff, a descendant of Elizabeth's. Other sources give this date as the day of her baptism, which would

have been just a few days after she was born. Shircliff, W. E. (1999). *Elizabeth Raffald: Her Biography and Family Tree*, p. 1.

2. Shipperbottom, R. in Raffald, E. and Shipperbottom, R. (1997). *The Experienced English Housekeeper with an Introduction by Roy Shipperbottom*. Southover Press, p. vii.

3. Shipperbottom, R. (1996). 'Elizabeth Raffald', in Walker, H. (ed.), *Cooks & Other People: Proceedings of the Oxford Symposium on Food and Cookery, 1995*. Oxford Symposium, p. 233.

4. Houston, R. A. (1982). 'The development of literacy: Northern England, 1640–1750', *Economic History Review*, p. 199.

5. Day, I. (1997). *The Art of Confectionery*.

6. Harland, J. (1867). *Collectanea Relating to Manchester and Its Neighbourhood, at Various Periods*, Volume 72. Chetham Society, p. 148.

7. Raffald, E. (1769). *The Experienced English Housekeeper*. J. Harrop, p. 253.

8. Ibid., pp. i–ii.

9. Booker, K. (2017). *Menials: Domestic Service and the Cultural Transformation of British Society, 1650–1850*. Bucknell University Press, p. 108.

10. Hecht, J. J. (1956). *The Domestic Servant Class in Eighteenth Century England*. Routledge & Kegan Paul, p. 123.

11. Booker (2017), p. 46.

12. Hecht (1956), p. 101.

13. *The London Magazine* (1756), 'To Joseph D'Anvers, Esq.' May, pp. 225–226.

14. Hill, B. (1996). *Servants: English Domestics in the Eighteenth Century*. Clarendon Press, Oxford, pp. 4, 6.

15. Ibid., pp. 37–38. But then he did tax anything he possibly could including – infamously – windows all to pay for the various wars and spats against the French.

16. There is widely held belief that beer was drunk because the water was dirty. While it is true that the microbes in small beer outcompeted any pathogenic microbes, making it safe to drink, it was favoured for its nutrition; essentially liquid bread. Drinking water, or 'fair water' as it is often referred to, crops up all the time in historical cookery books.

17. Hill (1996), p. 74.

18. Shipperbottom (1997), p. viii.

19. Alcock, T. (1752). *Observations on the Defects of the Poor Laws, and on the Causes and Consequences of the Great Increase and Burden of the Poor*. R. Baldwin, p. 45.
20. Woodforde, J. (1999). *The Diary of a Country Parson*. Edited by J. Beresford. Canterbury Press, pp. 86–87.
21. Alcock (1752), p. 48.
22. Dickson Wright, C. (2011). *A History of English Food*. Random House, p. 264; Hecht (1956), p. 162.
23. Hecht (1956), p. 155.
24. Ibid., p. 161.
25. Hill (1996), pp. 76–77, 86.
26. Ibid., p. 155.
27. Quote originally from a discussion in *Bulletin of the Society for the Study of Labour History*, volume 26, 1973 but found via Hill (1996), p. 93.
28. Ibid., p. 1.
29. Quote via Hill (1996), p. 94.
30. Ibid., p. 97; Hecht (1956), p. 84.
31. Hecht (1956), p. 79.
32. Miege, G. (1702). *The New State of England, Under Our Present Sovereign Queen Anne. In Three Parts*. R. J. Vol. II, p. 175.
33. Foster, C. F. (2002). *Seven Households: Life in Cheshire and Lancashire 1582 to 1774*. Arley Hall Press, p. 204.
34. Hecht (1956), p. 178.
35. Ibid., p. 149.
36. Hill (1996), p. 26.
37. Hecht (1956), pp. 46–47. The butler at this point was not the figure we imagine today, his position evolving from the original task of looking after the wine barrels, or butts, hence the word buttery (*butterie*) for the room in which barrels of alcohol were stored.
38. Raffald (1769), pp. 43–45.
39. Lofts, N. (1976). *Domestic Life in England*. Morrison & Gibb, p. 164.
40. Hartley, D. (1954). *Food in England*. Little, Brown & Company, pp. 36–38.
41. Brears, P. (2014). *Traditional Food in Yorkshire*. Prospect Books, p. 85–87.
42. Dickson Wright (2011), pp. 257–258.
43. Lofts (1976), p. 163.
44. Raffald (1769), pp. 55–56. Rees are female ruffs. There is a striking sexual dimorphism in the species, the males being larger with an

impressive summer plumage that includes a ruff of feathers around their neck, hence their name.

45. Borsay, P. (2003). 'Politeness and elegance: the cultural re-fashioning of eighteenth-century York', in Hallett, M. and Rendall, J. (eds), *Eighteenth-century York Culture, Space and Society*. Borthwick Publications, University of York, p. 3.

46. Borsay (2003), p. 5; Strevens, S. (2014). *The Birth of the Chocolate City: Life in Georgian York*. Amberley, Chapter 1 (e-book).

47. Borsay (2003), pp. 7, 9.

48. Ibid., p. 9.

49. Hill (1996), p. 15; Armstrong, A. (1974). *Stability and Change in an English County Town: A Social Study of York 1801–51*. Cambridge University Press, p. 29. At the turn of the eighteenth century, across the country there were 300,000 female servants and 260,000 male; however, if one looks at the fashionable towns and cities, there is a pronounced difference. It was most obvious in London, where it is estimated that there were four female servants for every male. Hill (1996), p. 42.

50. Shipperbottom (1997), p. viii.

51. Calcott, W. (1769). *A Candid Disquisition of the Principles and Practices of the Most Ancient and Honourable Society of Free and Accepted Masons*. Calcott, Wellins, p. i.

52. Brown, P. (2006). 'The Real Thing? Understanding the Archive at Fairfax House, York', in Hosking, R. (ed.), *Authenticity in the Kitchen: Proceedings of the Oxford Symposium on Food and Cookery 2005*. Prospect Books, p. 106.

53. Ibid., p. 10.

54. Raffald (1769), p. 237; curd cheese tarts had been enjoyed for centuries; Henry VIII had a favourite which he called maids-of-honour. Yorkshire curd tarts very similar to Elizabeth's recipe are still available throughout Yorkshire and are particularly popular in York.

Chapter 2: Arley Hall (1760–1763)

1. Shipperbottom, R. in Raffald, E. and Shipperbottom, R. (1997), *The Experienced English Housekeeper with an Introduction by Roy Shipperbottom*. Southover Press, p. viii.

2. Foster, C. F. (2002). *Seven Households: Life in Cheshire and Lancashire 1582 to 1774*. Arley Hall Press, p. 229.
3. Ibid., p. 24.
4. Ibid., p. 181.
5. Ibid., pp. 197–198.
6. This network was made up of the Sankey, Bridgewater, Trent and Mersey canals.
7. Arley Hall Archives 1750–90: Life on a Cheshire Country Estate (2019). Arley Hall website. Available at: https://arleyhallarchives.co.uk.
8. Foster, C. F. (1982). *Arley Hall, Cheshire*. Martin's of Berwick, p. 26.
9. Hecht, J. J. (1956). *The Domestic Servant Class in Eighteenth Century England*. Routledge & Kegan Paul, p. 64.
10. From Charles Foster's personal archive. This point is discussed in correspondence between Charles Foster and Roy Shipperbottom in the early 1990s.
11. Roy Shipperbottom wrote: 'it may well have been that he already met and fancied Elizabeth at that time, and that he recommended her for her position as Arley's Housekeeper.' Shipperbottom (1997), p. ix.
12. The salaries of several of Arley's staff can be seen online on Arley Hall Archives online: The Staff Employed at Arley Hall 1750–1790 at https://arleyhallarchives.co.uk/staff.htm.
13. Hecht (1956), pp. 69–70.
14. This is not an exhaustive list of staff working at Arley, the fullest list can be found on the Arley Hall Archives website at www.arleyhallarchives.co.uk/staff.htm. The examples used were all contemporaries of Elizabeth's. It would appear that the list on the site is incomplete, as there are several missing roles. For example, there is no butler listed in the years Elizabeth worked at Arley, and there are no ladies-in-waiting listed at all.
15. Hill, B. (1996). *Servants: English Domestics in the Eighteenth Century*. Clarendon Press, Oxford, p. 8.
16. In fact, the Warburtons seem to be paying their female staff slightly higher than the average at that time. These differences pale in comparison when one compares these salaries to the earnings of their employers, of course.
17. Quote from Turner, E. S. (1962). *What the Butler Saw: Two Hundred and Fifty Years of the Servant Problem*. Faber & Faber, Chapter 2 (e-book); point made in Hill (1996), pp. 24–25.

18. This is also true on websites such as Trip Advisor, etc. People are more likely to leave a comment if things have not gone well, yet less likely when things went swimmingly. Nothing has changed.

19. Hill (1996), p. 3.

20. Rovee, C. K. (2006). *Imagining the Gallery: The Social Body of British Romanticism*. Stanford University Press, p. 15; William Hogarth website: www.williamhogarth.org.

21. Elizabeth certainly displayed behaviour later in life that some would consider crass, so even she wasn't immune to this phenomenon.

22. Hecht (1956), p. 208.

23. Ibid., p. 228.

24. Quote from *Daily Advertiser*, 1771, no. 12534, February, via Hecht (1965), p. 64.

25. Shipperbottom (1997), p. ix.

26. Foster (2002), p. 200. Small game birds were often caught in nets by stretching them between trees, entangling the birds as they were scared away by shouts, gunshots or barking dogs.

27. Arley Hall archives: www.arleyhallarchives.co.uk/stafffood.htm.

28. Shipperbottom (1997), p. ix.

29. Raffald, E. (1769). *The Experienced English Housekeeper*. J. Harrop, pp. 273–274.

30. Thirsk, J. (1998). 'Preserving the Fruit and Vegetable Harvest, 1600–1700', in Wilson, C. A. (ed.), *The Country House Kitchen Garden 1600–1950*. The History Press, pp. 146–151.

31. Raffald (1769), p. ii.

32. '… her [Lady Betty's] sisters included Lady Charlotte, who eloped with John Burgoyne, dramatist and soldier who was successful in becoming Member of Parliament for Preston, Lancashire but is usually remembered as the general who was defeated at Saratoga.' Shipperbottom, R. (1996) 'Elizabeth Raffald', in Walker, H. (ed.), *Cooks & Other People: Proceedings of the Oxford Symposium on Food and Cookery*, 1995. Oxford Symposium, p. 233.

33. Foster (2002), p. 197.

34. The dedication appears just before the introduction in Raffald (1769).

35. Foster (2002), pp. 186–188.

36. The first, a daughter named Elizabeth, was born the next year but sadly died at the age of 12. The Warburtons had four more daughters and one

son, whom they named Peter. Tragedy struck again when their second daughter Anne died of smallpox at the age of 21, 'despite intensive nursing'. The remaining four siblings, however, went on to live to a ripe old age. Foster (2002), pp. 186–188.

37. Hill (1996), p. 56.
38. Booker, K. (2017). *Menials: Domestic Service and the Cultural Transformation of British Society, 1650–1850.* Bucknell University Press, p. 44. Booker is quoting from Haywood, E. F. (1743), *A Present for a Servant-maid*, T. Gardner.
39. Hill (1996), p. 51.
40. Ibid., p. 51.
41. Harland, J. (1867). *Collectanea Relating to Manchester and Its Neighbourhood, at Various Periods*, Volume 72. Chetham Society, pp. 145–146, 151.
42. Shipperbottom (1997), p. ix.
43. Arley Hall Archives website: https://arleyhallarchives.co.uk
44. As it turned out, the refurbishment would be a disaster, with the roof developing cracks, as well as a rat problem, that required much repair by 1818. Then the whole building had to be completely refurbished again in the mid-nineteenth century. In 1968, the 'rear of building comprising kitchens, servants' quarters, nurseries etc., in all some seventy rooms, was demolished to reduce the costs of maintenance.' Foster (1982), pp. 4–6.
45. Appleton, S. (2017a). *Introduction to Elizabeth Raffald*, p. 20.
46. Harland (1867), pp. 144–145.

Chapter 3: Feeding the Upstairs

1. Men too had to look and act the part, and there are extant recipes of in-law George Dockwra who bought 'A new Wigg' and 'A new Hatt' in 1742, and 'A full Grisel Bobwigg' in 1743. In that same year, he also spent 10s 6d at his barber of choice, from whom he received regular shaves with additional wig dressing and powdering to ensure he was perceived to be 'very much the gentleman'. Foster, C. F. (2002). *Seven Households: Life in Cheshire and Lancashire 1582 to 1774*. Arley Hall Press, p. 177.
2. This concept is known as honest signalling in evolutionary biology. The time and energy one can spend taking part in such costly, pointless theatre

demonstrating to anyone watching one's wealth and personal wellbeing, and therefore that one is good marriage material. In Darwinian terms, it increases your fitness. Even if you are already married off yourself, you still need to go through it, because it raises the social status of your family and therefore the prospects of your children or grandchildren.

3. Raffald, E. (1769). *The Experienced English Housekeeper*. J. Harrop, p. 242; *Guardian* (1986), 'Kissin' don't last but cookin' do', 9 April.

4. Raffald (1769). p. 245.

5. Foster (2002), p. 204.

6. Flower, M. (1984). *Arley Hall Gardens, Cheshire*. Beric Tempest & Co Ltd, p. 4.

7. Hecht, J. J. (1956). *The Domestic Servant Class in Eighteenth Century England*. Routledge & Kegan Paul, p. 48. Unfortunately, John Raffald missed out on working with the 'well-known landscape gardener William Emes to improve the park and the surroundings of the house'; that task was left to his replacement, Thomas Young. See Maps, Arley Hall Archives online: www.arleyhallarchives.co.uk/map7.htm

8. Coulton, R. (2018). 'Curiosity, Commerce, and Conversation: Nursery-Gardens and Nurserymen in Eighteenth-Century London', *The London Journal*. Routledge, 43(1), pp. 17–35.

9. Arley Hall Archives receipt dated 23 April 1762.

10. Arley Hall Archives receipt dated 16 July 1761.

11. Arley Hall Archives receipt dated 18 August 1759.

12. Gray, T. (1998). 'Walled gardens and the cultivation of orchard fruit in the south-west of England', in Wilson, C. A. (ed.), *The Country House Kitchen Garden 1600–1950*. The History Press, p. 102.

13. The hot walls are still extant in Arley's gardens and were renovated in the 1980s. Unfortunately, they are no longer fired up.

14. The modern gardeners' favourite, the tomato, was regarded with a great deal of distrust, and though available, it was a rarity in the eighteenth-century garden.

15. Campbell, S. (2011). *Walled Kitchen Gardens*. Replika Press Private Ltd, p. 32.

16. Thanks to the head gardener at Arley for this information. These dishes are extant in the hall's hothouse, now used as a large greenhouse. By the way, the first pineapple was successfully grown in England by this method in 1718.

17. The lesser-known vegetables such as these and seakale – mentioned above – are still available if one cares to keep an eye out in independent garden centres and traditional greengrocers and farmers' markets. My greengrocer has managed to source rarities such as blanched seakale and cardoons, so if intrigued by these vegetables, do ask, you never know. However, expect to purchase a whole tray, as the grocer would be unlikely to shift these unfamiliar foods in their shop.

18. Raffald (1769), pp. 350–351.

19. Foster (2002), p. 203.

20. Mr Kalm also noted, however, that women were idle compared to his home country of Sweden because they don't have to bake, brew, spin or weave, so he may have been simplifying things somewhat. Quote via Lofts, N. (1976). *Domestic Life in England*. Morrison & Gibb, p. 167.

21. Raffald (1769), p. 148.

22. Ibid., pp. 184–185.

23. Colquhoun, K. (2012). *Taste: The Story of Britain Through Its Cooking*. Bloomsbury, Chapter 12 (e-book).

24. Raffald (1769), p. 228.

25. In French cookery, this sauce is known as *beurre blanc*. Oddly there is no recipe for this ubiquitous sauce in Elizabeth's book, perhaps because it was so common it was therefore deemed unnecessary. There is a good recipe on p. 5 in Glasse, H. (1747). *The Art of Cookery Made Plain and Easy*. Prospect Books.

26. Johnson, S. (2005). *Johnson's Dictionary: A Modern Selection*. Edited by E. L. McAdam and G. Milne. Dover Publications, p. 240.

27. Bickham, T. (2020). *Eating the Empire: Food and Society in Eighteenth-Century Britain*. Reaktion Books, pp. 67–68.

28. Dickson Wright, C. (2011). *A History of English Food*. Random House, p. 267.

29. He also says that 'nothing is considered as a greater mark of ill-breeding, than for a person to interrupt this order, or seat himself higher than he ought.' Trusler, J. (1791). *The Honours of the Table, Or, Rules for Behaviour During Meals*. Published by the author, p. 6.

30. Dickson Wright (2011), p. 227.

31. Sometimes the first course was already waiting for guests as they arrived, covered with cloches to prevent food from cooling too quickly

or forming a skin. Guests waited for everyone to be ready before the cloches were removed by servants.

32. Raffald (1769), p. 361.

33. Ibid., pp. 361–362.

34. Adams, J. (1789). *Curious Thoughts on the History of Man*, pp. 167–168.

35. Raffald (1769), pp. 75–76.

36. Ibid., pp. 71–73.

37. Acton, E. (1845). *Modern Cookery for Private Families*. Quadrille, pp. 26–27. Mock turtle soup became so popular that Heinz would go on to produce it in tins.

38. Raffald (1769), pp. 123–124.

39. Ibid., pp. 115–116.

40. Ibid., p. 232.

41. Dickson Wright (2011), p. 226.

42. Raffald (1769), p. 181–182.

43. Ibid., p. 162.

44. There is no recipe for this form of flummery in Elizabeth's book, but there is guidance on the procedure in Hannah Glasse's *The Art of Cookery Made Plain and Easy*, written twenty-two years prior to *The Experienced English Housekeeper*, where both types of flummery are represented (p. 148).

45. Modern blancmanges are more often set with cornflour rather than gelatine, but essentially, in the eighteenth and nineteenth centuries, flummery and blancmange were the same creature.

46. Day, I. (1997). *The Art of Confectionery*, p. 28.

47. Raffald (1769), pp. 167–168.

48. Ibid., pp. 179–80.

49. This dish has been reproduced by Ivan Day (2011), *Solomon's Temple in Flummery: A Culinary Mobile*, *Food History Jottings*. Available at: http://foodhistorjottings.blogspot.com/2011/10/solomons-temple-in-flummery-culinary.html, and updated to modern tastes by Regula Ysewijn (2015), *Pride and Pudding: The History of British Puddings Savoury and Sweet*. Murdoch Books, pp. 272–273.

50. In the Old Testament, Solomon, son of David, built the temple inside which housed the Ark of the Covenant.

51. Day (2011).

52. Raffald (1769), p. 180.
53. Bickham (2020), p. 185.

Chapter 4: Fennel Street (1763–1766)

1. Sanders, J. (1967). *Manchester*. C. Tinling & Co, p. 57.
2. Ibid., pp. 57-58; the 1638 quote by Leland appears in Axon, W. E. A. (1886). *Annals of Manchester*. John Heywood, p. vi.
3. One hundred years later, Manchester would be home to over 340,000 inhabitants and Salford home to 176,000; Axon (1886), p. v.
4. Shipperbottom, R. (1996). 'Elizabeth Raffald', in Walker, H. (ed.), *Cooks & Other People: Proceedings of the Oxford Symposium on Food and Cookery, 1995*. Oxford Symposium, p. 234.
5. The exact proportion is 25.4 per cent: 248 of 975 sampled names in Elizabeth's alphabetical list of occupants in her 1772 directory.
6. Sanders (1967), pp. 58–59.
7. Lofts, N. (1976). *Domestic Life in England*. Morrison & Gibb, p. 145.
8. Workhouses have been around since the sixteenth century and weren't the regimented 'prison-like institutions of the sort that became commonplace in the mid nineteenth century'. The poor who lived there were not imprisoned or restrained. 'Instead, workhouses were general parish institutions that took on the character of emergency wards, casual night shelters, of creches and orphanages, almshouses and geriatric wards.' Hitchcock, T. (2004). *Down and Out in Eighteenth-Century London*. Bloomsbury, p. 133.
9. They were situated in Deansgate, Great Turner Street, Alport Lane, Hatters Lane and 'behind Cross – Salford'. Raffald, E. (1772). *Elizabeth Raffald's Directory of Manchester and Salford 1772*. Neil Richardson.
10. This was not the only source of milk; asses' milk was a popular alternative, presumably because they were already found in towns and cities doing the bulk of the heavy lifting and pulling, and if it was good enough for Cleopatra to bathe in, it was good enough for children and invalids. Lofts (1976), pp. 148–149.
11. Dickson Wright, C. (2011). *A History of English Food*. Random House, p. 291.

12. Then, between 1764 and 1779, imports would increase by 70 per cent. Timperley, C. H. (1839). *Annals of Manchester: Biographical, Historical, Ecclesiastical, and Commercial, from the Earliest Period to the Close of the Year 1839.* Bancks and Company, pp. 51, 56.
13. Timperley (1839), p. 56.
14. Ibid., p. 49.
15. Sanders (1967), pp. 68–69.
16. Nasmyth, J. (1883). *James Nasmyth Engineer: An Autobiography.* Edited by S. Smiles. Harper & Bros, pp. 199–200.
17. Ackroyd, P. (2017). *The History of England IV: Revolution.* Pan, p. 262.
18. Sanders (1967), p. 84.
19. Shipperbottom (1996), p. 234.
20. Lofts (1976), pp. 138–139.
21. Some servants became farmers, there is even one case of a servant who trained as a surgeon after they left domestic service. Hecht, J. J. (1956), *The Domestic Servant Class in Eighteenth Century England.* Routledge & Kegan Paul, pp. 188–190.
22. Shipperbottom (1997), p. x.
23. Raffald, E. (1769). *The Experienced English Housekeeper.* J. Harrop, pp. 33–34.
24. Ibid., pp. 3–4. Believe it or not, the recipe has been heavily edited, the recipe being around twice as long as presented here. Elizabeth has since been heralded as the inventor of both the stock cube and Cup-a-Soup.
25. Shipperbottom, R. (1997). *The Experienced English Housekeeper with an Introduction by Roy Shipperbottom.* Southover Press, p. x.
26. Fielding, H. (1751). *A Plan of the Universal Register-Office, opposite Cecil-Street in the Strand.* Self-published, pp. 4–6.
27. Philanthropus (1757). *An Appeal to the Public; Against the Growing Evil of Universal Register-offices.* Self-published, p. 21.
28. This point and quotes from the *Ipswich Journal* can be found in Hill, B. (1996). *Servants: English Domestics in the Eighteenth Century.* Clarendon Press, Oxford, pp. 23–24.
29. Reed, J. (1761). *The Register-office: A Farce of Two Acts.* T. Davies, pp. 3, 47.
30. Hecht (1956), pp. 30–31.
31. Shipperbottom (1997), p. xi.

32. Dickson Wright (2011), p. 308.
33. *Manchester Mercury*, 4 December 1764.
34. Shipperbottom (1997), p. ix.

Chapter 5: Market Place (1766–1772)

1. Shipperbottom, R. (1997). *The Experienced English Housekeeper with an Introduction by Roy Shipperbottom*. Southover Press, p. xi.
2. Shipperbottom, R. (1996). 'Elizabeth Raffald', in Walker, H. (ed.), *Cooks & Other People: Proceedings of the Oxford Symposium on Food and Cookery, 1995*. Oxford Symposium, p. 235; Shipperbottom (1997), p. xii.
3. This receipt can be viewed on the Arley Hall Archives website. In the eighteenth century, there were twelve pence in a shilling and twenty shillings per pound. There is a second receipt from Elizabeth in that year for 'Bedwashing & Calendering [pressing]', 3 November 1770.
4. Harland, J. (1867). *Collectanea Relating to Manchester and Its Neighbourhood, at Various Periods*, Volume 72, pp. 152–154.
5. Shipperbottom (1997), p. xi.
6. Harland (1867), p. 152.
7. Cuisine and civility became directly correlated at this time. For example, Scottish cookery was derided as too simple and barbarian and thus reflected 'the poor state of Scotland's civilization at the time'. There were no pots and pans or leavened breads, 'just cattle boiled in their hides'. After the battle of Pinkie, the English saw a variety of foods: cheeses, butter, bread, even 'silver plate and chalices'. The Scots had become more civilised, and their cuisine now reflected that. Bickham, T. (2020). *Eating the Empire: Food and Society in Eighteenth-Century Britain*. Reaktion Books, pp. 127–128.
8. This term was coined by Troy Bickham (2020). He uses the term 'ingestibles' because it also includes tobacco, which is neither eaten nor drunk. As far as I can see, Elizabeth did not buy and sell tobacco products.
9. Bickham (2020), p. 66.
10. Ibid., p. 60.
11. Raffald, E. (1769). *The Experienced English Housekeeper*. J. Harrop, p. 141.
12. Harland, J. (1852). 'Local Gleanings No. XXXII: Mrs. Raffald's Works', *Manchester Guardian*, 19 May, p. 3.
13. Ibid., pp. 157–158.

14. *Manchester Guardian* (1927), 'The Eighteenth-Century Girl in Manchester: HER ACCOMPLISHMENTS', 9 March, p. 3.

15. Appleton, S. (2017b). *The Manchester Directories 1772, 1773 & 1781 by Elizabeth Raffald.* www.lu-lu.com, p. 93.

16. *Manchester Guardian* (1927).

17. Shipperbottom (1997), p. xii.

18. *Manchester Mercury*, 21 April 1771.

19. She also wrote for it, though Suze Appleton could not find any evidence for this. Appleton, S. (2017a). *Introduction to Elizabeth Raffald.* www. lu-lu.com, p. 39.

20. *Manchester Guardian*, 9 March 1927, p. 3.

21. Harland (1867), p. 145.

22. Raffald, E. (1772). *Elizabeth Raffald's Directory of Manchester and Salford*, 1772. Neil Richardson.

23. Ibid.

24. Ibid.

25. Ibid.

26. 'Manchester in 1781', *Manchester Guardian*, 2 August 1843, p. 8.

27. 'An Old Manchester Directory', *Manchester Guardian*, 8 October 1845, p. 9.

28. This is not an exhaustive list of all the traders and inhabitants. There is also a yard merchant, saddler, cheesemonger, two more taverns called Three Boars Heads and Loxham's, a yarn merchant and a 'Frizemaker' (frize was a type of woollen fabric).

29. Dickson Wright, C. (2011) *A History of English Food.* Random House, p. 282.

30. Lofts, N. (1976). *Domestic Life in England.* Morrison & Gibb, p. 151.

31. Hobson, J. (2017). *Dark Days of Georgian Britain: Rethinking the Regency.* Pen and Sword History, p. 40.

32. Sanders, J. (1967). *Manchester.* C. Tinling & Co, pp. 85–86.

33. Axon, W. E. A. (1886). *Annals of Manchester.* John Heywood, p. 103.

34. Shipperbottom (1997), p. xii.

35. Shipperbottom (1996), p. 234.

Chapter 6: *The Experienced English Housekeeper*

1. Bickham, T. (2020). *Eating the Empire: Food and Society in Eighteenth-Century Britain.* Reaktion Books, pp. 137–138.

2. Taylor, D. (1957). 'OECONOMY WITH ELEGANCE: Watchword of an 18th-century paragon', *The Manchester Guardian*, 1 March, p. 6.

3. See also Elizabeth Moxon's *English Housewifry* (c.1741) and Susannah Carter's *The Frugal Housewife* (c.1765).

4. Smith, E. (1727). *The Compleat Housewife Or, Accomplish'd Gentlewoman's Companion*. Andrews McMeel. Preface.

5. Staid, J. (2012). 'Quizzing Glasse: Or Hannah Scrutinized', in *First Catch Your Hare: The Art of Cookery Made Plain and Easy*. Prospect Books, p. viii–x; Dickson Wright, C. (2011). *A History of English Food*. Random House, p. 295.

6. Books such as Patrick Lamb's *Royal Cookery; or, The Complete Court-Cook* (1710).

7. Glasse, H. (1747). *The Art of Cookery Made Plain and Easy*. Prospect Books, p. i.

8. Staid (2012), pp. xix–xx.

9. Glasse (1747), p. ii.

10. Verral, W. (1759). *A Complete System of Cookery*. William Verral.

11. Ibid., p. ii.

12. These female cooks always thanked him in floods of grateful tears too, of course.

13. Staid (2012), pp. xxii, xxx.

14. Bickham (2020), p.149. For example, there is *The Cotillons Made Plain and Easy* (1769) by Thomas Hurst and *Fractions Anatomized: or, The Doctrine of Parts Made Plain and Easy* (1762) by Richard Ramsbottom, to name but two.

15. Mary-Anne cooks up several of Elizabeth's recipes in her book *Deja Food* (2017), published by Random House.

16. Likewise, Eliza Smith and Mrs Beeton have been dubbed the Cradock, Smith and Lawson of the nineteenth century.

17. Raffald, E. (1769). *The Experienced English Housekeeper*. J. Harrop, p. iii.

18. Shipperbottom, R. (1996). 'Elizabeth Raffald', in Walker, H. (ed.), *Cooks & Other People: Proceedings of the Oxford Symposium on Food and Cookery, 1995*. Oxford Symposium, p. 233.

19. Shipperbottom, R. (1997). *The Experienced English Housekeeper with an Introduction by Roy Shipperbottom*. Southover Press, p. xiv.

20. Raffald (1769), p. ii.

21. Ibid., p. 193.

22. Ibid., pp. 85, 285, 286, 295.
23. Hannah's book had had six British editions published by 1769, but there were a further two editions printed in Dublin for an Irish readership.
24. Raffald, E. (1769), p. ii.
25. Ibid., p. iii.
26. Bickham (2020), pp. 129–130.
27. Raffald (1769), pp. 12–15.
28. Glasse (1747), p. ii.
29. Raffald (1769), p. 261.
30. Appleton, S. (2017a). *Introduction to Elizabeth Raffald.* www.lu-lu. com, pp. 98–99.
31. Raffald (1769), p. 244.
32. As far as I can see, her recipe is the second for piccalilli.
33. Raffald, E. (1769), p. 337–338. 'Alegar' used to be the word for malt vinegar: *ale-* because it's made from ale, and *-egar* because it is sour. Vinegar therefore is 'sour wine', and 'malt vinegar', then, means literally 'sour wine ale'.
34. Elizabeth David said that if you want to know what people were eating in any particular year, look at a cookery book that was printed twenty-five years after the date in question.
35. Driver, C. (1986). 'Kissin' don't last but cookin' do', *The Guardian*, 19 April, p. 9.
36. Raffald, E. (1769), p. 159.
37. Shipperbottom (1997), p. xiii.
38. Raffald (1769), p. 10.
39. Shipperbottom (1997), p. xiii.
40. Cole, M. (1791). *The Lady's Complete Guide*, G. Kearsley, p. vi.
41. Quotes via Merrett, R. J. (2012). 'The culinary art of eighteenth-century women cookbook authors', in Potter, T. (ed.), *Women, Popular Culture, and the Eighteenth Century.* University of Toronto Press, p. 126; and Staid (2012), p. xv, respectively.
42. Of 972 recipes, 342 were plagiarised; Bain, P. (2012). 'Recounting the chickens: Hannah further scrutinized', in *First Catch Your Hare: The Art of Cookery Made Plain and Easy.* Prospect Books, p. xxxv.
43. Robert Baldwin's publishing house was on Paternoster Row, London, adjacent to St Paul's Cathedral. He had inherited the business from his uncle Richard Baldwin, who often is confused with Robert.

44. Raffald, E. (1771). *The Experienced English Housekeeper*. 2nd edn. R. Baldwin.
45. Ibid., unnumbered appendix pages.
46. *Newcastle Courant*, 10 August 1771, via Appleton (2017a), p. 101.
47. Harland, J. (1867). *Collectanea Relating to Manchester and Its Neighbourhood, at Various Periods*, Volume 72. Chetham Society, pp. 146–147.
48. Harland (1867), p. 147.
49. Underwood, R. (2017). *Eighteenth-Century Women's Cookbooks: Authors and Copyright*. Texas Women's University, pp. 37–39.
50. Ibid., pp. 1–2.
51. In Underwood's study, 'Outside of London, seven of the eight women owned the copyright of their first editions. Clearly, the women who lived in developing industrial areas – Manchester, Newcastle, Leeds, and Doncaster – had a greater chance at retaining control over their intellectual property. The greater likelihood of an author retaining their copyright occurring outside of London may reflect a more lenient and tolerant attitude of those communities towards women owning property' (pp. 57, 58).
52. Ibid., p. 35.
53. Quote from Boswell, J. and Chapman, R. W. (no date), *Life of Johnson*. Oxford University Press, pp. 942–943. Johnson was also wrong. There is a difference; salt prunella comes in the form of tiny balls, the centre of which being nitrate, and the outside being nitrite (saltpetre is usually a powder and pure nitrate). This chemical difference, actually kick starts the preservation process, and is particularly useful on meat and fish that quickly deteriorates.
54. Underwood (2017), pp. 53–54.
55. Though Mary Cook raised a very good point that exposes Hannah, and asks just what a 'Lady' was doing 'swinking and sweating over a hot stove'? Via Staid (2012), p. xxviii.
56. Underwood (2017), p. 6.
57. Farley, J. (1783). *The London Art of Cookery, and Housekeeper's Complete Assistant*. Price, p. iv.
58. Henderson, W. A. (1805). *The Housekeeper's Instructor, Or, Universal Family Cook*. 12th edn. Edited by J. C. Schnebbelie. J. Stratford, p. 4.
59. Collingwood, F. and Woollams, J. (1806). *The Universal Cook, and City and Country Housekeeper*. 4th edn. Scatcherd & Letterman, p. 4.

They may mention them as influences in their introduction, but don't say when they have copied the recipes almost exactly. So she is not cited as the origin of their recipe for pigeons transmogrified, for example.

Chapter 7: The King's Head (1772–1779)

1. *Manchester Mercury*, 7 April 1772; Appleton, S. (2017a), *Introduction to Elizabeth Raffald.* www.lu-lu.com, p. 47.
2. *Manchester Mercury*, 12 May 1772. Mrs Cooper is listed as Widow Cooper in Elizabeth's directory.
3. King's Head Yard still exists, though sadly the tavern itself was demolished to make way for the railway. Appleton (2017a), p. 53.
4. Harland, J. (1867). *Collectanea Relating to Manchester and Its Neighbourhood, at Various Periods*, Volume 72. Chetham Society, p. 149.
5. Shipperbottom, R. (1997). *The Experienced English Housekeeper with an Introduction by Roy Shipperbottom.* Southover Press, p. xiv.
6. Harland (1867), p. 149.
7. For those unfamiliar with these terms, front of house is considered anywhere a patron is allowed to go: bar, restaurant, toilet, etc. Back of house is anywhere patrons do not go, such as the kitchens, scullery, offices, etc.
8. *Manchester Mercury*, 9 August 1774.
9. Harland (1867), p. 146.
10. Appleton (2017a), p. 50.
11. Harland (1867), p. 149.
12. Sonnelitter, K. (2016). *The Eighteenth-Century Revolution In Philanthropy, Histphil.* Available at: https://histphil.org/2016/08/10/the-eighteenth-century-revolution-in-philanthropy.
13. *Manchester Mercury*, 20 December 1774.
14. Oldfield, S. J. and Day, D. (2010). 'The Manchester public house: sport and the entrepreneur', *MMU Research Institute for Health & Social Change, Annual Conference*, p. 3.
15. Dickson Wright, C. (2011). *A History of English Food.* Random House, p. 289.
16. Raffald, E. (1769). *The Experienced English Housekeeper*, p. 114.
17. Harland (1867), p. 147.

18. Clarke (2000), p. 2.
19. Quote is by John Macky, but found in Clarke, P. (2000). *British Clubs and Societies 1580-1800: The Origins of an Associational World.* Oxford University Press, p. 1.
20. Borsay, P. (2003), 'Politeness and elegance: the cultural re-fashioning of eighteenth-century York', in Hallett, M. and Rendall, J. (eds), *Eighteenth-century York Culture, Space and Society.* Borthwick Publications, University of York, p. 9.
21. Andrews, C. E. (2007). 'Drinking and thinking: club life and convivial sociability in mid-eighteenth-century Edinburgh', *The Social History of Alcohol and Drugs*, 22(1), p. 77.
22. *Manchester Mercury*, 25 August 1772. A card assembly was a social card-playing club, where members played popular games such as Whist. The Raffalds would advertise Card Assemblies throughout their time at the King's Head, the latest of which I could find was dated 25 November 1777.
23. Duthille, R. (2018). 'Drinking and toasting in Georgian Britain: group identities and individual agency', *Pies in the Sky*, p. 10. An example, so you get the idea: an 'abnormal part of their revelry was the wearing of a wig made from the pubic hairs of Charles II, the libertine king's, mistress.' Milne, N. (2014). *Libertines and Harlots.* Paragon, p. 223.
24. Hill, B. (1996). *Servants: English Domestics in the Eighteenth Century.* Clarendon Press, Oxford, p. 46.
25. Quote from Boswell via Duthille (2018), p. 2.
26. Stephens (2011).
27. Duthille (2018), pp. 2, 8.
28. Two of these were advertised in the *Manchester Mercury*, 13 June 1775 and 1 January 1776.
29. Raffald (1769), p. 313.
30. Quote is Andre Simon from Ludington, C. (2016). *The Politics of Wine in Britain: A New Cultural History.* Palgrave Macmillan, p. 134.
31. Lofts, N. (1976). *Domestic Life in England.* Morrison & Gibb, p. 123.
32. Hirschfelder, G. (2014). 'The myth of "misery alcoholism" in early industrial England: the example of Manchester', in Schmid, S. and Schmidt-Haberkamp (eds), *Drink in the Eighteenth and Nineteenth Centuries.* Taylor & Francis Group (e-book).
33. Harland (1867), pp. 148–149.

34. Taylor, D. (1957). 'Watchword of a 18th century paragon', *Manchester Guardian*, 1 March.

35. Harland (1867), p. 148.

36. O'Flaherty, N. (2019). *Utilitarianism in the Age of Enlightenment: The Moral and Political Thought of William Paley*. Cambridge University Press, p. 123.

37. Shipperbottom (1997), p. xv.

38. The word 'Crawcrans' gave me a bit of bother. They appear to be a thin crisp made from a thinly rolled out paste of boiled-down milk and sugar which are baked and then placed upon sweetmeats to provide them with a pleasant crunch. Cook, A. H. (1760). *Professed Cookery*. Printed for and sold by the author, p. 152. My thanks to Katharina Reiche for hunting down this tricky to find delicacy.

39. *Manchester Mercury*, 25 November 1777.

40. *Manchester Mercury*, 10 May and 8 December 1778.

41. *Manchester Mercury*, 22 December 1778.

Chapter 8: The Exorcist and the Midwife

1. Harland, J. (1867). *Collectanea Relating to Manchester and Its Neighbourhood, at Various Periods*, Volume 72. Chetham Society, p. 148.

2. Handley, S. (2015). *Visions of an Unseen World: Ghost Beliefs and Ghost Stories in Eighteenth Century England*. Taylor & Francis Group, pp. 1–2.

3. Ibid., p. 1.

4. Clarke, R. (2012). *A Natural History of Ghosts: 500 Years of Hunting Proof*. Penguin, p. 293; Handley (2015), pp. 1–2, 5.

5. There is a Raffald family legend concerning John's brother James that illustrates this. The story goes that his only son was at sea – he'd desired to be a sailor ever since he was a lad. However, one day, his mother saw his apparition 'as if standing on the opposite side of the stall in the Market Place [at] one o'clock in the afternoon ... From the intelligence subsequently received, it was ascertained that on the very day and hour the youth was drowned.' Harland (1867), p. 153.

6. The first of these to catch public attention being the Hammersmith Ghost in 1803.

7. This account and others are described and discussed in Sangha, L. S. (2020). 'The social, personal, and spiritual dynamics of ghost stories in early modern England', *The Historical Journal*, 63(2), pp. 1–13. See also Handley (2015), p. 7.
8. This counted for something at the time because men's views were generally regarded as more convincing, honest, level-headed and accurate.
9. This account is described and discussed in Clarke (2012), pp. 35–60.
10. Harland (1867), p. 173.
11. Schnorrenberg, B. B. (1981). 'Is childbirth any place for a woman? The decline of midwifery in eighteenth-century England', *Studies in Eighteenth-Century Culture*, p. 394.
12. Lofts, N. (1976). *Domestic Life in England*. Morrison & Gibb, p. 151.
13. Hill points out that men actively excluded women from midwifery, but there was a feminisation of domestic service. This did not occur from actively pushing out men, but from the expectations of women *versus* men in the home: in other words, it was not women who stole the jobs of men in a domestic service context. Hill, B. (1996). *Servants: English Domestics in the Eighteenth Century*. Clarendon Press, Oxford, p. 37.
14. Schnorrenberg (1981), p. 394.
15. Behr, G. (1978). 'Charles White of Manchester: the 250th anniversary of his birth', *British Medical Journal* (Dec), pp. 1699–1700.
16. Behr (1978), p. 1700.
17. Suze Appleton, personal communication.
18. John Harland says that she wrote her book 'under the able guidance and superintendence of Mr. Charles White, the celebrated surgeon...' Harland (1867), p. 173.
19. We know this because he does credit his sources in the book. Entry also available at Wikisource: https://en.wikisource.org/wiki/Dictionary_of_National_Biography,_1885-1900/Raffald,_Elizabeth
20. Harland (1867), p. 145.
21. Appleton, S. (2018). *Elizabeth Raffald: The Experienced English Housekeeper of Manchester*. www.lu-lu.com, pp. 25, 36. Suze Appleton believes there may have been two more children, a daughter, Mary, who died in her infant years in 1771, and a boy simply noted as 'a Male' in the same year in the records of the Collegiate Church, now Manchester Cathedral.

22. Jaine, T. (2012). Introduction to *First Catch Your Hare: The Art of Cookery Made Plain and Easy*. Prospect Books, p. xi.

23. The mortality rate in London in the 1740s was 45 per cent; Davenport, 2015, p. 2. If Elizabeth gave birth to eight children, the mortality rate increases to 62.5 per cent, and if sixteen, 81.25 per cent.

24. It is highly likely that deaths were underreported in Manchester because the date are collected from the Collegiate Church's records; those born to parents of other religions, as well as home births, are not typically recorded. See Davenport (2015), pp. 10–13.

25. Ibid., p. 6.

26. Harland (1867), p. 146.

Chapter 9: The Exchange Coffee-House (1779–1781)

1. Raffald, E. (1769). *The Experienced English Housekeeper*. J. Harrop, p. 5.

2. Harland, J. (1867). *Collectanea Relating to Manchester and Its Neighbourhood, at Various Periods*, Volume 72. Chetham Society, p. 229.

3. Axon, W. E. A. (1886). *Annals of Manchester*. John Heywood, p. 105.

4. Shipperbottom, R. (1996). 'Elizabeth Raffald', in Walker, H. (ed.), *Cooks & Other People: Proceedings of the Oxford Symposium on Food and Cookery, 1995*. Oxford Symposium, p. 236.

5. Bickham, T. (2020). *Eating the Empire: Food and Society in Eighteenth-Century Britain*. Reaktion Books, p. 80; Ellis, M. (2017). *Eighteenth-Century Coffee-House Culture, Vol 1*. Taylor & Francis Group, p. xii. They would have been struck by the taste too: the coffee was very strong, the beans over roasted, extremely bitter and, apparently, sulphurous in flavour.

6. Quote via Ukers, W. H. (2009). *All About Coffee*. Gutenberg Press, p. 75. This is a comment widely quoted, but appears to have no source.

7. Tullett, W. (2019). *Smell in Eighteenth-century England: A Social Sense*. Oxford University Press, p. 136.

8. Hillier also lists the various coffee houses in London and what type of chat and rhetoric they specialise in. For example, at White's, 'Horse-matches, Tupees [and] Mortgages' are the topics of choice, whereas at Child's it is 'False-Polling' and 'Infant-Baptism'. Hilliar, A. (1730). *A Brief and Merry History of Great-Britain*. James Hoey, pp. 28–29.

9. 'By the King. A Proclamation for the Suppression of Coffee-houses'. Assigns of John Bill, and Christopher Barker, printers to the Kings most excellent Majesty.

10. Hilliar (1730), p. 28.

11. Intile, K. (2007). *The European Coffee-House: a Political History*. University of Oregon, p. 42.

12. Ibid., p. 48.

13. Dickson Wright, C. (2011). *A History of English Food*. Random House, p. 270.

14. Quote from an unknown source in Appleton, S. (2017a). *Introduction to Elizabeth Raffald*. www.lu-lu.com, p. 62.

15. Bickham (2020), p. 82.

16. *Manchester Mercury*, 4 July 1780.

17. Allen, M. (2017). *The 18th-Century Spy Who Gave Us Big Strawberries, Gastro Obscura*. Available at: www.atlasobscura.com/articles/big-strawberries-spy-chile-france.

18. In 1846, to be precise; Axon (1886), p. 33.

19. Barr, C., Masteralexis, L. and Hums, M. (eds) (2011). *Principles and Practice of Sport Management*. Jones & Bartlett Learning, p. 5.

20. Chase, L. and Holloway Scott, S. (2017). *Nude Male Races on Kersal Moor, 1777-1811, Two Nerdy Historian Girls*. Available at: https://twonerdyhistorygirls.blogspot.com/2017/05/nude-male-races-on-kersal-moor-1777-1811.html; Appleton, S. (2018). *Elizabeth Raffald: The Experienced English Housekeeper of Manchester*. www.lu-lu.com, p. 54.

21. Shipperbottom, R. (1997). *The Experienced English Housekeeper with an Introduction by Roy Shipperbottom*. Southover Press, p. xv.

Chapter 10: Suddenly Gone

1. Harland, J. (1867). *Collectanea Relating to Manchester and Its Neighbourhood, at Various Periods*, Volume 72. Chetham Society, pp. 149–150.

2. *Manchester Mercury*, 23 April 1781.

3. Appleton, S. (2017a). *Introduction to Elizabeth Raffald*. www.lu-lu.com, pp. 56–57; Appleton, S. (2018). *Elizabeth Raffald: The Experienced English Housekeeper of Manchester*. www.lu-lu.com, p. 54.

4. Procter, R. W. (1866). *Manchester in Holiday Dress*. Simpkin, Marshall & Co., p. 161.

5. Dickson Wright, C. (2011). *A History of English Food*. Random House, pp. 296–297.

6. *Manchester Mercury*, 1 May 1781.

7. Shipperbottom, R. (1997). *The Experienced English Housekeeper with an Introduction by Roy Shipperbottom*. Southover Press, p. xiv.

8. Harland (1867), pp. 150–151.

9. These opinions are discussed in letters between Roy Shipperbottom and Charles Foster in the early 1990s.

10. As an ex-restaurateur and head chef, I can sympathise; the workload and hours are immense, even with today's labour-saving devices.

11. Appleton (2017a), p. 57.

12. Harland (1867), pp. 151–152. There is some disagreement as to the year John died. Harland reckons he died at 89, but Roy Shipperbottom believes he died aged 85 in December 1809. Charles Foster gives 1811 as the year of his death.

13. There is only one reference to John interacting with his daughters after Elizabeth passed away, when Anna asked him to teach her astrology: 'he refused to teach this knowledge to his youngest daughter, Anna, telling her that it would do her no good, and intimating his regret that he had ever studied it.' There is doubt that this ever happened, of course. Harland (1867), p. 151.

14. Harland (1867), pp. 155–156.

15. Mr Thomas Munday was 'of the firm of Thweat, Galley and Munday, of No. 1, Blue Boar Court, Manchester, and No. 5, Bread Street, London, manufacturers of muslins, dimities, ginghams, &c.' Harland (1867), p. 156.

16. Harland (1867), p. 156.

17. Ibid., p. 165.

18. Ibid., pp. 168–169.

19. Ibid., p. 165.

20. There were several versions of her portrait. The 1784 edition had a poor artist's copy of the original; by 1791, obviously false portraits were used.

21. Harland (1867), pp. 165, 169.

22. She was by no means the only deceased author whose canon went under this treatment; the problem was endemic. Bickham, T. (2020). *Eating*

the Empire: Food and Society in Eighteenth-Century Britain*. Reaktion Books, pp. 154–155.

23. Harland, J. (1852). 'Local Gleanings No. XXXII: Mrs. Raffald's Works', *Manchester Guardian*, 19 May.
24. Axon, W. E. A. (1886). *Annals of Manchester*. John Heywood, p. 107.

11. Legacy

1. Harland, J. (1867). *Collectanea Relating to Manchester and Its Neighbourhood, at Various Periods*, Volume 72. Chetham Society, p. 173.
2. Bickham, T. (2020). *Eating the Empire: Food and Society in Eighteenth-Century Britain*. Reaktion Books, p. 126.
3. Raffald, E. (1769). *The Experienced English Housekeeper*. J. Harrop, p. ii.
4. Campbell, R. (1747). *The London Tradesman, Being a Compendious View of All the Trades, Professions, Arts, Both Liberal and Mechanic, Now Practised in the Cities of London and Westminster*. T. Gardener, pp. 276–277. Campbell goes on and on in this way for several pages and it's a great read. He was just so very annoyed.
5. Underwood, R. (2017). *Eighteenth-Century Women's Cookbooks: Authors and Copyright*. Texas Women's University, p. 69.
6. Ibid., pp. 69–70.
7. Bickham (2020), pp. 153–154.
8. Shipperbottom, R. (1997). *The Experienced English Housekeeper with an Introduction by Roy Shipperbottom*. Southover Press, p. xvi.
9. Bickham (2020), p. 150.
10. This isn't the case for all foods, of course. For example, Bakewell pudding (the forerunner to the Bakewell tart) is definitely from Bakewell in Cheshire.
11. Dickson Wright, C. (2011). *A History of English Food*. Random House, p. 373.
12. Eliza Acton was perhaps the one who lost out the most: a third of the recipes from her book *Modern Cookery for Private Families* (1845) were stolen.
13. Dickson Wright (2011), p. 372.

14. *Manchester Guardian* (1951), 'MISCELLANY: Many-Sided Performer', 17 August, p. 5.

15. Appleton, S. (2018). *Elizabeth Raffald: The Experienced English Housekeeper of Manchester*. www.lu-lu.com, p. 65.

16. The book is very rare; only nine handwritten copies exist, one of which can be viewed in Manchester Central Library.

17. Driver, C. and Arlott, J. (1981). 'It is hard enough to eat tolerably at a fair price in London, but how much better off are Manchester and Liverpool?: Good Food Guide', *The Guardian*, 27 November, p. 12.

18. White, F. (1932). *Good Things in England*. Persephone, p. 9.

19. David, E. (1977). *English Bread and Yeast Cookery*. Grub Street, pp. 480, 486.

20. Bilton, S. (2018). *The Origins of the Wedding Cake, English Heritage*. Available at: http://blog.english-heritage.org.uk/origins-of-the-wedding-cake

21. Sam Bilton, personal communication.

22. Mary-Ann Boermans, personal communication. Mary-Ann breathes life into several of Elizabeth's recipes in her book *Deja Food* (Random House, 2017) including macaroni with Parmesan, barbequed pork and Elizabeth's herb pie for Lent (which I have also made, and very good it is too).

23. This quote is from the first edition of *English Food*, but can be found in Grigson, J. (1992). *English Food*. 3rd edn. Penguin, p. xiii.

24. These include Eliza Acton's *Modern Cookery* by Quadrille, Florence White's *Good Things in England* by Persephone and Hannah Glasse's *The Art of Cookery Made Plain and Easy* by Prospect Books, as well as a whole series of books of classic British cookery writing by Penguin.

25. Henderson, F. (2012). *The Complete Nose to Tail: A Kind of British Cooking*. Bloomsbury, p. 5.

26. He is also a champion of the great British pudding, and he and his pastry chef Justin Gellatly produced some excellent traditional puddings and jellies.

27. Miller, N. (2007). 'Eating through the ages', *The Guardian*, 14 March. Available at: www.theguardian.com/books/2007/mar/14/booksonhealth.foodanddrink

28. McLagan, J. (2011). *Odd Bits: How to Cook the Rest of the Animal*. Jacqui Small LLP, p. 113.

29. I used to run very successful offal nights in my days of the pop-up restaurant, and then when I opened my eatery in 2016, I put out dishes using things like calf's head and sweetbreads. The enthusiasm *is* there.

30. *Manchester Evening News* (2010). 'Chef pays tribute to cooking legend', 7 October. Available at: www.manchestereveningnews.co.uk/news/local-news/chef-pays-tribute-to-cooking-legend-900563

31. Suze's books are available on Amazon and are well worth buying. If you want to see the primary and secondary sources yourself, may I suggest hunting out *The Complete Elizabeth Raffald* (2017).

32. Appleton, S. (2017a). *Introduction to Elizabeth Raffald*, p. 3.

33. Howarth, R. (2015). 'Elizabeth Gaskell and Elizabeth Raffald are in the running for commemorative statue in Manchester', *Knutsford Guardian*, 2 November. Available at: www.knutsfordguardian.co.uk/news/13931335.elizabeth-gaskell-and-elizabeth-raffald-are-in-the-running-for-commemorative-statue-in-manchester

34. I did most of my research for this book in Manchester Central Library, and every day I walked past the statue of Emmeline Pankhurst, and each time imagined what Elizabeth's statue would have been like had she won the poll.

Appendix: Cook Like It's 1769

1. My blogs' addresses are: britishfoodhistory.com and neilcooksgrigson.com

2. Staid, J. (2012). 'Quizzing Glasse: or Hannah scrutinized', in *First Catch Your Hare: The Art of Cookery Made Plain and Easy*. Prospect Books, p. xxix.

3. When it came to accurately measuring smaller amounts, the accepted method was to use a specific coin, for example in Elizabeth's recipe for a sauce with a cod's head, she asks for 'as much beaten Mace as will lie on a Six-pence'. Raffald, E. (1769). *The Experienced English Housekeeper*. J. Harrop, p. 18.

4. Grigson, J. (1992). *English Food*. 3rd edn. Penguin, p. 38.

5. There are several that *are* legal game but you might not expect to be: woodcock, snipe and rook can all be eaten legally today.

6. I have done this in the past, and haven't quite worked out if I should feel guilty about it. You see, I am very much against the farming of veal calves in crates, but then, none of those calves were raised for their heads, brains, tongues, testes, etc.; they were raised for their tender meat. Consequently, I believe I am not adding to the body count by eating those bits.

7. If you do fancy having a crack at making a pudding in a cloth, see my blog post on making a Dickensian Christmas Pudding. Buttery, N. (2021). *To Make a Christmas Pudding Part 1: Stir Up Sunday*, in *British Food, a History*. Available at: https://britishfoodhistory.com/2021/11/21/christmas-pudding-part-1-stir-up-sunday

8. Grigson (1992), p. 215.

Bibliography

Acton, E. (1845). *Modern Cookery for Private Families*. Quadrille.

Adams, J. (1789). *Curious Thoughts on the History of Man; Chiefly Abridged Or Selected from the Celebrated Works of Lord Kaimes, Lord Monboddo, Dr. Dunbar, and the Immortal Montesquieu...: Designed to Promote a Spirit of Enquiry in the British Youth of Both Sexes*. G. Kearsley.

Alcock, T. (1752). *Observations on the Defects of the Poor Laws, and on the Causes and Consequences of the Great Increase and Burden of the Poor*. R. Baldwin.

Appleton, S. (2017a). *Introduction to Elizabeth Raffald*. Amazon.

Appleton, S. (2017b). *The Manchester Directories 1772, 1773 & 1781 by Elizabeth Raffald*. CreateSpace Independent Publishing Platform.

Appleton, S. (2018). *Elizabeth Raffald: The Experienced English Housekeeper of Manchester*. Amazon.

Axon, W. E. A. (1886). *Annals of Manchester*. John Heywood.

Bain, P. (2012). 'Recounting the chickens: Hannah further scrutinized', in *First Catch Your Hare: The Art of Cookery Made Plain and Easy*. Prospect Books.

Beeton, I. (1861). *The Book of Household Management*. Lightning Source.

Bickham, T. (2020). *Eating the Empire: Food and Society in Eighteenth-Century Britain*. Reaktion Books.

Booker, K. (2017). *Menials: Domestic Service and the Cultural Transformation of British Society, 1650–1850*. Bucknell University Press.

Borsay, P. (2003). 'Politeness and elegance: the cultural re-fashioning of eighteenth-century York', in Hallett, M. and Rendall, J. (eds), *Eighteenth-century York Culture, Space and Society*. Borthwick Publications, University of York.

Boswell, J. & Chapman, R. W. (2008). *Life of Johnson*. Oxford University Press.

Brears, P. (2014). *Traditional Food in Yorkshire*. Prospect Books.

Brown, P. (2006). 'The real thing? Understanding the archive at Fairfax House, York', in Hosking, R. (ed.), *Authenticity in the Kitchen: Proceedings of the Oxford Symposium on Food and Cookery 2005*. Prospect Books.

Campbell, R. (1747). *The London Tradesman, Being a Compendious View of All the Trades, Professions, Arts, Both Liberal and Mechanic, Now Practised in the Cities of London and Westminster*. T. Gardener.

Campbell, S. (2011). *Walled Kitchen Gardens*. Replika Press Private Ltd.

Clarke, P. (2000). *British Clubs and Societies 1580–1800: The Origins of an Associational World*. Oxford University Press.

Clarke, R. (2012). *A Natural History of Ghosts: 500 Years of Hunting Proof.* Penguin.

Collingwood, F. & Woollams, J. (1806). *The Universal Cook, and City and Country Housekeeper* (4th edition). Scatcherd & Letterman.

Colquhoun, K. (2012). *Taste: The Story of Britain Through Its Cooking*. Bloomsbury.

David, E. (1977). *English Bread and Yeast Cookery*. Grub Street.

Dickson Wright, C. (2011). *A History of English Food*. Random House.

Duthille, R. (2018). 'Drinking and toasting in Georgian Britain: group identities and individual agency', *Pies in the Sky*.

Ellis, M. (2017). *Eighteenth-Century Coffee-House Culture, Vol 1*. Taylor & Francis Group.

Farley, J. (1783). *The London Art of Cookery, and Housekeeper's Complete Assistant*. Price.

Fielding, H. (1751). *A Plan of the Universal Register-Office, opposite Cecil-Street in the Strand*.

Flower, M. (1984). *Arley Hall Gardens, Cheshire*. Beric Tempest & Co Ltd.

Foster, C. F. (1982). *Arley Hall, Cheshire*. Martin's of Berwick.

Foster, C. F. (2002). *Seven Households: Life in Cheshire and Lancashire 1582 to 1774*. Arley Hall Press.

Glasse, H. (1747). *The Art of Cookery Made Plain and Easy*. Prospect Books.

Gray, T. (1998). 'Walled gardens and the cultivation of orchard fruit in the south-west of England', in Wilson, C. A. (ed.), *The Country House Kitchen Garden 1600–1950*. The History Press.

Grigson, J. (1992). *English Food* (3rd edition). Penguin.

Handley, S. (2015). *Visions of an Unseen World: Ghost Beliefs and Ghost Stories in Eighteenth Century England*. Taylor & Francis Group.

Harland, J. (1867). *Collectanea Relating to Manchester and Its Neighbourhood, at Various Periods, Volume 72*. Chetham Society.

Hartley, D. (1954). *Food in England*. Little, Brown & Company.

Hecht, J. J. (1956). *The Domestic Servant Class in Eighteenth Century England*. Routledge & Kegan Paul.

Henderson, F. (2012). *The Complete Nose to Tail: A Kind of British Cooking*. Bloomsbury.

Hill, B. (1996). *Servants: English Domestics in the Eighteenth Century*. Clarendon Press.

Hilliar, A. (1730). *A Brief and Merry History of Great-Britain*. James Hoey.

Hirschfelder, G. (2014). 'The myth of "misery alcoholism" in early industrial England: the example of Manchester', in Schmid, S. and Schmidt-Haberkamp, B. (eds), *Drink in the Eighteenth and Nineteenth Centuries*. Taylor & Francis Group.

Hitchcock, T. (2004). *Down and Out in Eighteenth-Century London*. Bloomsbury.

Intile, K. (2007). *The European Coffee-House: A Political History*. University of Oregon.

Jaine, T. (2012). 'Introduction', in *First Catch Your Hare: The Art of Cookery Made Plain and Easy*. Prospect Books.

Johnson, S. (2005). *Johnson's Dictionary: A Modern Selection*. Edited by E. L. McAdam and G. Milne. Dover Publications.

King of England (1675). 'By the King. A Proclamation for the Suppression of Coffee-houses', assigns of John Bill, and Christopher Barker, printers to the Kings most excellent Majesty.

Lofts, N. (1976). *Domestic Life in England*. Morrison & Gibb.

McLagan, J. (2011). *Odd Bits: How to Cook the Rest of the Animal*. Jacqui Small LLP.

O'Flaherty, N. (2019). *Utilitarianism in the Age of Enlightenment: The Moral and Political Thought of William Paley*. Cambridge University Press.

Philanthropus (1757). *An Appeal to the Public; Against the Growing Evil of Universal Register-offices*. Self-published.

Procter, R. W. (1866). *Manchester in Holiday Dress*. Simpkin, Marshall & Co.

Raffald, E. (1769). *The Experienced English Housekeeper* (1st edition). J. Harrop.

Raffald, E. (1771). *The Experienced English Housekeeper* (2nd edition). R. Baldwin.

Raffald, E. (1772). *Elizabeth Raffald's Directory of Manchester and Salford 1772*. Neil Richardson.

Raffald, E. & Shipperbottom, R. (1997). *The Experienced English Housekeeper with an introduction by Roy Shipperbottom*. 1997 reprint. Southover Press.

Reed, J. (1761). *The Register-office: A Farce of Two Acts*. T. Davies.

Rovee, C. K. (2006). *Imagining the Gallery: The Social Body of British Romanticism*. Stanford University Press.

Sanders, J. (1967). *Manchester*. C. Tinling & Co.

Shipperbottom, R. (1996). 'Elizabeth Raffald', in Walker, H. (ed.), *Cooks & Other People: Proceedings of the Oxford Symposium on Food and Cookery, 1995*. Oxford Symposium.

Shircliff, W. E. (1999). *Elizabeth Raffald: Her Biography and Family Tree*. Self-published.

Smith, E. (1727). *The Compleat Housewife Or, Accomplish'd Gentlewoman's Companion*. Andrews McMeel.

Staid, J. (2012). 'Quizzing Glasse: or Hannah scrutinized', in *First Catch Your Hare: The Art of Cookery Made Plain and Easy*. Prospect Books.

Strevens, S. (2014). *The Birth of the Chocolate City: Life in Georgian York*. Amberley.

Thirsk, J. (1998). 'Preserving the fruit and vegetable harvest, 1600–1700', in Wilson, C. A. (ed.), *The Country House Kitchen Garden 1600–1950*. The History Press.

Timperley, C. H. (1839). *Annals of Manchester: Biographical, Historical, Ecclesiastical, and Commercial, from the Earliest Period to the Close of the Year 1839*. Bancks and Company.

Trusler, J. (1791). *The Honours of the Table, Or, Rules for Behaviour During Meals*. Published by the author.

Tullett, W. (2019). *Smell in Eighteenth-century England: A Social Sense*. Oxford University Press.

Verral, W. (1759). *A Complete System of Cookery*. William Verral.

White, F. (1932). *Good Things in England*. Persephone.

Woodforde, J. (1999). *The Diary of a Country Parson*. Edited by J. Beresford. Canterbury Press.

Ysewijn, R. (2015). *Pride and Pudding: The History of British Puddings Savoury and Sweet*. Murdoch Books.

Journals and Newspapers

Andrews, C. E. (2007). 'Drinking and thinking: club life and convivial sociability in mid- eighteenth-century Edinburgh', *The Social History of Alcohol and Drugs*, 22(1), pp. 65–82.

Coulton, R. (2018). 'Curiosity, commerce, and conversation: nursery-gardens and nurserymen in eighteenth-century London', *The London Journal*, 43(1), pp. 17–35.

Davenport, R. (2015). 'The first stage of the epidemiological transition in British cities: a comparison of Manchester and London, 1750–1820', *Cambridge Group for the History of Population and Social Structure*.

Day, I. (1997). *The Art of Confectionery*. Available at: www.historicfood. com/The Art of Confectionery.pdf.

Driver, C. (1986). 'Kissin' don't last but cookin' do', *The Guardian*, 19 April, p. 9.

Driver, C. & Arlott, J. (1981). 'It is hard enough to eat tolerably at a fair price in London, but how much better off are Manchester and Liverpool?: Good Food Guide', *The Guardian*, 27 November, p. 12.

Duthille, R. (2018). 'Drinking and toasting in Georgian Britain: group identities and individual agency', *Pies in the Sky*.

Harland, J. (1852). 'Local Gleanings No. XXXII: Mrs. Raffald's Works', *Manchester Guardian*, 19 May.

Houston, R. A. (1982). 'The development of literacy: Northern England, 1640–1750', *Economic History Review*, pp. 199–216.

Manchester Guardian (1843). 'Manchester in 1781', 2 August.

Manchester Guardian (1845). 'An Old Manchester Directory', 8 October.

Manchester Guardian (1927). 'The eighteenth-century girl in Manchester: HER ACCOMPLISHMENTS', 9 March, p. 3.

Manchester Guardian (1951) 'MISCELLANY: Many-Sided Performer', 17 August, p. 5.

Manchester Mercury

Miller, N. (2007). 'Eating through the ages', *The Guardian*, 14 March.

Oldfield, S. J. & Day, D. (2010). 'The Manchester Public House: Sport and the Entrepreneur', *MMU Research Institute for Health & Social Change, Annual Conference*.

Sangha, L. S. (2020). 'The social, personal, and spiritual dynamics of ghost stories in early modern England', *The Historical Journal*, 63(2), pp. 339–359.

Schnorrenberg, B. B. (1981). 'Is childbirth any place for a woman? The decline of midwifery in eighteenth-century England', *Studies in Eighteenth-Century Culture*, 10, pp. 393–408.

Taylor, D. (1957). 'OECONOMY WITH ELEGANCE: Watchword of an 18th-century paragon', *The Manchester Guardian*, 1 March, p. 6.

The London Magazine (1756). 'To Joseph D'Anvers, Esq.', May, pp. 225–226.

The Observer (1936). 'Housekeeping in the old days: 18th century recipes Mrs. Raffald's book a best sellar', 13 December, p. 10.

Underwood, R. (2017). *Eighteenth-Century Women's Cookbooks: Authors and Copyright*. Texas Women's University.

Websites

Allen, M. (2017). *The 18th-Century Spy Who Gave Us Big Strawberries, Gastro Obscura*. Available at: www.atlasobscura.com/articles/big-strawberries-spy-chile-france

Arley Hall Archives 1750–90: Life on a Cheshire Country Estate (2019). Available at: https://arleyhallarchives.co.uk

Bilton, S. (2018). *The Origins of the Wedding Cake, English Heritage*. Available at: http://blog.english-heritage.org.uk/origins-of-the-wedding-cake

Chase, L. & Holloway Scott, S. (2017) *Nude Male Races on Kersal Moor, 1777–1811, Two Nerdy Historian Girls*. Available at: https://twonerdyhistorygirls.blogspot.com/2017/05/nude-male-races-on-kersal-moor-1777-1811.html

Day, I. (2011). *Solomon's Temple in Flummery – A Culinary Mobile, Food History Jottings*. Available at: http://foodhistorjottings.blogspot.com/2011/10/solomons-temple-in-flummery-culinary.html

Sonnelitter, K. (2016). *The Eighteenth-Century Revolution in Philanthropy, Histphil*. Available at: https://histphil.org/2016/08/10/the-eighteenth-century-revolution-in-philanthropy

Index

Page numbers in **bold** refer to pages in the notes section.